THE BOOK OF
SWIMBRIDGE

A North Devon Village in the Twentieth Century

St James Church, Swimbridge

PHILIP DALLING

HALSGROVE

First published in Great Britain in 2015

Copyright © Philip Dalling

Title page illustration: *A pen and ink drawing of St James'church by Swimbridge artist Cecil E Dunn*

British Library Cataloguing-in-Publication Data
A CIP record for this title is available from the British Library

ISBN 978 0 85704 270 5

HALSGROVE
Halsgrove House,
Ryelands Business Park,
Bagley Road, Wellington, Somerset TA21 9PZ
Tel: 01823 653777   Fax: 01823 216796
email: sales@halsgrove.com

Part of the Halsgrove group of companies.
Information on all Halsgrove titles is available at: www.halsgrove.com

Printed and bound in the UK by The Short Run Press, Exeter

By the same author

Local history & topography

*Erewash Valley Portrait – the
changing face of the DH Lawrence country*

Sports history

Nottingham and Long Eaton Speedway 1928-1967

The Golden Age of Speedway

Speedway The Classic Era

Classic Speedway Venues

CONTENTS

Preface

The inspiration for this work can be found in the impressive collection of material relating to the life and times of Swimbridge assembled over a lifetime by my cousin, Mervyn Dalling.

On Mervyn's death in March 2013 the material – photographs and other illustrative items, public and private documents, press cuttings, programmes of events ranging from church anniversaries to carnivals; posters, fixture cards for sports clubs, invoices and statements of account, and even railway tickets – passed into my keeping.

It would be understating and undervaluing Mervyn's passion for anything and everything relating to the place where he was born, where he lived for all but a few months of his life, and where he died, to view his collection merely in terms of the thousands of material items he so painstakingly collected.

The most interesting items relate to the personal reminiscences he collected and documented from the people he lived amongst for so long. For although the researcher can learn much from delving into official records of the county, district, the parish, both civil and ecclesiastic, and other public documents, the real story of Swimbridge lies in the glimpses Mervyn's collection allows of the people, whether high or low, rich or poor.

I had obviously seen and read much of the material in the collection before Mervyn's death. He was generous in allowing access to his work, not only to family members and friends, but also to the substantial number of people who wrote to him from all over the world, or who in many cases rang the doorbell at his home at Church Cottages, seeking details of the role their own relatives had played in the development of the village.

The time and energy Mervyn expended in responding to these queries is evident through the copies he made and filed of his replies to letters, in which he routinely enclosed copies of documents and/or copious notes he compiled from his own researches and was happy to share.

As far back as 1965 Mervyn published his own invaluable book (updated from time to time) of facts and statistics which still today provides an ideal introduction to Swimbridge.

As a journalist and author, my immediate thought when receiving his legacy was that the most suitable tribute to his memory and to the fruits of his life's work would be to tell the story of Swimbridge and its people in the twentieth century, the period in which Mervyn personally, his parents and grandparents (my grandparents too) played their own part in the life of the parish.

It has been a great pleasure for me, starting out from the hugely advantageous position of having Mervyn's superb collection as a continuous source of golden nuggets of information, to follow up by meeting and talking to dozens of Swimbridge residents, present and past, whilst pursuing my own researches.

I have recorded my thanks in the acknowledgements section of this book to all those who have taken the time to talk to me.

Although I was not born in Swimbridge, I was brought to the village to what were then Coombe Cottages, at Tordown, for the first time at the age of six months, and have scarcely missed at least an annual visit throughout my life.

I am proud to be a part of a family that can trace its connections with the village and parish back to the latter years of the seventeenth century.

Philip Dalling
Barbrook, Exmoor 2015

Mervyn Charles Dalling
1941 - 2013

As a genealogist, historian, author, story-teller, musician and composer, photographer, printer, and keen gardener, Mervyn Dalling packed more into his life than some people would believe possible.

Despite the breadth of his interests, everything Mervyn did was centred on his love for his home village. He was born and died in Swimbridge (or Swymbridge, to use the spelling he preferred), in a house close to the parish church of St James, and left the village for only a brief spell to work elsewhere.

He was educated at the village school, later moving to Barnstaple Boys Grammar School. He spent his working life with the County Court Service, in Barnstaple and, for a brief spell, in Trowbridge in Wiltshire.

He took early retirement some twenty years ago after a serious illness which involved the removal of a lung, and devoted the rest of his life to his myriad interests and to acting as an unofficial ambassador for Swimbridge. He had an encyclopaedic knowledge of the village, the wider parish, and its inhabitants.

Family history was a passion for Mervyn, and he enjoyed great success in tracing the family trees of the Dalling and Morrish families – his paternal grandmother was a Morrish. In the case of the Morrish family he established that they had lived in Swimbridge since the late seventeenth century.

Despite cancer being diagnosed in his remaining lung towards the end of 2012, he continued to pursue his interests.

In 1965 he published a book full of fascinating facts about the village and he was always in demand as a speaker for a variety of organisations. In recent years he had produced several photographic displays for exhibition in the parish church, particularly of men from Swimbridge who died in the two world wars of the twentieth century and in later conflicts.

An accomplished organist, who played on occasions at Swimbridge and Gunn churches and elsewhere, he wrote both words and music for a number of hymns, particularly for harvest celebrations and to be sung at the weddings of people he knew personally.

Mervyn acquired a small letterpress printing machine, and produced a variety of material, including orders of service. He later switched to computer technology, turning out invitations to family events and more substantial material, including a history of Barnstaple Boys Grammar School, of which he was a proud old boy.

On his 68th birthday he organised a celebration at the Jack Russell in Swimbridge (formerly the New Inn) to mark his half century as a regular at the pub, where he knew and was greeted by almost all the customers.

He had a very distinctive sense of humour and the ability to hold an audience rapt with his stories and songs in local dialect, performed at harvest suppers and elsewhere.

Mervyn was the elder son of Owen and Blanche Dalling. He leaves a brother, Colin, and two sisters, Lorna Jones and Jo Masters. His eldest sister, Diana, died in 1999.

Both Mervyn and his father served as members of Swimbridge parish council. Mervyn also had a spell as parish clerk and was also clerk to the Feoffees.

A week before Mervyn's death, his next-door neighbour for more than seventy years, Anthony Yeo, died. Both men are buried in Swimbridge churchyard, which their homes overlooked.

(This appreciation of the life of Mervyn Dalling, written by the author of this book) first appeared in the North Devon Journal *following Mervyn's death in March 2013).*

Author's Note

This volume sets out to profile both the village and the wider parish of Swimbridge. References in the text to 'Swimbridge parish' in almost all instances refer to the parish as it existed prior to the boundary changes of 2003 and 2015, and include in that definition the outlying settlements of Accott, Bydown, Cobbaton, Travellers Rest, Dennington, Irishborough/Ernesborough, Gunn, Hannaford, Kerscott, Riverton, Tordown, Stone Cross, Yeoland, et al.

Although it is primarily intended to reflect local life in the hundred years from 1900 onwards, those tumultuous decades of the recent past can only be fully understood if they are considered in the light of earlier events. Many of the acute social changes that reached fulfilment in the years from 1900, and the attitudes and beliefs that led to their implementation, had their roots in the Victorian era.

Dates alone can be confusing; the closing years of Queen Victoria's reign and the first decade or so of the twentieth century have much in common, just as at a later date the so-called 'Swinging Sixties' did not really begin until the middle of that decade, with the early 1960s having far more in common with the 1950s.

Equally, it would be wrong to end the narrative at the point where the last stroke of midnight on 31 December 1999 signalled the start of a new century and a new millennium. It is important to review the way in which Swimbridge has faced the transition into the twenty-first century, and has responded to social changes perhaps even more sweeping than those of the previous hundred years.

In attempting to interpret the era I have chosen not to adopt a chronological sequence, working one by one through the decades under review. After first looking at how the village and wider parish are products of their natural environment, I have explored how people lived at the start of the twentieth century, gradually tracing the enormous changes local society has experienced over the course of a century.

Having set the scene, both in terms of how Swimbridge as a place fitted in to its physical surroundings, and how its inhabitants lived day-to-day, I have gone on to study the area topic by topic – the village and parish at work, at play, enjoying its leisure etc. The very considerable impact upon Swimbridge of the two World Wars of the twentieth century is also covered in detail.

It may also be helpful at the start to clarify the way in which the name of the village will be used throughout the text. Mervyn Dalling always insisted on the version of the name with a *y* – ie Swymbridge, which was in fairly general use throughout the nineteenth century and, in some contexts, well into the twentieth century.

Although the author is a great respecter of tradition, it is his decision to spell the name in the modern fashion, ie with an *i* – Swimbridge. He believes this will be readily accepted by those who lived in the village through much of the period under review and those who are essentially children of the very late twentieth and indeed the twenty-first, centuries.

Acknowledgements

The debt owed by this book to the lifetime work of Mervyn Dalling has already been acknowledged. The priceless store of photographs and historical documents he amassed over the years, together with the fruits of the original research he pursued, will hopefully continue to be preserved and, where possible, made available to the public.

I am personally indebted to a great many people who have helped in my own task of supplementing and interpreting Mervyn's work.

On many occasions over the past two years, when I have needed to identify a photograph or clarify a point raised by a document, my initial reaction has been simply to 'ask Mervyn'. Sadly, after just a moment's reflection, the realisation has dawned that his knowledge is no longer directly available.

Happily for me, a substantial number of people from the village and the wider parish have gone to considerable lengths to answer my queries and attempt as far as possible to fill the gap. I am very grateful to them for the information given and also for the hospitality they have extended to me.

The individuals to whom I have turned for information and advice include the following, in each case listed in alphabetical order.

From Mervyn Dalling's family: Colin and Angela Dalling, Jo Masters, and Lorna and Pat Jones.

From Swimbridge and neighbouring parishes: John and Barbara Ackland, Bill and Win Babb, Emeritus Professor Richard Balment, John, Margaret and James Bartlett, Bert and Mel Bartlett, Mavis and Matt Bluge, the Rev Peter Bowers, David and Penny Clapp, Mike and Maureen Clift, Lindsey Cooper, Gavin Coulstock, Paul, Melissa and Jill Darch, Ken Dennis, Geoff Dodd, Jessica and Peter Duncan, Eddie Dymond, Richard Edgell, Charles and Brenda Elworthy, Lorna Elworthy, Colin Elworthy, Christopher and Janet Elworthy, Sophia Elworthy, Lyn and Michael Essery, Sid and Maureen Facey, Enid Harding, Mark and Rosemary Haworth-Booth, John and Anne Hayes, Maureen Hayward, Bill Hedge, Denzil, Carol and Patrick Holland, Richard Howe, Preston Isaacs, Martin James, Vera Knight, Raymond Liverton, David Luggar, Ian and Amy McLaughlin, David Netherway, Tom Oliver, the Rev Shaun O'Rourke, Janet and Jeffrey Patton, Liz Pile, Garry Reed, George and Nancy Shapland, Sheila and George Snell, John and Barbara Squire, Gordon and Dulcie Tucker, Colin and Lee Wadsworth, Julie and Malcolm Whitton.

From local and national organisations: Nicola Allen (Woburn Abbey Archives), Ken Baker, Bob Crawley and Peter Dyer (re bus services in North Devon), Barnstaple Heritage Centre, Professor John Beckett (The University of Nottingham), Amy Bingham (Media Relations Manager, North Devon District Council), Berwick Coates (West Buckland School), Colin MacDonald and colleagues at the North Devon Record Office, Ather Mirza and Peter Thorley (University of Leicester), Mervyn Mugford (Devon County Library Service), North Devon Football League Archives, Charles Sale (Gravestone Photographic Resource).

Special thanks to Keith and Vivien Thomas of Dean Steep, Lynton, for the map of Swimbridge Parish which appears on page eight. The map greatly enhances the book and provides a valuable visual reference for readers not familiar with every corner of the parish.

The author extends apologies to anyone who may have been missed from the acknowledgements.

Finally, this work would never have been completed without the devotion of Brenda Dyer (née Huxtable of Yeoland, Swimbridge), who spent many hours taking, sourcing and processing photographs, tracking down information, particularly for use in photographic captions, making countless useful suggestions and enduring the occasional (?) irascibility of the author.

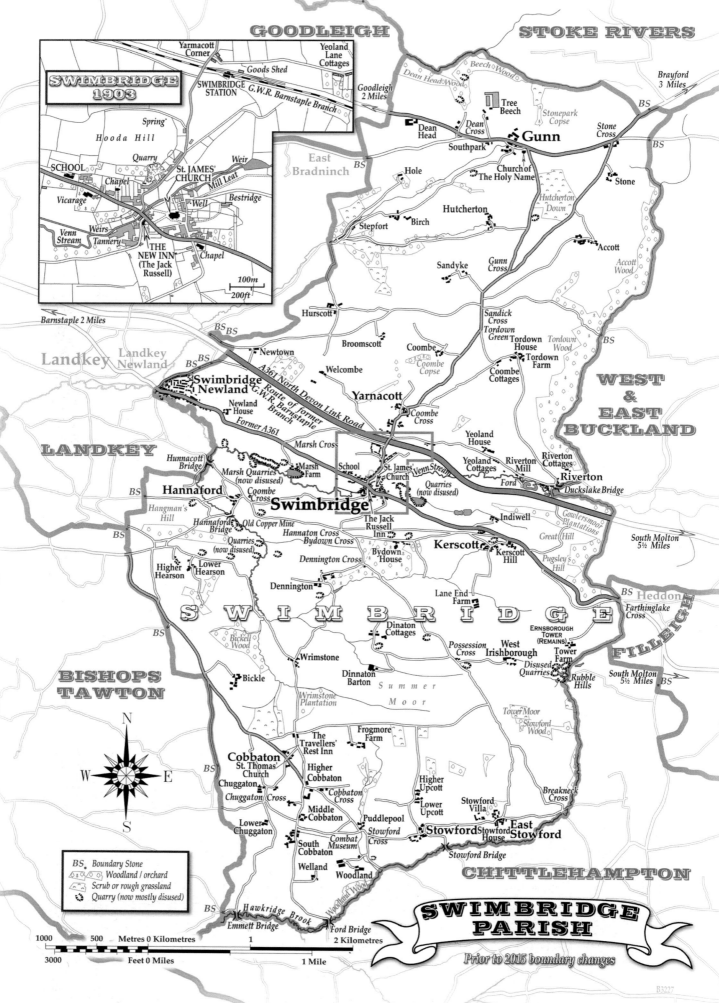

GOODLEIGH

STOKE RIVERS

Brayford 3 Miles

BS

BS

Beech Wood

Dean Head Wood

Stonepark Copse

Tree Beech

Stone Cross

Dean Cross

Gunn

Stone

Dean Head

Southpark

Church of The Holy Name

Goodleigh 2 Miles

Hole

Hutcherton

Hutcherton Down

Accott

Accott Wood

East Bradninch

BS

Stepfort

Birch

Sandyke

Gunn Cross

Hurscott

Broomscott

Coombe

Sandick Cross

Tordown Green

Tordown House

Tordown Wood

BS

WEST & EAST BUCKLAND

BS BS

Barnstaple 2 Miles

BS

Newtown

Welcombe

Coombe Copse

Coombe Cottages

Tordown Farm

Landkey

Landkey Newland

BS

Swimbridge Newland

Yarnacott

Yeoland House

Riverton Cottages

Riverton

LANDKEY

Newland House

Former A361

A361 North Devon Link Road Route of former G.W.R. Barnstaple Branch

Marsh Cross

Coombe Cross

School

St. James' Church

Venn Stream

Yeoland Cottages

Riverton Mill

Ford

Duckslake Bridge

Hunnacott Bridge

Marsh Quarries (now disused)

Marsh Farm

Quarries (now disused)

Hannaford

Coombe Cross

Swimbridge

Hangman's Hill

Hannaford Bridge

Old Copper Mine

Hannaton Cross

The Jack Russell Inn

Indiwell

Gowlersmoor Plantations

South Molton 5½ Miles

BS

Quarries (now disused)

Bydown Cross

Kerscott

Kerscott Hill

Great Hill

Pugsley's Hill

BS Heddon

Higher Hearson

Lower Hearson

Dennington Cross

Bydown House

Farthinglake Cross

FILLEIGH

Dennington

S W I M B R I D G E

Lane End Farm

Ernsborough Tower (Remains)

Tower Farm

Bickell Wood

Dinaton Cottages

Possession Cross

West Irishborough

Disused Quarries

Rubble Hills

South Molton 5½ Miles

BS

BISHOPS TAWTON

Wrimstone

Dinnaton Barton

Summer Moor

Tower Moor

Stowford Wood

Breakneck Cross

Bickle

N

Wrimstone Plantation

Frogmore Farm

Stowford Villa

W E

BS

The Travellers' Rest Inn

Higher Upcott

S

Cobbaton

St. Thomas' Church

Higher Cobbaton

Lower Upcott

Stowford Villa

Stowford House

East Stowford

Chuggaton

Cobbaton Cross

Higher Upcott

Stowford

Chuggaton Cross

Middle Cobbaton

Puddlepool

Stowford Cross

Lower Chuggaton

South Cobbaton

Combat Museum

Stowford Bridge

CHITTLEHAMPTON

BS Boundary Stone

Woodland / orchard

Scrub or rough grassland

Quarry (now mostly disused)

Welland

Woodland

Woodland Wood

SWIMBRIDGE PARISH

BS

Hawkridge Brook

Ford Bridge

Prior to 2015 boundary changes

Emmett Bridge

1000 500 Metres 0 Kilometres   1   2 Kilometres

3000 Feet 0 Miles   1 Mile

B3227

SWIMBRIDGE 1903

SWIMBRIDGE 1903

Yarmacott Corner

Goods Shed

Yeoland Lane Cottages

SWIMBRIDGE STATION

G.W.R. Barnstaple Branch

Goodleigh 2 Miles

Spring

Hooda Hill

Quarry

Weir

SCHOOL

St. JAMES' CHURCH

Chapel

Mill Leat

Vicarage

Well

Bestridge

Venn Stream

Weirs

Tannery

THE NEW INN (The Jack Russell)

Chapel

100m

200ft

Chapter 1

A Village in Context

Swimbridge in the Landscape

Official documents are often justifiably criticised for their turgid prose and use of obscure jargon.

Full marks then to the anonymous writer who, in 1990, as the twentieth century prepared to enter its final decade, sat down to write the text that underpinned the case for the designation of most of Swimbridge village as a conservation area.

As an unspoilt village in attractive surroundings, it is no surprise that guide books over the years have fallen over themselves to heap praise on Swimbridge, using a range of adjectives from 'charming', to 'delightful' and describing the parish church of St James as 'a gem' and `a treasure house'.

Even the rather dry *Buildings of England* series, created by the austere German-born Sir Nikolaus Pevsner, devotes three pages to Swimbridge and uses descriptions such as 'grand', 'glorious', 'remarkable' and 'uncommonly lavish' in its critiques of the parish's grander buildings.

Tracking down enthusiastic descriptions of Swimbridge proved enjoyable and informative. But after sampling each new discovery, the author found himself returning again and again to the appraisal of the village produced by such an unlikely source (from a literary point of view) as North Devon District Council.

As a study of the potential Swimbridge offered for conservation area status, the council's appraisal naturally concentrated on the village's splendid setting in the North Devon landscape and on the quality and

The heart of Swimbridge for more than a thousand years, the bridge across the Venn Stream and the church of St James.

variety of its buildings.

Those who know and love Swimbridge hardly need reminding of the natural beauty of its surroundings, but it is encouraging to know that it can be appreciated even by detached and sometimes dour officialdom.

The village, attractive and thriving as it is, needs to be seen in a larger context, that of the wider civil and

The north-eastern extremities of the parish of Swimbridge lie on the fringes of Exmoor. Looking north east across the hamlet of Kerscott, the snow-dusted foothills of the moor are visible in the distance. (Jessica Duncan)

The view north west from Bydown across the neighbouring parish of Landkey to the Taw Estuary and the market town of Barnstaple on the right hand side of the view.

Looking north from Hannaford Lane across the village of Swimbridge to the hamlet of Yarnacott and the hills beyond.

ecclesiastical parish which until boundary changes in 2003 and in 2015, bore the Swimbridge name.

Civil parishes were formed in England under the Local Government Act of 1894, to take over local oversight of civic duties in rural towns and villages. The act created parish councils and district councils to rationalise the large number of bodies which had been created for a variety of activities such as public health, secular burials, water supply and drainage. It also finally removed secular duties from the ecclesiastical parish and gave them to the new parish councils.

The civil parish of Swimbridge as created by the 1894 act – the parish council actually met for the first time on December 31 of that year, chaired by Mr H. Chichester of Tree – was (and is, notwithstanding the boundary changes) bordered by no fewer than seven neighbouring parishes.

Working clockwise around Swimbridge from the north west, these are Goodleigh, Stoke Rivers, East and West Buckland, Filleigh, Chittlehampton, Bishops Tawton, and Landkey.

At the end of the twentieth century Swimbridge parish extended to 11.375 square miles or 7,280 acres (2,946 hectares). Since the year 2000 two significant boundary changes have taken place, depriving Swimbridge of approximately seventeen and a half per cent of its territory.

In 2003 Swimbridge Newland, to the west of Swimbridge, was transferred to Landkey, a parish to which it was physically attached. The move cost Swimbridge parish 174 acres (70 hectares) or approximately a quarter of a square mile.

In May 2015 a further and much larger change occurred, with a substantial section of the southern part of Swimbridge parish, taking in Cobbaton, Travellers Rest and Stowford, becoming part of Chittlehampton. With this transfer Swimbridge lost 1,250 acres (505 hectares) or just under two square miles.

Since the millennium Swimbridge has thus lost 1,424 acres (576 hectares) or two and a quarter square miles from its territory.

The boundary changes which took effect in 2003 and 2015 had in both instances been requested by residents, of Swimbridge Newland and the settlements in the southern part of the parish respectively, and then ratified by a referendum.

In both instances a majority of voters felt a closer attachment to, in the first case Landkey and in the second to Chittlehampton.

The voting figures for the transfer of Swimbridge Newland were 168 in favour of linking with Landkey and 78 against, with a reported 75 per cent turn-out.

The figures in respect of the Cobbaton/Travellers Rest/Stowford area were 70 in favour of leaving and 42 who wished to retain the status quo.

In 2003 the membership of Swimbridge parish council was reduced from eleven to eight councillors, to reflect the decrease in the size of the parish. No decrease in the number of councillors is expected to result from the 2015 boundary change, as Swimbridge council is now close to the minimum number of members.

An earlier attempt to transfer Swimbridge Newland to Landkey, in 1902, had been rebuffed. Legal representation hired by Swimbridge at that time cost £5.9s and 9d – just under £5.50p!

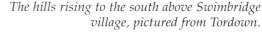

The hills rising to the south above Swimbridge village, pictured from Tordown.

The compact core of the village in the 1970s, showing St James' church and churchyard, Dennington Hill in the centre with the then still active Methodist chapel of 1898 on the corner. To the right of the junction of Dennington Hill and the main A361 road as it was at the time are Swimbridge's original council houses, built in the 1930s.

The Venn Stream, once liable to overflow, has been tamed by flood prevention works. The stream is placid in this shot as it wanders past the allotments on the side of Station Hill.

The eastern part of the village in the 1970s, showing the steep Kerscott Hill in the centre of the photograph. The first phase of the housing development to the north of the road (The Orchards) is complete. Bestridge Meadow, to the left of The Orchards, was later developed as housing.

Despite these changes Swimbridge remains one of the larger parishes within North Devon. The northernmost point of the parish remains the boundary with Stoke Rivers, situated to the north of the unclassified road which runs from the A399 at Brayford, through the hamlets of Stone Cross and Gunn to Goodleigh, and eventually on to Barnstaple.

The population of Swimbridge parish has varied throughout the twentieth century and the first decade or so of the twenty-first century. Figures provided by the Office for National Statistics following the 2011 Census give the population of the parish as 1,005 – 506 males and 499 females. It is expected that the loss of the southern part of the parish will reduce the population by around 180 people.

The 2011 Census figures revealed that more than 97 per cent of the population gave their ethnic status as being of English, Scottish, Welsh or Northern Irish origin.

About nine per cent of the population at that time classed themselves as disabled in the sense of a disability limiting day-to-day activities or a long-term health problem. In terms of age groups, 23.87 per cent of the population were aged between 0 and 24 years, 52.74 per cent between 25 and 64 years and 23.39 per cent were over 65.

From its northern boundary with Stoke Rivers, Swimbridge parish runs in a southerly direction, past the settlements of Accott, Tordown and Yarnacott, into the valley of the Venn Stream, a tributary of the River Taw. The entrance to the village proper is marked by the physical dividing line of the North Devon Link Road, once the track of the Taunton to Barnstaple railway line.

In the centre of the village, situated on the valley floor, the former A361 road between South Molton and Barnstaple, unclassified since the opening of the Link Road, forms an east-west channel of communication across the parish.

Steep and narrow lanes climb from the main road to the ridge which forms the village's southern horizon, leading to the settlements of Kerscott, Bydown, Dennington, and Hannaford, all still part of Swimbridge parish despite the 2015 boundary amendments.

The parish as originally constituted fell away from the high ground, taking in Irishborough/Ernesborough, Stowford and eventually Cobbaton/Travellers Rest. The pre-2015 southern boundary lay along the course of another tributary of the Taw, the Hawkridge Brook, between the villages of Chittlehampton to the east and Umberleigh to the west.

From east to west the greatest width of Swimbridge parish in 2015, is around 4 miles, lying either side of the former A361, from the boundary with Filleigh, to the east of Kerscott, to a point close to the summit of Hangman's Hill and the boundary with Landkey.

Looking west up Barnstaple Hill, traffic-free except for a horse and cart, about to pass the Baptist chapel on the right of the photograph. The view dates from 1933 and although light by later standards, motor traffic did use the road, as evidenced by the petrol pumps at the village post office and stores.

The village of Swimbridge lies at the foot of the shallow valley formed by the watercourse of the Venn Stream, which runs diagonally from northeast to southwest through what is essentially a compact settlement clustered around its major architectural feature, the parish church.

Fertile, and in many instances gently-sloping agricultural land, an abundant supply of water for both people and livestock, together with a river small enough to be forded and eventually bridged, but with sufficient force to act as a source of power, are ample reasons for the suitability of the site for human settlement.

The first people to establish themselves on the banks of the Venn were probably Saxons. The settlement existed prior to the Norman conquest in 1066, with a church and a resident priest, although the first written record of the existence of a village came two decades later, after the Normans had surveyed their newly acquired assets and documented them in the Domesday Book of 1086.

The most authoritative interpretation of both the development of Swimbridge as a settlement, and the origin of its name, stem from William George Hoskins (1908-1992), a proud Devonian who is widely recognised as the father of the academic discipline of English local history.

Although the bulk of Hoskins' professional career was spent at the universities of Leicester and Oxford, the history of his native county was always at the

Professor William George Hoskins, the father of English local history, encouraged Swimbridge historian Cecil Grimmett in the early 1950s. (Leicester University)

heart of his research and writings. Born at Cullompton and educated at the University College of South West England (now the University of Exeter) he was first Reader in, and later Professor of, English Local History at Leicester.

Hoskins reached the conclusion that the key to understanding local history was the land. He argued his views in what is regarded as perhaps his major work, *The Making of the English Landscape*, published in 1955.

He gloried in being descended from six centuries of Devonshire yeomen farmers, churchwardens, constables, overseers, bailiffs – with his forebears rarely, as he admitted, rising much above these modest stations in life.

Hoskins was a great encourager not just of those who shared his interests professionally, but also of local historians. He corresponded regularly with Cecil Grimmett, who was Swimbridge's resident policeman in the middle years of the twentieth century, and a keen historian who can be seen as a forerunner to Mervyn Dalling in the role of village chronicler.

Following the Norman invasion the office of priest in Swimbridge was held by a man called Sawin (or Saewin), who is believed to have succeeded an uncle (Brictferth) in the post. Writing to Cecil Grimmett in 1955, Hoskins confirmed the origins of the Swimbridge name and its gradual evolution, saying:

"There is no mystery about the name Swimbridge. There was evidently a bridge here in Saxon times, over the tributary of the Taw, and the estate was called Bridge (like Bridgerule on the Tamar).

"The Saxon word for bridge is BRYCG. Birige, as Swimbridge is referred to in the Domesday Book, is a corruption.

"Later, to distinguish it from other estates called Bridge, it was given the name of Sawin's Birige, Sawin being the office holder in 1066, and so eventually we get Swimbridge."

The fact that the church was the landowner at Swimbridge in those early Norman times, and for many generations to come, prevented the establishment of a dominating manor house in the village.

When the Lordship of the Manor passed from the hands of the Church it was assumed by the Russell family, Dukes of Bedford, who were major local landowners in Devon but never established a residence in the north of the county.

A well-defined social hierarchy did nevertheless develop in Swimbridge parish (explored in more detail in Chapter One, *A Village and its People*), headed by landowners drawn from the aristocracy, in the case of the Russells and the Fortescues of Castle Hill in the neighbouring village of Filleigh.

Other local families also enjoyed substantial land holdings, including the Chichesters of Hall in the parish of Bishops Tawton, and the Rolles of Stevenstone.

Within the boundaries of Swimbridge parish itself, gentry and yeoman families including the Notts and the Burys built or acquired mansion houses in outlying hamlets, and the village itself saw the construction of substantial domestic properties of the townhouse style linked to professional people, the clergy, prosperous farming families and, from the nineteenth century onwards, the proprietors of the tannery business once it had been established on an industrial scale rather than as a cottage industry.

Away from the initial settlement on the banks of the stream, the village and the wider parish of Swimbridge developed gradually over the centuries. Employing the W. G. Hoskins theory of local history being inextricably linked to the landscape, the inhabitants harnessed the natural advantages of their environment to the evolving skills of agricultural husbandry, and the technology which enabled the development of related pursuits such as milling and leather tanning, and the extraction of the area's abundant mineral wealth.

The high ground that surrounds the village reaches its ultimate height, and most would say the peak of its

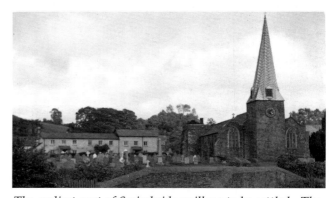

The earliest part of Swimbridge village to be settled. The church of St James, with Church Cottages to the left and the bridge in the foreground, is part of the village conservation area, although some changes have been made to the appearance of properties.

The well-wooded chert hills to the south west of Swimbridge, photographed from Bydown.

visual beauty, to the south and south west, in the form of Hangman's Hill, Coddon Hill and Hearson Hill.

Swimbridge is on a geological divide, with the northern part of the parish containing rocks of the older Devonian geological period, with the southern area based upon the Culm Measures of the Upper Carboniferous era.

The high ground to the south, with its whale-backed hills including Hangman's Hill and Hearson Hill were created by chert* rocks, which extend south to Codden Hill, outside the parish boundary but visible from some viewpoints and the highest point in the area.

The core of the village itself, in the valley bottom, stands on a narrow band at the junction of the two geological regions, made up of sandstone, limestone and slate of the Lower Carboniferous era.

The centre of the village, The Square, photographed from Hooda Hill before the opening in 1988 of the North Devon Link Road. The road through the village was then the main A361 road from Barnstaple to Taunton. The shop on the south side of the road is still open. The tannery buildings behind the shop have been partly cleared.

The location of the village ensures that, viewed from any direction, from its streets, from the centrally-situated square, from the extensive church-yard, the forecourt of the surviving public house, and from the ancient (pedestrian) bridge over the Venn which has traditionally represented an important meeting place for villagers, the backcloth is formed by unspoilt green hillsides.

If the village and its residents can hardly fail to look upwards to the hills, the traveller approaching Swimbridge from either direction along the Barnstaple-South Molton road has an elevated view across the settlement, looking down and across the varied assortment of buildings.

Although superficially the heart of the Swimbridge of today (2015) appears remarkably similar to the village depicted on photographs taken in the early part of the twentieth century (and indeed consider-ably earlier), in reality the differences between the two eras are very marked.

The twenty-first century Swimbridge is essentially residential, a popular destination for those who have come from other parts of the country to live in North Devon and to work in the regional centre of Barnstaple, just 4½ miles away, with adequate road access to the town and, by rural standards in North Devon, a good bus service.

The part of the village with the most urban appearance, High Street , was in the past the location for a pub, a school and shops. It is today wholly residential.

The village's proximity to Barnstaple (and to a lesser extent to South Molton, 7 miles distant), meant that true self-sufficiency as a village community disappeared long before the start of the twentieth century.

Although a certain amount of buying and selling traditionally took place within the parish boundaries, farmers and their wives were for the most part reliant for trade on the markets in Barnstaple and, to a lesser degree, South Molton, with goods being carried from the village initially in panniers and baskets slung on pack animals and later carried by horse-drawn trap and cart.

The Pannier Market in Barnstaple and the adjacent Butchers Row, designed to accommodate more than 30 shops, opened in 1855 and succeeded less formal markets in the High Street. South Molton's Pannier Market was opened in 1864.

Access to traps and other wheeled vehicles meant that, for the better off in particular, shopping and social activities in an urban setting were possible.

---

*Chert is a fine-grained silica-rich microcrystalline, cryptocrystalline or microfibrous sedimentary rock that may contain small fossils. In some areas, chert is common as stream gravel and fieldstone and is currently used as construction material and road surfacing. Part of chert's popularity in road surfacing or driveway construction is that rain tends to firm and compact chert while other fill often gets muddy when wet.

For the cottagers, the development of carrier services between the village and the towns offered an alternative to walking, and the coming of the railway in 1877 and of regular bus services in the 1920s opened up local travel to all but the very poorest residents.

The transfer of education for senior pupils from the village school to Barnstaple or South Molton at the end of World War Two and, as the twentieth century progressed, and the shrinking number of employment opportunities in agriculture, quarrying and the tannery industry forced more and more village people to seek employment in the towns.

Before the growth in private car ownership in the late 1950s/early 1960s, The Square in Swimbridge in the early morning presented quite a bustling scene, with significant numbers of schoolchildren and workers waiting for buses to town. Public transport still plays a role, despite the massive increase in car ownership.

Looking down Barnstaple Hill to The Square, which at the time of the photograph, believed to be in the Edwardian era, was the location of cottages, visible in the centre. To the right of the cottages, demolished after World War Two, is the road bridge and the former shop premises, which at this period were thatched.

During the first half of the century, the mix in the village of housing, commercial premises and industrial sites, all cheek by jowl within a relatively confined area, was significant.

Hooda Quarry and the tannery (both described in greater detail in a later chapter) were both within a stone's throw of The Square and the parish church. Interspersed among the houses were the workshops and yards of craftsmen, including blacksmiths, a wheelwright and carpenter, and a stonemason, and stabling for a haulage and contracting business employing heavy draught horses.

The village at the dawn of the twentieth century was comparatively self-sufficient, with at least three grocery shops, a butcher's shop with its own slaughterhouse attached, a post office, a tailor, two shoe and boot makers, several dairies offering milk deliveries, three public houses, three places of worship, a school,

a boarding house, and a railway station offering passenger, parcels and goods services.

In the outlying hamlets were four other places of worship, another school, at least two more licensed houses, and a flourishing rural self-help economy with a variety of self-employed craftsmen and tradesmen offering their services to farmers and others.

The village today remains in a far more favourable position than many equivalent settlements, retaining an excellent school, a lively parish church community, a pub, an enlarged village hall, and a post office/store, but much of its former vitality, in an economic if not a cultural sense, has been lost.

A modern view looking down Barnstaple Hill towards The Square, with the tower and steeple of St James' church in the background.

A tour of the village presents not just a snapshot of its present-day character as a thriving community, but also reveals a great deal of its more recent past, in the shape of public, commercial and industrial buildings which have survived the loss of their original purpose to play a continuing role.

The heart of the village, and the natural place for the start of a tour, is the area around The Square, taking in the parish church, pub and post office. Although the village core is compact, what can fairly be described as minor ribbon development has, for at least two centuries, served to stretch Swimbridge outwards and upwards.

The road to Barnstaple, as it climbs out of The Square, is a microcosm of how the village has expanded and developed over the course of a couple of centuries.

Barnstaple Hill is the location for some of the most

The western end of Swimbridge village, The school is towards the top of the picture, with the Victorian former Vicarage, now divided into two dwellings, in the centre. In the bottom right hand corner are new homes in Liverton Drive.

interesting domestic architecture of the early nine-teenth century, taking in the late Georgian period, the twentieth century and, in contrast, for a largely sympathetic twenty-first century housing development. It contains a substantial red brick Victorian house, which for nearly a century was the vicarage but which is now divided into two apartments – the fate of many parsonage houses throughout the country.

The main road on the Barnstaple side of the village is also rich in public buildings.

It boasts the late 1930s village hall (greatly extended in 2015), an early-nineteenth-century Baptist chapel (now converted to a dwelling) and, as the road leaves the built-up area, the Victorian school and the original residence of the headteacher, now used as additional teaching accommodation.

In the opposite direction leading out of The Square, towards South Molton, the streets and lanes north and south leading off the main road represent the main core of the village, situated closest to the church.

To the north of the main road can be found narrow thoroughfares including Church Lane (known locally as Ching Chang's Alley, a nomenclature believed to derive from Anglo-Saxon). At the junction of Church Lane and the main road are the buildings which once

The old forge, before the construction of St Honorine du Fay Close on the other side of the main road. One of the taps which formed the old water supply, with a B denoting the donor, the 9th Duke of Bedford, is visible at the road junction in front of the forge.

constituted the village's last working blacksmith's forge.

Further along the main road on its north side is the junction with the High Street, which presents an almost urban appearance and which in the past was the site not only of residences but also of commercial premises, including the Lamb and Flag Inn (licence revoked in 1909).

Another public house stood at the corner of High Street and the main road. The Coach and Horses, dates from the era when the main highway between Barnstaple and South Molton, which formerly ran along the high ground through Bydown and Kerscott, was diverted to pass through the village. The pub, which once had a thatched roof, survived a major fire in 1953 but closed its doors as a licensed house circa 1970.

Chapel Court, which leads off the High Street shortly after its junction with the main road, was the site of the village's original Wesleyan chapel, opened in 1816, which closed in 1898 and was converted into a dwelling.

High Street leads on to Watergate, which in turn gives access to Mill Court, the last real working farm to operate (until the end of the 1960s) in the village centre. Both the farmhouse and the farm buildings were later converted for residential purposes.

On the south side of the main road in the South Molton direction, leading upwards to settlements including Bydown, Dennington and Hannaford, are lanes of a much more rural character.

house in the village, built circa 1830 and now listed.

Following the road along from The Square in the direction of South Molton, a substantial site on the corner of Dennington Hill is occupied by the village's second Wesleyan Methodist chapel, opened in 1898. Like its Baptist counterpart, the chapel and adjoining schoolroom is now a private dwelling.

The first major twentieth century developments in the village are on the South Molton side of The Square, including on the south side of the main road two pairs of semi-detached council houses from the 1950s at High Cross and a 1980s' development of private and social housing at Honorine du Fay Close, named after Swimbridge's French twin town.

On the north side of the main road, past the former Coach and Horses pub, is the site of Town Tenement, another farm/dairy business which operated in the village centre well into the twentieth century. Further along the north side is The Orchards/Bestridge Meadows development. The first family to move in to the new bungalows in February 1971 were the Knights – Vera and Dennis and their children Raymond, Marilyn and Julie.

The churchyard, again pictured before the development of St Honorine du Fay Close. The Venn Stream flows in the foreground but is hidden by vegetation.

The Orchards housing development, of the early 1970s.

The Jack Russell (the New Inn until 1962) is the only one of the three licensed premises which existed in the village itself into the twentieth century to survive to the present day, and is a focal point for village life. It occupies a prominent position on the main road, opposite the main entrance to the parish church and stands on the corner of Hannaford Lane, which was the main access to the site of the tannery, closed in the 1960s and since then used, with fluctuating success, for light industry.

The tannery proprietors, like the mill owners of more industrial areas of Britain, lived for well over a century adjacent to their works, chiefly in Tannery House, in what is perhaps the most distinguished

The allotments by the side of the Venn Stream have provided a major source of food for local residents. Hooda Hill broods over the scene

Station Hill led, logically, to the village's railway station. The down platform used by trains to Barnstaple is shown, with the signal box to the left, and the booking office and waiting area to the right. On the road above, close to the road bridge, is the former station master's house, demolished to make way for the North Devon Link Road.

Returning to The Square itself, once occupied by cottages (as was part of the churchyard) a road is thrown off to the north. Station Hill, from 1877 to 1966 led to the railway station, and also gave access to a quarry active until the 1950s.

Despite its many impressive vistas, and notwithstanding the impressive presence of the parish church, the most dominant image of Swimbridge taken away by visitors is the view (from several vantage points) of Station Hill.

It is this view that inspired the author of the Swimbridge Conservation Area Character Appraisal to come up with a description that the author wishes he had thought of himself: "Hooda Hill, to the north-east of the parish church, is a prominent natural landmark on the edge of the village, with a single line of housing development seeming to *wrap itself around its lower slopes.*"

The best descriptions always seem obvious once you have discovered them.

Simple as it may be, the unknown writer's view of Station Hill makes the description in the Devon volume of *The King's England*, of 'a row of charming cottages climbing around the hillside' seem almost banal.

Station Hill also leads to another development of council housing, Archipark, built in 1951. Many of the properties are now in private ownership.

Continuing towards the site of the former railway station, on the west side of the road and overshadowed by the bulk of Hooda Hill, is another modern development of bungalows, known as Hooda Close.

On the eastern side of Station Hill are two connected houses built in 1911 by the prominent Dunn family, farmers, dairymen, landowners, and staunch supporters of the Methodist cause in the village.

A detached house built by the Great Western Railway in the 1930s for its Swimbridge stationmaster stood at the junction of Station Hill and Road Lane, a thoroughfare which gives direct access from

The finger post at Bydown Cross points not only to the neighbouring villages and parishes of Landkey and Chittlehampton but also to three hamlets traditionally contained within Swimbridge parish – Dennnington, Cobbaton and Hannaford.   Cobbaton was transferred to Chittlehampton in May 2015.

Accott Manor, one of the earliest sites of human habitation in Swimbridge, pictured when it was no longer a dwelling, simply being used for storage.

The ruins of Accott Manor have been turned by owners Tom Oliver and Liz Pile into an attractive and highly imaginative garden, retaining many of the features from its time as a farmhouse.

the northern half of the village and the hamlets of Yarnacott and Riverton to the South Molton – Barnstaple road at Marsh Cross.

The actual village of Swimbridge is, despite boundary changes, still only a relatively small part of the greater ecclesiastical and civil parish which bears the same name.

Describing an imaginary walk around the comparatively compact area of the village is an easier task than attempting to repeat the exercise within the boundaries of the wider parish, certainly as they existed for the greater part of the twentieth century.

To the north of the Link Road the countryside around the settlements of Yarnacott, Yeoland, Riverton, Tordown, Coombe, Sandyke, Accott and Stone Cross, and the considerable hamlet of Gunn is satisfying walking country, with extensive views from the high ground to the Taw estuary, the North Devon coast and further afield to the hills of Dartmoor.

A circular route that takes in several of these settlements can be achieved by following the road from The Square in Swimbridge, via Station Hill and Yarnacott to Tordown Green, and then turning right to Tordown House and Tordown Farm. A further right turn leads to the narrow lane leading to Riverton and a return to the village via Yeoland Lane and Yarnacott again.

The lanes climbing out of the village to the south give access to the settlements of Kerscott, Bydown, and Hannaford, and eventually to Dennington, Cobbaton and Travellers Rest.

This southern part, much of it lost to Swimbridge parish under the 2015 boundary changes, contains many of the hamlets, sizeable farms, gentry houses, former churches, chapels and a school (at Travellers Rest), which have contributed so much to the history of Swimbridge.

Altogether Swimbridge parish before the recent boundary changes contained some 50 listed buildings – the parish church of St James is Grade One and the others Grade Two.

Chapter 2

A Village and its People
Swimbridge and Society

The bells that rang out from the tower of Swimbridge parish church to herald the dawn of the twentieth century resounded across a village which, like its counterparts elsewhere in North Devon and in other rural parts of England, was still marked by rigid class division.

The ringers in the church tower, and others throughout the village and wider parish who listened at midnight on 31 December 1899 for the peals that would mark a new century, had little reason at the time to suspect that they were standing on the cusp of major social change and upheaval.

Seen from the viewpoint of Swimbridge at the birth of the new century, the gulf between the social classes remained as wide as ever, although there were some small indicators of change.

Few villagers living at the lower end of the social scale in North Devon would have been more than vaguely aware that, elsewhere in the country, the age-old structures of society under which they lived their everyday lives had become much more fragile.

'Up country' (to use a traditional and often dismissive Devonian description of anywhere north of Bristol), a great many people now lived in towns and industrialised villages where almost the entire population was working class, with only a sprinkling of professionals and small tradespeople.

In many heavy industrial areas, the aristocracy and gentry, who had once lived in fairly close proximity to their servants and tenants (albeit behind the high walls of the parkland surrounding their halls and manors), together with the men who had made fortunes from the results of the industrial revolution – coal-owners, iron and steelmakers, mill proprietors and the higher ranks of business and trades people – had moved well out of the manufacturing towns and villages, to live 'above the smoke'.

The landowners and early industrialists had pocketed the profits from their pits' blast furnaces, and mills, and in the case of the landed classes their earnings from the ownership of the mineral rights lying under their broad acres, and had moved to a more acceptable environment.

In some cases they had little choice but to abandon their ancestral seats, when the coal seams which had brought them new riches ironically led to these same homes being destroyed by subsidence, or made virtually uninhabitable by smoke and dirt.

The bells of St James' rang out on New Year's Eve 1899 across a parish still marked by rigid social divisions.

Links between the gentry and working people in rural areas like Swimbridge were closer than those in the industrial midlands and north. The author D. H. Lawrence described the gulf between miners and coal owners as 'impassable'.

In the emerging mono-cultural industrial towns and villages, the traditional deference shown by the have-nots to the haves was rapidly breaking down.

The novelist D.H. Lawrence, born into a mining family in the Erewash Valley, on the Nottinghamshire/Derbyshire border, vividly described the attitude of the colliers to any surviving gentry.

"There was no communication between the hall and the mining village, none. No caps were touched, no curtseys bobbed. Gulf impassable, with a quiet sort of resentment on either side."

Caps were definitely still touched, if the occasion demanded, in Swimbridge and throughout North Devon. Social change would indeed come to rural villages in remote parts of England as the twentieth century progressed, but it arrived much later than in the industrial north and midlands.

Swimbridge in 1900 did not owe allegiance to any one dominating aristocratic landowning family. For the most part the major landowners in the parish had their residences outside its boundaries.

It was not the case that wealthy and influential families had been driven away by a deteriorating environment or economic disaster; they had never lived in Swimbridge in the first place.

For centuries the Lordship of the Manor was in the hands of the established church rather than those of any lay landowner. In pre-Reformation times, when 'church' meant Roman Catholic, a simple dwelling in the village rather than any grand mansion was all that was considered necessary for the resident (unmarried) priest.

When the title did eventually pass into secular hands, the new Lords of the Manor, the Russell family, Dukes of Bedford, were well established in their ancestral home at Woburn Abbey in

The family seat of Hugh, 4th Earl Fortescue, was in the neighbouring parish of Filleigh but the family owned land and exerted influence in Swimbridge

Herbrand, 11th Duke of Bedford, was a major benefactor to Swimbridge.

Bedfordshire, 350 miles from North Devon.

The Fortescue family, of Castle Hill, just 3 miles away, did have land and property holdings in Swimbridge parish, but in terms of influence they looked more towards their home village of Filleigh

The Palladian mansion of Castle Hill, Filleigh, the seat of the Earls Fortescue at the start of the twentieth century and still owned today by a branch of the family.

and to the market town (and for many years parliamentary borough) of South Molton.

Other major landowners in the parish in the nineteenth century whose wealth and position qualified them for inclusion among the ranks of the landed gentry, included the Hon Mark Rolle, whose seat was at Stevenstone, St Giles in the Wood, near Torrington, and the Chichesters, of Hall, near Bishops Tawton and Youlstone, near Shirwell.

The absence of a seat of the aristocracy in Swimbridge did not mean that there were no wealthy and influential families living within the parish boundaries. If the aristocrats occupied the highest point on the social ladder in the locality in the years before and after the turn of the 19th/20th centuries, on the rung just below them were the gentry families, themselves often long-established and wealthy.

The Notts of Bydown, Cobbaton, and Tordown, the Burys of Dennington, and others occupied lands and houses around the fringes of the village and were still a power (albeit a diminishing one) locally as the nineteenth century turned into the twentieth.

The land-owning aristocracy and gentry were joined on their lofty rung of the ladder by other individuals who claimed the rank of gentleman by virtue of birth, education, or the accumulation of wealth.

This category included the vicar, other professional people, and a considerable number of retired military officers (or their widows) living on their pensions. The higher reaches of local society also included

Tordown House, home in 1900 of the Harding-Notts and once occupied by the Rev John Russell.

Relative prosperity and Edwardian respectability in the Swimbridge farming community, displayed by Abner Tucker of Yarnacott and his family.

Frederick Richard Harding-Nott, his wife Leila and their daughter Florence, a gentry family pictured just before the start of the twentieth century at their Swimbridge home, Tordown House. The Harding-Notts of Tordown were a branch of the Nott family of Bydown.

those with private, unearned incomes, often originally derived from trade, and local entrepreneurs, including the owners of the tannery and local quarries, and a small number of the wealthier farmers, particularly those who owned their own land.

The bulk of the farmers across the parish, whether tenants of the major landowners, or landowners in their own right, essentially constituted a class of their own, although there were significant differences of status within their ranks.

Some were prosperous, farming large holdings and employing substantial numbers of employees. They often had other interests, in property or commercial ventures, quite separate from their primary agricultural activities. Others struggled to establish themselves and make farming pay.

A rung or two further down the ladder came those who enjoyed some form of authority in the community, among whom would be numbered the school master, the nonconformist clergymen, the postmaster and the Great Western Railway company's station master.

A trade in their hands. Wheelwright and carpenter William Henry Holland and his sons Jack (centre) and Tom (right).

Hard work for Vic Smart (left) and Ern Cox, handling hides at Swimbridge tannery

A flourishing business, in a largely self-sufficient community. Jim Balment delivers meat for his brother Charles' Swimbridge-based butchery.

The Swimbridge-based track gang work on the turnouts at the eastern end of the village railway station.

Swimbridge also had a substantial number of small-time business people, shopkeepers and self-employed craftsmen, who also formed a distinct class. Like the more prosperous farmers, they probably enjoyed larger incomes than many of the retired residents and those with limited unearned incomes but, in 1900, the fact that they had to earn a living from trade gave them a lower status than that enjoyed by the leisured classes.

Status meant something even towards the foot of the social ladder, occupied by those paid for their labour either weekly or, in some instances, by the day.

In agriculture, those skilled in handling stock, cowmen and shepherds, had better earnings and conditions than the general labourers, as did the foremen and more skilled workers in the tannery and the quarries.

On the railway, footplatemen, signalmen and booking clerks had greater responsibility and thus higher earnings and greater status than the porters and platelayers.

A sub-section of those at the bottom of the social pyramid was formed by those in domestic service of one kind or another. Here too there were further social divisions, with higher servants enjoying greater status than those who rarely appeared 'upstairs' in the grander houses.

Young people from Swimbridge crossed the parish boundaries to seek positions as either indoor or outdoor servants at the big houses like Castle Hill and Hall. The gentry houses in the parish itself, at Bydown, Dennington, Hannaford, Tordown, Yeoland and elsewhere would, at least in the first few decades of the twentieth century, have continued to employ substantial numbers of domestic staff, coachmen, grooms, gardeners and perhaps gamekeepers.

Domestic help would not have been restricted to

the gentry; the more prosperous farmers would have employed help inside the farmhouse as well as on the land and those professional and business people the directories of the time classed as 'Private Citizens' would also have had their domestics.

At the very foot of the ladder, below even the general labourers, were the elderly and those unfit or unwilling to work, who in the days before the introduction of pensions and other benefits were dependent upon help from their children or the generosity (or otherwise) of the Poor Law Guardians.

If the children themselves were unable to assist and the meagre official handouts of the day were insufficient, the poor could obtain assistance from village charities controlled by the Feoffees. Feoffee is a Middle English term, derived from Anglo-Norman French, denoting trustees holding freehold property for charitable purposes.

The Feoffees still function in Swimbridge as a charitable organisation, although no longer owning property in the village to fund their good works.

If all other official or charitable sources proved insufficient for a poverty-stricken individual or family, the last resort was the dreaded workhouse.

It is time to examine in more detail the families and individuals living in Swimbridge parish as the twentieth century began, dividing them into four sections – firstly the aristocracy, gentry, professionals and large-scale employers of labour; the farmers; the tradespeople, skilled craftsmen and those in positions of authority; and finally those who earned their living from manual labour, including most of those in domestic service.

At the top of the social ladder

The fact that most of the great landowners in Swimbridge in the latter years of the nineteenth century and the opening decade of the twentieth century did not actually reside in the village or parish did not mean that they were without influence, much of it of a beneficial nature.

In the last decade of the nineteenth century the Dukes of Bedford sold most of their land holdings in Swimbridge parish. It would be fair to say that in 1900 their influence was waning, but it would be unfair not to acknowledge the fact that the Russells gave a great deal to Swimbridge over a long period of time, with the range and practicality of their benefactions indicating an informed interest in village life. The Fortescues of Castle Hill also made generous benefactions.

When the Lordship of the Manor of Swimbridge passed into the secular hands of the Russell family, successive Dukes of Bedford, there was no question of their main home at Woburn being superseded.

Despite their extensive land holdings and mining interests in Devon, the Russells contented themselves with a town house in Exeter and with what was somewhat ingenuously termed a 'cottage' at Endsleigh, above the Tamar valley, which stood in a park of 3,400 acres!

The Bedford land holdings across Devon had been extensive, estimated in the last quarter of the nineteenth century as embracing more than 22,000 acres and producing an income of nearly £50,000 a year.

Although the return from their North Devon lands around Bydown and Dennington, at Smalldon and in other parts of Swimbridge parish was not insignificant, the income was much less than that which flowed from holdings and mineral rights in and around Tavistock, a town effectively 'owned' by the Russell family until shortly before the 1914-18 War.

The Russells' recorded benefactions to Swimbridge began in the mid-nineteenth century. Swimbridge School, on Barnstaple Hill, was opened in 1866, built on land given by the 8th duke, William Russell. He died in May 1872, unmarried and the title passed to a cousin, Francis Hastings Russell, a Liberal politician.

A year after succeeding to the title, the 9th Duke visited Swimbridge School – a rare example of a visit to the parish by a member of the Russell family. The school in turn marked significant Russell family events, giving tea to the children in October 1876 to mark the marriage of the 9th Duke's son.

The Russell family also supported both the established and the dissenting churches. In 1877 the ninth Duke gave land for the enlargement of the churchyard, and when the parish church of St James was extensively restored in 1880 he donated the substantial sum of £500 towards the cost.

The 11th Duke, Herbrand Arthur Russell, who held the title for almost half a century until his death in 1940, was the last Russell to hold the title of Lord of the Manor of Swimbridge, selling off a large part of the family property in the parish in 1898. The final significant benefaction came during the same year when Herbrand donated a site for a new Methodist chapel off the main road through the village, at its junction with Dennington Hill.

Perhaps the greatest gift of the Russell family to Swimbridge was the provision in 1870 of a public supply of water, piped from Indiwell, east of the village, to six taps placed at strategic points.

The taps, all long removed, were located close to the old Forge; by the Methodist chapel; at Watergate in the heart of the old village; on Barnstaple Hill, to the west of the village centre; close to an entrance to Hooda Quarry on Station Hill; and adjacent to what is now the bus shelter and the Jubilee Hall.

The taps had a keystone with the date of their installation and a large letter B, for Bedford. They served the village until mains water arrived in 1950-51, at which point the Indiwell supply was discontinued. The use of the water supply for some eighty

Drawing water from the tap near the old forge, one of the six water points in the village donated by the 9th Duke of Bedford. Pictured with the bucket, shortly before mains water came to Swimbridge in 1951, is Mrs Elizabeth Ann Scott. Talking to Mrs Scott is Mrs Julia Vellacott, whilst blacksmith Bernard Ley and a young Ralph Sampson watch from behind the forge wall.

years, the school and the Methodist chapel ensured that the Russell family legacy has endured in Swimbridge.

The fame and fortune of the Fortescue family is said to date from the Battle of Hastings in 1066, when a Norman invader, Richard le Fort, saved the life of William the Conqueror by covering him with his shield. Richard was henceforth known, in Norman French, as *Fort-Escu* or, in the English translation, 'strong shield'.

At the start of the twentieth century the seat of the earldom was the Palladian mansion of Castle Hill at Filleigh.

Castle Hill was built in 1730 by Hugh Fortescue, 14th Baron Clinton, who in 1751 was created 1st Baron Fortescue and 1st Earl of Clinton. The house dominates the view from the road between Swimbridge and South Molton, which until the opening of the present A361 North Devon Link Road was the main highway from Barnstaple to Taunton.

The Fortescues, like their fellow North Devon landowners the Dukes of Bedford, were active in public and political life. Like the Russell family, they were on occasions generous benefactors to Swimbridge, but their main influence was, understandably, based upon Filleigh, where they built the church of St Paul, the school and other buildings, to the hinterland of the estate village, and to South Molton.

Hugh, the 4th Earl Fortescue who, as Viscount Ebrington (the courtesy title borne by the heir to the earldom) lived for a while at Bydown House in Swimbridge parish, was a Liberal politician who sat in the House of Commons until inheriting, and later took his place in the House of Lords.

Noted as a sportsman, particularly in the hunting-field, he died in 1932. He was succeeded as the 5th Earl Fortescue by his son, Hugh William who, in contrast to his father, was a Conservative politician.

During a distinguished parliamentary career he served under successive prime ministers Stanley Baldwin, Neville Chamberlain and Winston Churchill as a Lord-in-Waiting (government whip in the House of Lords), and during the period 1936 to 1945 as Captain of the Honourable Corps of Gentlemen-at-Arms (chief government whip in the House of Lords).

After Clement Attlee and the Labour Party won power in the general election of 1945, Lord Fortescue was chief opposition whip in the House of Lords. He was again Captain of the Honourable Corps of Gentlemen-at-Arms, under Churchill from 1951 to 1955 and under Sir Anthony Eden from 1955 to 1957. He was admitted to the Privy Council in 1952 and made a Knight of the Garter in 1951.

He married the Hon. Margaret, daughter of Wentworth Beaumont, 1st Viscount Allendale, in 1917 and the couple had four children. The heir, Hugh Peter Fortescue, Viscount Ebrington (1920–1942), was killed in action at the battle of El Alamein.

The 5th Earl died in June 1958, aged seventy, just four days after the death of his wife. As he had no surviving male issue, the 5th Earl was succeeded by his younger brother, Denzil. Although the title passed to his brother on his death, the 5th Earl left his principal seat, Castle Hill, to his elder surviving daughter, the late Lady Margaret Fortescue.

Lady Margaret held many appointments with various bodies and organisations in North Devon, and was a patron of the living of St James' church. Castle Hill is now the home of her daughter Eleanor, Countess of Arran. The other historic family residence, Ebrington Manor, Gloucestershire, is now the seat of the Earls Fortescue.

The present Queen Elizabeth II, as Princess Elizabeth, stayed at Castle Hill before succeeding to the throne.

If at the start of the twentieth century Swimbridge and its widespread parish lacked a single dominating seat of the aristocracy, it certainly possessed a substantial number of houses which the influential *Buildings of Britain* series, cataloguing the more distinguished architecture of the nation county by county, categorises as 'mansion' houses, often of considerable size and aesthetic value.

These properties were to be found on the fringes of the village itself, chiefly on the ridge of high land to the south, at Bydown, Denning and Hanniford, and to the north of the railway line, at Yeocot, Tordown, and Yeoland.

As the twentieth century was ushered in by the Swimbridge church bells, the majority of these houses were still in use as private homes, although in many cases changing economic and social circumstances had obliged their gentry owners to either sell or let the properties for occupation by people whose incomes were derived from trade and commerce as opposed to long-term land ownership.

In the case of the three gentry houses on the southern fringe of Swimbridge, Bydown, Dennington and Hannaford, the long–standing tradition of properties being handed down through successive generations of families was superseded, at first when the houses were let to tenants and, eventually, when they were bought and sold on the open market.

Unlike other outposts of Swimbridge parish such as Gunn and Cobbaton, these three southern hamlets, reached from the village by steep and narrow lanes, never possessed churches, chapels, schools or public houses.

Even today, in a twenty-first century which has brought an element of bustle even to North Devon, they exude a pleasant atmosphere of solitude and detachment.

The land surrounding the mansions at Bydown and Dennington has been farmed for centuries, under

The magnificent west front of Bydown House.

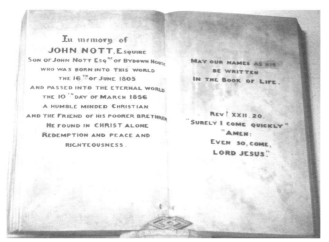

The memorial to John Nott of Bydown in Swimbridge church. Part of the inscription (top right) may have been deliberately obscured.

the successive ownership of families such as the Dukes of Bedford, the Maynes, Chichester and Rolles.

Each settlement had, in addition to the respective 'big house', dependent farmsteads and cottages, surrounded by well-tended farmland and rolling, well-wooded hills.

Bydown House is arguably, from an aesthetic and architectural point of view, the finest house in Swimbridge parish. The Bydown estate is believed to have originally belonged to the Mayne and Chichester families but later passed into the hands of the Notts, who were to have a long and, for a while, stormy association with Swimbridge.

In the mid-nineteenth century, Bydown was the property of John Nott who, although not the largest landowner in the area, was the only one of the local magnates to actually live within Swimbridge parish, with the result that he was regarded as the squire and the effective leader of local society.

Nott's land holdings in Swimbridge parish totalled some 900 acres, a figure roughly equal to the acreage owned by the Dukes of Bedford. In terms of acreage, the Chichester family owned around 1,000 acres, the Hon Mark Rolle had 750, whilst the Fortescues had around 60 acres.

John Nott was also leaseholder of the tithes, the taxes payable by farmers and others to the established Anglican Church, which he was required to collected and pay to the Dean and Chapter of the Exeter Diocese. Both positions, of squire and leaseholder of the tithes, were to bring Nott into conflict with the Rev. John Russell (a story told in full in chapter three of this book, *A Village at Prayer*).

Although earlier dwellings undoubtedly existed on the site, the present Bydown House, according to the British Survey of Listed Buildings, dates from the early nineteenth century (circa 1820-1830). The Devon volume of *The Buildings of England*, by Professor Nikolaus Pevsner and Bridget Cherry, devotes a specific entry to Bydown House, completely separate from the main Swimbridge section.

Pevsner and Cherry describe Bydown as a trim neo-Grecian mansion, standing in a small park, with two immaculate white stucco frontages, probably built at some time in the period 1820-1830. The house contains two date stones, one of 1758 and one of 1789, which had been re-set in the new house when it replaced an earlier dwelling on the site.

'Trim' and 'immaculate' are not the only positive adjectives to be used by Pevsner and Cherry in connection with the house. The entrance hall and central stair-hall merit the description 'handsome'.

At the start of the twentieth century Bydown was still owned by the Pyke-Nott family (the Pyke had been added to the Nott name as a result of a marriage and subsequent inheritance), but was occupied by Robert Jameson, a member of the Irish whisky distilling family, who later bought the property outright. He served in the Army in the 1914-18 war, and after being invalided out drove cars for the Red Cross in France.

The Pyke-Nott family produced a notable twentieth century artist and portrait painter, Evelyn Caroline Eunice Pyke-Nott (1870-1959), later known as Evelyn C. E. Shaw. In 1899 she married Byam Shaw, a painter, illustrator, designer and teacher.

Bydown was again on the market in 1917, when it was described as a residential estate with a main house and subsidiary buildings. No bid was forthcoming and the property was withdrawn.

Bydown House was later the home of Captain Frederick Phillips, who played an active role in the life of the village and was chairman of the parish council from 1919 to 1927. After his death in 1927 the property was put on the market again by his executors. The details advertised by the agents were more complete than at the previous sale a decade earlier, describing 'an integrated estate with, in addition to the main house, five cottages, extensive outbuildings and what was described as 'a capital farmery, with complete set of buildings'.

The new owner was a Mr Herbert May, who farmed the land throughout the 1930s but allowed the main house to remain empty.

The deteriorating situation in Europe and the outbreak of World War Two brought very different occupants to Bydown. Nazi persecution led to the widespread emigration of Jewish people from Germany and Austria, as Adolf Hitler's grip strengthened. Circumstances in late 1938 meant that it became imperative to send Jewish children abroad.

The Auslandhascharah movement was the overseas arm of the Youth Aliyah organisation, which aimed to train children and young people in Britain and elsewhere, with a view to their eventually emigrating to Palestine. The London office soon became the organisation's busiest, reflecting the popularity of Britain as a destination.

Youth Aliyah was created by Recha Freier, the wife of a Berlin Rabbi, in 1932 and combined productive agricultural training with educational and Zionist values, in a community which was a model for the latter kibbutzim in the post-war state of Israel,

The first settlement in England was at Great Engeham Farm, Kent, opened in June 1939 but when the English Channel county of Kent was designated off-limits to aliens, the group moved to the isolation of Bydown.

The headmaster at Bydown was Dr Fridolin M. Friedmann, a former headmaster of the Landschulheim of Caputh, near Berlin. Friedmann was a strict disciplinarian and life at Bydown was far from harmonious.

The Auslandhascharah movement was the overseas arm of Youth Aliyah which trained young Jewish refugees from Nazi Germany, with a view to them emigrating to Palestine. Bydown House was its British base during the early part of World War Two.

Bydown House in the modern era was divided into separate apartments. Businessman Martin James, the present owner, has bought back 95 per cent of the properties to recreate Bydown in its full glory.

Some of the young people put together a wall newspaper, described as 'betraying a subversive and even revolutionary streak among the young residents'.

The centre's lease on Bydown expired at the beginning of October 1941 and it was not renewed.

In later years the house was divided into apartments and the agricultural outbuildings also converted to housing. In recent years however the present owner of Bydown, businessman Martin James, has gradually bought back the apartments in a bid to restore the house to its original status as a

Dennington House, pictured in the 1940s. The Rev John Russell lived at Dennington after marrying Penelope, daughter of the Bury family who owned the property.

single dwelling. At the time of writing (2015) he had reclaimed 95 per cent of the property.

In sharp contrast to the separate section devoted to Bydown by Pevsner and Cherry in *The Buildings of England* Devon volume, the second mansion-style house on the southern outskirts of Swimbridge, Dennington House, fails to receive a mention of any kind.

This is perhaps particularly surprising given the house's connections with the Rev. John Russell.

The development of the Dennington estate over the centuries followed a similar pattern to that of its close neighbour at Bydown and the present house, built upon the site of earlier dwellings, is believed to date from the same period (1820-1830).

In 1656 following ownership by the Handford family and a branch of the Chichesters, the property came to be owned by the Burys, a connection that was to endure for more than 200 years.

When the direct Bury line died out in the mid-eighteenth century, the property passed to a distant relative from the Braunton area, Richard Incledon, who assumed the name of Bury in order to inherit.

Richard Incledon Bury was a distinguished officer of the Royal Navy who rose to the rank of Vice-Admiral of the Blue. He died, aged eighty, in 1825, following a fall from his carriage on his own driveway at Dennington. A year later, with Richard Incledon Bury's wife Jane still in possession of the property, their daughter Penelope married the Rev. John Russell.

When Parson Russell and his wife moved to the northern fringe of Swimbridge parish, becoming the tenant of Tordown House, Dennington became the home of their son, Richard Bury Russell, the head of a Barnstaple bank. Bury Russell and his father both died in 1883, the son at the early age of fifty-five, and Dennington and its estate was, for the first time in many generations, sold on the open market as opposed to being inherited.

The purchaser was the Rev. William Henry Thompson, who from 1868 had been Vicar of the Church of England parish of Exmoor. Exmoor Parish, the largest in Somerset, had been created in 1856 and the parish church of St Luke built at Simonsbath by Sir Frederic Knight, whose father John Knight had bought the old Royal Forest of Exmoor and, with the help of his son, had set about the task of reclaiming the rough grazing of the high moors to arable production, building farmsteads and attempting to exploit the minerals to be found on the moor.

At Dennington Thompson farmed an estate of more than 800 acres, living at Dennington House until the death of his wife in 1896, when he moved to Parracombe Rectory to live with his son-in-law and daughter, the Rev. John Frederick Chanter and his wife Rose Edith.

The Rev Thompson took a keen interest in agricul-

The Rev. John Russell pictured booted and spurred.

The Rev W H Thompson, former Vicar of Exmoor, who bought the Dennington Estate.

ture and this led indirectly to his death in the winter of 1908, at the age of seventy-six. He was noted for his weekly visit to Barnstaple livestock market, where he caught a cold which developed into bronchial pneumonia.

Chanter was the author of an early guide book to Swimbridge church, and later became Prebendary and Treasurer of Exeter Cathedral. Rose inherited Dennington on the death of her father. After the Rev. Thompson left Dennington for Parracombe the house was let to tenants including, for a short period, Viscount Ebrington, the heir to the Fortescue earldom.

In 1895 the house was leased to William Oliver Harris of Wootton Hall in Northamptonshire for a rental of £1,000 a year, which included rights of shooting and fishing on the Dennington estate. Harris died at Dennington in 1907 and from that point onwards the house changed hands quite frequently. Occupants during the first half of the twentieth century included a Major H.A.P. Littledale, Neville Waterfield, Lt Col W.R. Battye and a Miss

Charlotte Hogg, who founded a boarding school at the property.

North Devon in general, and Swimbridge in particular, was frequently chosen as a suitable place to live by former military men, when they retired back to England after serving the Empire, often in some of its most far flung and exotic outposts.

One of the more interesting occupants of Dennington House in the years between the two world wars of the twentieth century was Walter Rothney Battye, born in Rawalpindi, India, in 1874, the son of an officer of the Indian Army. Battye received his medical training at St Bartholomew's and St Thomas's Hospitals in London and won the Parkes Memorial Medal at the Army Medical School, Netley in 1898, passing in second place into the Indian Medical Service.

He was posted to an Indian Cavalry regiment and took part in the international expeditionary force to China which put down the Boxer Rebellion in 1900. He was transferred to the coveted political section of the Indian Civil Service in 1903 and served in Persia and Rajputana.

During World War One Battye, once again in the Indian Medical Service and now holding the rank of major, served at Gallipoli, where he was awarded the Distinguished Service Order (DSO), in France and in Mesopotamia (modern-day Iraq). Promoted Lieutenant-Colonel in 1918, he returned to India at the end of hostilities and was chief medical officer for central India before retiring in 1929.

Battye died in Bournemouth in 1943, having left Dennington prior to it being converted by Miss Hogg into a school – the fate of many substantial country houses at a time when their owners were finding such properties increasingly expensive to maintain as family homes.

Miss Hogg was succeeded at Dennington House by Percy and Mary Tisdall, who ran the school as a facility specialising in educating children whose parents were working abroad. The pupils became a familiar site in Swimbridge, as they were taken each Sunday to morning service at the parish church of St James.

Mr and Mrs Tisdall retired in the early 1960s and Dennington's time as a school came to a temporary close. The house was then the home of a Major Murphy, who played a role in Swimbridge life including acting as a mounted marshal for the village carnival procession.

The property reverted to educational use in 1967, when Colin and Barbara Osborne ran Dennington as a school for boys with behavioural problems.

From 1989 to the present day Dennington has focused on behavioural problems of a different, adult nature. It is the home of the Francis House hostel, which specialises in the rehabilitation of those with alcohol and drug-related issues.

Although Bydown and Dennington were the properties which could lay claim to the status of mansion-style houses, several other houses within the parish boundaries were and are worthy of note.

Hannaford House or Greater Hannaford, an eighteenth century building, stuccoed like Bydown and Dennington, with a central Venetian window and a ground floor room had a ceiling with rococo flourishes and an Adam fireplace, was occupied for several generations by the Hole family.

Dennington was not the only substantial property in Swimbridge to be ignored by Pevsner and Cherry. Tordown House, some two miles to the north of the village centre, was the one-time home of the Rev. John Russell, who rented the property in the absence at the time of a clergy house in Swimbridge.

The outbuildings at Tordown also appear to have been used by Russell to house his controversial pack of hounds. By 1906 Tordown was the home of Frederick Richard Harding-Nott, a member of a branch of the original Nott family of Bydown.

The Hole family relax on the lawns of their home, Hannaford House, during the long Edwardian summer. Rides in the pony cart were a popular diversion.

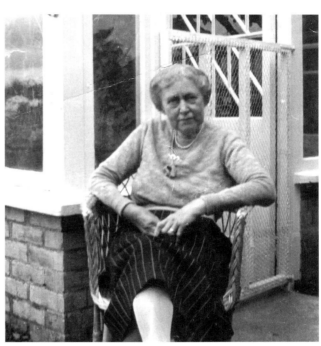

Mrs Leila Harding-Nott, at Tordown House in the late 1930s.

The village of Swimbridge itself has several dwellings of considerable interest. Tannery House, and Orchard House, a separate detached property further along Hannaford Lane were, until the final closure of the business in 1965, occupied by the successive owners/managers of the tannery.

The stuccoed, four-bay Tannery House, with a Doric porch with two columns, dates from the period, circa 1830, when leather working, a traditional village craft, was first industrialised.

A third property in Hannaford Lane, Tannery Cottage, formed the residence of the tannery foreman.

The farming community

The works of Thomas Hardy, the Dorset poet and novelist who understood the West Country and its way of life as well as any man, are proof that beneath the tranquillity of the countryside and its measured seasonal rhythms lurk tales of human triumph and tragedy equal to anything experienced in allegedly more lurid and edgy urban surroundings.

Thomas Hardy would have relished the themes of many of the stories that have been passed down from generation to generation within Swimbridge's farming families.

He would have recognised, even a century ago, that it took a stubborn attachment to the land and to a certain way of life to enable the farming industry to survive in a society which is usually ignorant of or indifferent to its economic importance, and often openly hostile to its practices and way of life.

The last hundred years or so has seen the aristocratic and gentry families that dominated life in rural villages and parishes like Swimbridge for generations either disappear from view or at the very least experience a significant loss of influence on day-to-day life.

The number of farming families has admittedly also declined, as economics have dictated that larger and more mechanised farm units are necessary for the industry to remain viable.

Yet whilst the names that dominated land ownership in Swimbridge in the nineteenth century – the Dukes of Bedford, the Notts and Pyke-Notts, the Hon Mark Rolle and others – are no longer influential, many of the farming families established in the parish a century or more ago are still working the land and playing significant roles in village life.

The Bartletts, the Balments, the Dallyns, the Elworthys (at both Dennington Barton and Bickle), the Shaplands (of Newtown), the Snells, and the Squire family (of Yarnacott) still till the land and raise their livestock in the parish. Others, like the Tuckers of Frogmore Farm, Cobbaton, no longer actively farm, but still live on the land their family has held and worked for generations.

Intermarriage within the community means that although several of the family names listed in the directories published during the early part of the twentieth century are no longer directly active in local agriculture today – the Westaways, the Squires (of Accott), the Symons, the Dunns, the Shaplands (of

The Squire family at Accott, circa 1875.

Above left: *The Elworthy family moved to Swimbridge and Dennington Barton as tenants of the Rev W. H. Thompson when he bought the Dennington estate. The Elworthys married members of other local farming families. Arthur Elworthy is seen with wife Marjory (née Symons) formerly of Marsh Farm.*

Above right: *Albert Westaway, his wife May and daughter Phyllis at Combe Farm.*

Left: *Phyllis Bartlett, nee Westaway, and her husband Sid, at Combe Farm.*

Kerscott) and several strands of the once extensive Yeo family – their descendants still live and often still farm in Swimbridge.

Thomas Hardy was right when he predicted that farming, one of the oldest occupations known to man, would always survive, whatever apocalyptic events shook the world.

As he foretold in *In the Time of the Breaking of Nations*, written in 1915 when Europe was in flames and and its empires and monarchies were threatened with extinction, it would be the farmer, 'harrowing clods in a slow silent walk' that would survive, 'though dynasties pass'.

For more than a century the farming families of Swimbridge have provided a valuable thread of continuity within a community which has seen much change during that time, including the virtual extinction of its once vibrant industrial base.

Some of those farmers have been landowners in their own right, often purchasing their farms during the period, around the turn of the nineteenth/ twentieth centuries when for various reasons the major landowners were selling their holdings.

Their individual family histories represent a price-less factual record, as opposed to largely romanti-cised fictional accounts, of how people actually lived, in good times and in bad times, in poverty and in comparative wealth, affected both by local factors which they could help to influence and by national and international events, such as economic depressions, world wars and changing social beliefs, over which they had no control.

Throughout the twentieth century, as in earlier times, men and women who could gain the use of a few acres of land on which to grow crops and raise livestock at least had a chance to raise their status.

The early years of the century saw many instances of men from the labouring classes acquiring some land, a factor which partially explains why the numbers of registered farms and smallholdings in Swimbridge expanded quite rapidly at the time.

The process of establishing a farm virtually from scratch was a far harder task than simply inheriting a holding from a previous generation as the experiences of those who took the first step towards agricultural prosperity often illustrate.

When Sergeant Albert Westaway's period of service as a regular soldier with the Royal North Devon Hussars came to an end in 1912, he was pleased to be able to get a foot on the farming ladder by securing the tenancy of Coombe Farm, which stands on the hills to the north of Swimbridge village.

Not long after getting the keys to the farmhouse, Albert's wife May gave birth to a child. It was a difficult delivery and she was unable to feed the baby herself.

Desperate for milk for the child, Albert set off on his bicycle to the livestock market at Blackmoor Gate, where he bought a cow and its calf.

The purchase complete, he started out on the 9 mile trek back to the farm.

The cow he drove in front of him; the calf, which could never have covered the distance unaided, he placed on the crossbar and seat of his bike, and pushed it all the way home.

The Westaways were to establish an alliance through marriage with another prominent farming family which had become established locally around the turn of the nineteenth/twentieth centuries.

The Bartlett family had farmed from the mid-eighteenth century in the parish of Clovelly, but moved to Swimbridge parish when James Laramy Bartlett bought Tree, at Gunn, from the Chichester family.

James Laramy Bartlett's son Sidney, born in 1913, married Phyllis Westaway of Combe, and the couple had three children, Albert (Bert), John and Christine. Sidney Bartlett purchased the nearby Sandyke Farm for £30,000 in 1968.

Today, Combe Farm is occupied by Bert Bartlett, whilst Sandyke is in the ownership of John Bartlett, who took over the farm after several years working for the Ministry of Agriculture, Fisheries and Food in the north west of England.

John later purchased the land which had previ-

Sid Bartlett's son John and his wife Margaret. John, who with son James farms Sandyke and land formerly attached to Accott has, like his father, chaired Swimbridge parish council and other village organisations.

ously been part of Accott Manor and today his son James is carrying on the family farming tradition at Sandyke.

(John Bartlett's knowledge of farming in Swimbridge parish and an account of his grandfather Albert Westaway's role with the local War Agriculture Committee during World War Two feature in *A Village at Work* chapter, which considers the more technical, as opposed to personal aspects of farming in Swimbridge parish.)

Farming has always been (and continues to be) a precarious business, dependent not just upon many factors, including the vagaries of the weather and an unpredictable demand for its products, to which in recent decades can be added increased interference from government and other bodies and a lack of public understanding of the industry's importance to the wellbeing of the nation.

The story of the Symons family, formerly of Marsh Farm, illustrates the life-changing potential of unforeseen external factors, such as the destructive effects of war.

Farming families such as the Symons, still mostly tenants rather than landowners, were well established and modestly prosperous in the early years of the twentieth century, with little reason to believe that within a relatively short time their lives would be completely disrupted by circumstances over which they had no control.

For the family at Marsh in the 1900s, which would eventually consist of seven children, five girls and two boys, day-to-day life offered hard work, ample if plain food, some domestic help in the farmhouse and simple, usually outdoor amusements. It was not a luxurious or easy life, but was far superior to the

The Shapland family of Newton, pictured in the early 1900s. Father John and mother Penelope are pictured at their respective ends of the front row, with daughter Penelope and son Christopher in between. Their children in the back row are, l-r, Lilian, Richard, John and George Henry.

Left: *Although many farming families in the early years of the twentieth century were comfortably off by the standards of the day, they were not immune from tragedy. Emily Symons, the wife of Walter Symons of Marsh Farm died in childbirth, leaving behind seven children.*

Below: *The Symons family at Marsh before World War One. Standing, l-r, Albert, Ernest (in his Volunteer uniform)., and Lillian. Sitting, l-r, Gertrude, Elsie, Kate, Walter Symons, and Marjorie.*

conditions experienced by the families of labourers.

Although most of the children walked the short distance each weekday to Swimbridge School the eldest son, Ernest, was educated from the age of twelve at West Buckland School, which had been established in 1858 for the sons of farmers and the middle class. The boy's fees were paid by a great uncle.

For the eldest girl in the family, Elsie Symons, born in 1893, childhood came to an abrupt end on Good Friday 1906, when she was thirteen. Premature (and by today's standards often avoidable) death was no stranger to the family, as it was to so many others rich and poor in that era. In addition to the surviving children, two other boys having died in infancy.

On that day her mother was brought to bed for the birth of a further child. In the absence of a telephone, a rarity in 1906, her husband, Walter, put his pony into the trap and drove to Barnstaple to fetch a doctor. Elsie, to the day of her death in 1975 at the age of eighty-two, remembered the minute detail of a day that was the first of several blows which over a decade or so were to shatter the family's existence.

She remembered that, perhaps unseasonably, the sun shone all day. She recalled her mother, despite her confinement, telling her how to make parsley sauce for the fish that was the traditional Good Friday meal.

The nurse in attendance at the birth constantly called for hot water, and Elsie remembered her frustration with the fire in the open fireplace that never seemed to heat the kettle quickly enough.

The new baby – another daughter – died. Elsie's mother lived until the evening, in agony for most of the time. The doctor, perhaps hardened to deaths in childbirth, asked the grieving Elsie her name and pulled her ear. "I always hated him after that," Elsie confessed when, many years later, she penned her account of the day.

For the next three years aunts and a housekeeper looked after Walter Symons and the children until, as Elsie recalled "I was sixteen and then we managed on our own."

For some time after her mother's death Elsie drove in the pony cart to Barnstaple Pannier Market to sell produce. "No-one had cars then, at least not farmers. The first time father saw one on the road he teased us all, saying he had seen a cart going along the road without a horse. We kept guessing until he relented and told us it was the new fangled motor car.

"The dust the cars caused was awful when one passed along the road and the children at Swimbridge school would run to the gates to see one pass."

Elsie Symons was eventually to marry John Herbert Squire, from a farming family able to trace its descent in Swimbridge parish back to 1509. Although life for her was to be long and fulfilling, tragedy was to continue to dog the Symons and lead

to them abandoning Marsh and farming altogether (see the chapter *A Village at War*).

The story of the Squire family is closely bound up with the history of Accott Manor, situated to the north of Swimbridge village, and one of the oldest settlements in the parish. Reputedly named after a Saxon landowner named Acca (also the source of the name of Acland, Landkey) the Accott lands originally comprised several farms and, like other holdings in Swimbridge, formed part of the Episcopal Manor of Bishops Tawton, with the first references recorded in the twelfth century.

Over the centuries Accott, still divided into separate farmsteads, came into the ownership of first the Giffard family and later the Chichesters of Hall, who held the property until the early 1900s and let it out to tenants.

One of these tenants was to be John Squire (1842-1924) who lived at Accott Manor for seventy years, never sleeping away from his home in all that time. Alliances between local families were commonplace, and John married Maria, a member of another local farming family, the Irwins.

After the Squire family had left Accott Manor the property was tenanted by James Mortimer, with East Accott farmed by William Lee. Shortly before World War One the Chichester family sold the Accott properties for estate duty reasons and they were bought by the Lee family

Because the new owners only required one farmhouse, the Manor House was used for storage. The thatch was neglected during the agricultural depression of the 1930s and in the 1950s the then owner, Wilfred Lee, son of William, abandoned the building altogether and pulled down the main chimney for safety reasons.

Wilfred Lee, during World War Two trapped for food the rabbits that were plentiful on the Accott fields and sent them to London by train from Swimbridge Station.

When Wilfred died in 1976 the Accott land, totalling 318 acres and including extensive woodlands, were purchased by Sid Bartlett. The buildings comprising Accott Manor were subsequently sold in 2006 and converted into dwellings. The ruins of the old manor house have been attractively landscaped.

Another family of long-standing in the parish is that of Elworthy of Dennington Barton and Bickle. The branch of the Elworthys at Dennington acquired their holding as a result of the purchase of Dennington House and the estate containing the Barton farm by the Rev. W. H. Thompson, mentioned earlier in this chapter.

In the last decade of the nineteenth century William Elworthy, the second son of Thomas Elworthy of Lower House, Simonsbath, worked as coachman, groom and gardener to the Rev. Thompson.

Members of the Yeo family at Yeoland in 1884. Thomas and Elizabeth Yeo (née Richards), who were married by the Rev. John Russell, are surrounded by their children, including William, Mary Margaret, Thomas, Grace, James (who emigrated to Australia) and Elizabeth.

An old and rare photograph of another branch of the Yeo family, at Bydown Farm. The farm disappeared during the course of the nineteenth century and the family is widely dispersed across the Commonwealth.

In 1883 (in the same year that saw the death of his father, the Rev. John Russell), the Barnstaple banker Richard Bury Russell died, aged fifty-five. Dennington, the family home of the Burys and subsequently the Russells, and latterly occupied by Bury Russell, was sold to the Rev. Thompson.

Some years after Thompson's purchase of the Dennington estate, William Elworthy, his wife Francis and their family moved to Swimbridge parish, with William becoming farm bailiff and tenant of Dennington Barton, which adjoined Dennington House.

William had twin sons, Arthur and Frederick. William's son Arthur, his grandson Charles, and now his great-grandson Spencer have carried on the family tradition at Dennington Barton into the fourth generation.

The Elworthy's have farmed Dennington Barton without a break for well over a century, staying put as Dennington House itself saw repeated changes of both ownership and use – a prime example of the continuity enjoyed by several farming families in Swimbridge parish.

The other twin, Frederick, after service in the 1914-18 war, took over Bickle from the Tossell family. The farm was continued by his son, also Frederick, and is now worked by his grandsons Christopher and Colin.

Perhaps the longest pedigree in the annals of agriculture in Swimbridge is claimed by the Yeo family. Although the name of Yeo can still be found on the electoral register and is inscribed on the headstones of a prominent cluster of graves in the parish churchyard, the clan's direct links with farming locally, which had endured for some 300 years, came to an end relatively early in the twentieth century.

Members of the Yeo family, of Bydown, Dennington, Yeoland and Yeocot, donated the bus shelter to Swimbridge in 1952. One of the last members of the farming family to live locally, Miss Grace Yeo of Yeocott (pictured holding a bouquet) formally opened the shelter. She later went to live in Australia.

For generations members of the family, either because of the tradition of handing over farms to eldest sons, restricting the farming opportunities open to younger siblings or, on occasions, the pressures exerted by depressions in English agricultural, had emigrated to the British dominions of Australia, New Zealand and Canada.

Perhaps the greatest contribution made by the Yeo family, apart from leaving their name scattered around Swimbridge parish, was to help develop the British Empire, where they gained a substantial reputation in their new homes not just for their farming achievements but for their work in importing high quality Devon livestock for breeding purposes.

The wedding of Hubert Snell of Tordown Farm and Mary Harriett Hubber, of Lower Hearson in Swimbridge parish. Beside the groom is his brother Walter. Next to the bride is her father, William Hubber, whilst on the right is the bride's sister, Winnie Hubber.

One of the last members of the Yeo family to follow in the steps of her forebears and emigrate to Australia was Miss Grace Yeo. In 1952, before leaving the village for a new life, Miss Yeo performed the opening ceremony for a new stone-built bus shelter in Swimbridge Square, a facility much appreciated then and now in inclement weather by local people waiting for a bus to Barnstaple.

A slate plaque in the shelter records that the facility was 'erected by the descendants of the Yeo family, of Bydown, Dennington, Yeoland and Yeocot.'

The Yeo family traced its descent from a Thomas Smale, who died at Swimbridge in 1573 and whose granddaughter, Cathryn, baptised in 1577, married a Roger Yeo.

By the middle of the nineteenth century, a James Yeo farmed a smallholding at the first named of the family holdings on the bus shelter plaque, Bydown. Situated not far from the Nott family's mansion of Bydown House, but separate from the 'big house' and owned by Dukes of Bedford, Bydown Farm is described as a tenanted smallholding of between 35 and 40 acres, with a farmhouse and outbuildings, orchards, meadows and areas of arable.

James Yeo, who died in 1874, married an Elizabeth Shapland, another name prominent in the history of farming in Swimbridge, in two separate branches. The couple had two daughters, Hannah Shapland Yeo and Elizabeth East.

Although the daughters are believed to have occupied the Bydown farmhouse for some time after James Yeo's death, the house disappeared at some point in the late nineteenth century, the Ordnance Survey map of 1891 showing no sign of the building.

The Yeo connection with the second holding named on the plaque, Dennington Barton, was severed not long after when, as recorded earlier in this chapter, the Elworthys moved from Simonsbath to take over the farm, which in its turn was part of the estate connected to Dennington House.

The third of the Yeo family holdings in Swimbridge to be recorded for posterity on the bus shelter plaque was also by far the most impressive. Yeoland House, a mile from the village in a north-easterly direction, on a minor road leading to the hamlet of Riverton and onwards to West Buckland, is an impressive late-Georgian period dwelling, clearly designed as a gentleman's residence.

When a branch of the Yeo family built Yeoland House (circa 1830) the site, on a south-facing slope with extensive views across the valley of the Venn Stream, was already occupied by a much older cottage, believed to have been constructed at some point in the seventeenth century.

The cottage, later known as Little Yeoland, may have been the sole surviving domestic property from what may have been a hamlet. It was re-modelled at the same time as the new house was being built and for many years the two properties were interconnected, with Little Yeoland accommodating servants working in the main house.

In the latter part of the nineteenth century and the first years of the twentieth century, Yeoland was still in the possession of the Yeo family, being shown as occupied at various times by the Misses Yeo and, in 1906, by Thomas Yeo.

As the twentieth century progressed Yeoland was farmed successively by the Tucker, Richards and Huxtable families, and for a time was owned by the Rev. Bruce Willis, chaplain at West Buckland School.

The house is built of rendered and painted stone, with hipped slate roofs. The two-storey building is symmetrical with a double-depth central staircase and a central porch with Tuscan columns and engaged pilasters flanking a round-arched doorway with a plain fanlight. There is a small cupola to the centre of the front range of the house, with a bellcote supported on timber struts.

In the twentieth century Little Yeoland was let to tenants as an separate dwelling, with an independent entrance. The connection with Yeoland House was ultimately broken when the two properties were sold separately.

Little Yeoland has been suggested as the home of the highwayman Tom Faggus, from R. D. Blackmore's Exmoor novel *Lorna Doone*. Faggus, like many other people who feature in the book, may have been based upon a real-life character.

It has been claimed that Little Yeoland was the scene of a daring escape by Faggus from the hands of the law. The house was surrounded but Faggus escaped by thrusting his hat on a pole up a chimney to draw the fire of his pursuers. When they were reloading their muzzle-loading firearms Faggus ran out

Yeoland House was owned in the late 1950s and 1960s by George Huxtable, another farmer who chaired Swimbridge Parish Council and was very active in village life. The family is seen on a visit to the Devon County Show. L-r, daughters Vera (Mrs Knight) and, in the pushchair, Brenda (Mrs Dyer), Mrs Amy Huxtable, and daughter Win (Mrs Babb). Behind Win is George Huxtable, in trilby hat, with son Arthur by his side. Arthur Huxtable and his family still own land at Yeoland.

of the house to his horse and made good his escape.

Today, the conversion of former farm buildings means there are four separate dwellings on the Yeoland site. The Huxtable family still own and farm the pastures in front of Yeoland House, stretching down to the Venn Stream.

The fourth Yeo family property on the plaque is Yeocot, situated on what is today the north side of the North Devon Link Road. This was the home of Miss Grace Yeo, unveiler of the bus shelter plaque, before she left for Australia. The house is now unrecognisable, being greatly extended to house a nursing home.

Kerscott, situated just off the Swimbridge to South Molton road at the top of the hill which bears the same name, is effectively a separate hamlet, now consisting of five separate properties.

For the greater part of the twentieth century Kerscott was associated with the Shapland family. William Shapland was established there as a farmer in 1902, having succeeded the Burden family.

By the mid-1920s the Shapland lands and properties had been divided; West Kerscott was farmed by William Russell Shapland Senior and East Kerscott by his son, William Russell Shapland Junior.

More relaxation from what was still the back-breaking work of hay harvest in the mid-twentieth century.. The Richards family of Mill Court Farm enjoy a break for tea in 1956. The group includes Mrs Frederick Richards, Mrs A. Richards, Leonard Dalling, Ernie Mogridge, Frederick Richards.

The Shapland family was active in the Methodist community and in village life in general throughout the twentieth century. William Shapland was chairman of Swimbridge parish council in 1917 and

Richard Lepper, once of the Royal Navy, retired to North Devon, and eventually to Swimbridge, like many other former officers. He is pictured while serving in India, accompanied by his turbaned groom.

William Russell Shapland Senior held the same position in 1949. The tradition was continued by William Russell Shapland Junior, chairman of the council in 1957 and 1962.

The former West Kerscott Farm, the most impressive of the properties at Kerscott, is today known as Kerscott House. Although the exact date at which the property was built is not known, it is thought to be the oldest inhabited site in the hamlet.

Formerly owned by the Dukes of Bedford, the property is known to have been remodelled in the late sixteenth century and extended in the seventeenth century.

It retains a wealth of character and is particularly noted for two ceilings in the drawing room and a bedroom. The ceilings have ornate plaster mouldings and are believed to date from circa 1590 and 1620 respectively. The main heavy oak entrance door has an ancient lock and key that is still operational.

Today Kerscott House is also renowned for its gardens and grounds, developed by the owners, Jessica and Duncan, from farmland. The gardens and grounds, which occupy some 14 acres, with landscaped woodlands, a water meadow and spring-fed ponds, have featured as a cover for the Royal Horticultural Society's magazine.

East Kerscott is the second grade two listed property in the hamlet. The house, of painted rendered stone rubble and cob, was remodelled in the seventeenth century and enlarged in the nineteenth century. It is noted for a surviving fire insurance plaque marked 'West of England, Exeter' located between central first floor windows.

Indiwell, formerly a farmhouse nestled in the valley below the road to Filleigh and South Molton off Kerscott Hill, was destroyed by fire in 1913 (illustrated on page 92). Villagers flocked to remove furniture and valuables from the property, which at the time was part of the Fortescue estate. The thatched roof collapsed leaving just the four walls standing. The house was later rebuilt.

Other notable buildings in the parish originally built as gentry residences but later farmed include Stowford and Irishborough (formerly Ernesborough). The former Irishborough Manor House was the birthplace in 1554 of John Cowell, Master of Trinity Hall, Cambridge and author of a dictionary of law terms.

Trade, craft or profession

Social status was of immense importance in the nineteenth and early twentieth centuries, to no lesser extent in North Devon than anywhere else in England. Novelists, particularly Anthony Trollope, whose works were later turned into popular television series such as *The Pallisers* and *The Barchester Chronicles*, wrote millions of words revolving around the all-embracing issue of class.

The distinction between a true gentleman or lady, and those slightly doubtful personal or business acquaintances regarded as the sort of people you might invite to dinner but would not dream of marrying, was narrow and occasionally complicated, and money talked, often blurring any issue of class distinction.

Swimbridge, at least until social barriers began to

It was not just retired military men who retired to Swimbridge on pensions or private incomes. Miss Risdon, who lived at Endsleigh, close to the railway station, was able to employ three village girls, working shifts, as her full-time carers. Miss Risdon is pictured left, with, l-r, Thirza Smith, Joan Dalling and Rose Dalling.

loosen somewhat, particularly after World War Two, was home to a fairly small number of people who sat somewhere below the ranks of the acknowledged gentry yet somewhat above the tradesmen, shop-keepers and skilled craftsmen and far above the mass of the labourers, tannery and quarry employees and other manual workers.

In the earlier decades of the century this profes-sional element within Swimbridge society was virtu-ally non-existent (directories for 1850 and again in 1878 list a surgeon) although the parish was favoured by retired military men of all ranks and maiden ladies (often sisters) living on unearned incomes.

The vicar (and probably his curate) would certainly have ranked as gentleman and would have been on visiting terms with the gentry. At a slightly lower social level would have been ranked the head-master of Swimbridge School and his counterpart at Travellers Rest School, together with their assistants, and the nonconformist ministers associated with the Methodist and Baptist chapels,

The village postmaster and the stationmaster employed by the Great Western Railway – in the early

Miss Penelope Shapland was one of the village's most prominent residents for much of the twentieth century. Born in 1874, she was baptised by the Rev. John Russell. She was a lifelong worker for St James' church and very active in the Conservative and Unionist cause. Her home at The Cottage (later known as Chapel House) was used as the Conservative committee rooms for the village.

Cecil Dunn, a talented artist whose water colours of Swimbridge are highly valued, worked in his family's dairy business until the end of World War Two. He is seen on Station Hill, delivering milk straight from his large can to customers' own jugs.

1920s this individual rejoiced in the splendid name of Jethro Chubb – would have enjoyed status as a result of their positions of authority. Another figure of authority, the resident policeman, was often seen as a man apart, no doubt respected by most but regarded with suspicion by others.

Villages, especially relatively large settlements like Swimbridge, were substantially self-sufficient in 1900. The commercial directories of the time identify a considerable number of trades people and self-employed craftsmen, ranging from the landlords of the four public houses operating in the parish at the time, the butchers, boarding house keepers, and general shopkeepers, to carpenters, wheelwrights, hauliers and contractors, boot and shoe makers, stone masons and rabbit catchers.

The trades people, shop-keepers and skilled crafts-men formed a bridge between the monied and leisured classes of society and the mass of the farm labourers, tannery employees, quarry workers, rail-waymen and other manual workers.

Until social barriers began to loosen in the middle years of the twentieth century, the trades people in particular had to be constantly aware of the need to offer an efficient service and, perhaps above all, a civil approach, whilst at the same time retaining a degree of independence and a social status in the community often well above that of their labouring neighbours.

It was by no means unusual for tradespeople in the parish to achieve prosperity and status in the community. One family prominent in the commercial life of Swimbridge through much of the twentieth century (and with descendants still living in the village in 2015) were the Dunns.

Originally farmers in the parish, in the early years of the twentieth century Henry Dunn owned the village stores in The Square and subsequently became the village postmaster. Henry prospered and in 1911 built a pair of distinctive houses (Endsleigh and Valle Vue) at the top of Station Hill, standing at right angles to the road, which at the time of writing (the early spring of 2015) were still in the possession of members of the family.

One of the houses was constructed for Henry's son, William Henry, who succeeded his father as postmaster and proprietor of both the general stores and of an associated dairying business. William Henry Dunn had two sons, Cecil and Ivan, both of who achieved considerable success in their chosen careers.

Cecil originally worked in the family business and delivered milk in the village. Following World War Two he took advantage of a fast-track scheme for training schoolteachers. After studying in St Albans, he went to Australia to teach art and married an Australian. Cecil and his wife later moved to Canada, where they worked with Cree Indians in the

After World War Two Cecil Dunn qualified as a teacher. He emigrated to Canada, where he taught Cree Indians, and later to Australia.

state of Ontario.

Cecil Dunn was a talented artist and amongst his substantial output were a number of water colours of scenes in and around Swimbridge. These works are highly prized by those who are fortunate enough to own them. Ivan Dunn worked in the postal service and rose to become head postmaster in Barnstaple.

The Dunn family were prominent members of the Swimbridge Methodist society. William Henry Dunn was a lay preacher and Ivan Dunn played the organ at the chapel.

William Brayley, who preceded Henry Dunn as postmaster, doubled up in 1906 as a tailor and the village had two butchers (one in Swimbridge Newland), two dairymen and a second general shop keeper. There were three blacksmiths listed (one at Cobbaton), and three carpenters.

For thirty-eight years from 1870 the mail cart between Swimbridge and Barnstaple was driven by George Chapple, who retired in 1908 on what was described as 'a well-earned pension.' When Chapple had first started work for the Post Office his daily delivery round involved a walk of 17 miles, as far as West Buckland and for the first two years he was required to work on alternate Sundays.

Promoted eventually to drive the mail cart, George

Above: *The Balment family has been active in Swimbridge life for decades, as farmers, butchers and running the post office. The photograph shows Charles Henry Balment's butcher's shop in The Square, later run by his son Harry and daughter -in-law Kathlyne.*

Left: *The Holland family and horse and cart.*

The Yeo brothers, hauliers and contractors, l-r Henry, George, Charles and James (Jim).

The Dunn family also operated a dairy from the Post Office and Stores premises, as evidenced by the milk churns visible in this shot. Petrol was also sold, from the pump to the right of the building.

The Balment family butchery business also had two shop units in Barnstaple's Butchers' Row. Charles Henry Balment is pictured on the left (in the cap) with his brother Jim on the right.

Kathlyne and Harry Balment pictured in their Swimbridge shop.

Sub-postmaster, shopkeeper and dairyman Bill Dunn pictured in the 1930 outside Swimbridge Post Office and Stores. In addition to the jars of sweets, visible above the door is a sign advertising mineral waters by Dornats of Barnstaple.

The Boxall family played a significant part in village life as well as keeping the village shop. L-r, Mr N. Boxall, Robin and Cherry.

In the middle years of the twentieth century Swimbridge has a second general stores, kept by Mrs Elizabeth Skinner and situated by the main road bridge over the stream, opposite Hannaford Lane.

Based not in Swimbridge but in neighbouring Landkey, Darch's bakery nevertheless delivered daily to households in the village and parish, and demands to be included!

Henry Dunn built the pair of houses shown to the right of the picture, in 1911. His descendants owned and lived in the properties at the time of writing.

Chapple at the end of his service reckoned that he had covered more than 225,000 miles carrying mail.

Commercial listings in the opening years of the century included mentions of another prominent local business family, the Balments, whose farming activities at Yarnacott had first been mentioned in the mid-nineteenth century. By the early 1920s Charles Henry Balment had established his butchery business, which at its peak had a shop in The Square, Swimbridge, two units in Barnstaple's Butchers Row and an extensive delivery round, made by horse and trap.

The butchery business was later taken over by Charles Henry Balment's elder son Harry and his wife Kathlyne, with the farm at Yarnacott passing to the younger son William (Bill). After Harry Balment's death the Swimbridge butcher's shop was acquired by Fred Hunt, who ran it until his retirement. After the closure of the butchery the premises were used for a time as a tearoom.

The original village post office and stores, which in the first half of the century also sold petrol from pumps which lingered on outside the building long after the last gallon had been dispensed, passed in due course from the Dunns to the Berry family, the Aclands, the Boxalls, and others, before its eventual closure.

The present-day post office, which also serves the village by selling newspaper and a range of grocery and other items, is situated on the opposite side of The Square. This ensures Swimbridge has an advantage over villages of a similar size which have lost their retail outlets.

PC Grimmett's profession in the 1950s was that of keeping the peace in Swimbridge (not too difficult a job). Also a noted amateur historian, he bought his own motorcycle on which he patrolled the parish beat. He is pictured behind the old police house, now a private dwelling, which stands opposite The Jack Russell.

Sam Snell of Tordown, father of Herbert (seen in an earlier picture in this chapter) was born into great poverty but overcame all obstacles to become a respected farmer and churchwarden.

After working while still a child for the previous tenant, Sam Snell was able to take over Tordown Farm, now owned by Sam's grandson George and his wife Sheila. The farmhouse is shown after the original thatched roof was removed.

During the middle years of the century the village's second general stores, next to the bridge over the Venn Stream (now a private dwelling) was kept by Mrs Elizabeth Skinner.

By the sweat of their brow

At the base of the rigid social pyramid in Swimbridge at the start of the twentieth century were to be found a further two distinct social categories.

On the one hand were the unskilled workers, virtually all male, earning a meagre wage simply through the strength of their arm and the sweat of their brow. On the other was almost the only category of employment open at the time to women, that of domestic service.

Unskilled males were to be found working outdoors whatever the weather, on the land, at the quarry face, and, as maintenance staff, along the main highways and the railway line. Long hours were the norm, holidays were minimal, no protective clothing was supplied, and in general safety provision was, at best, sketchy.

The workers employed at the tannery were for the most part sheltered from the worst of the elements, but conditions in the tanning shed, handling and processing raw hides, could be pretty grim, as surviv-

ing photographs bear effective witness.

The cottages to which the labourers returned at the end of the working day, situated either in terraces in the centre of the village or in small groups scattered around the parish and its hamlets, accommodated in many (perhaps in most) cases large families. By later standards these homes were ill-lit, poorly heated and insanitary, with water having to be carried considerable distances from communal taps.

An account of a court case involving sheep stealing from Hearson, part of Swimbridge parish, is valuable for its description of the living conditions which at the time often prevailed for manual workers and their families.

Home in the hamlet of Travellers Rest for a farm labourer accused of the crime and his family was a cottage with just one bedroom. This contained five beds, occupied by the man, his wife, their seven children and another labourer, who was a lodger with the family. The accused man told the court: "We live like a nest of rats."

The recollections of life for a tenant farmer and his family, noted by Elsie Symons, and reproduced earlier in this chapter, provide a valuable record of life at a rung on the social ladder considerably higher than that occupied by labourers of various kinds and their families.

More eyewitness recollections, in this instance of life for the family of a farm labourer, are vividly captured in the remarkable memoirs of Sam Snell, which cover the final years of the Victorian period and the subsequent Edwardian era in Swimbridge parish.

Born in 1885 into extreme poverty, and being expected to work to help maintain his family from an early age, Sam Snell managed by sheer determination and hard work to haul himself up the social ladder and become in later life a farmer in his own right and a highly-respected churchwarden.

Before his death, in a letter to village historian Cecil Grimmett, Sam Snell recalled his early life, ensuring that the experiences of the less-privileged residents of Swimbridge were preserved for future generations. Sam recalled that the house where he had been born was 'more like a linhay, with rough slabs of stone for a floor, and no ceilings upstairs or down.' Lying in bed, Sam and his brothers and sisters could look both up into the thatch of the roof and down into the living quarters through the big gaps in the floorboards.

Sam's father, who was 'more or less an invalid' and who died when Sam was just two years old, was one of many from the labouring classes who had to apply to the parish for help to feed and clothe himself, his wife and their six children.

After his father's death, and with two of his older siblings already out at work, Sam's mother was allowed six shillings a week (30 pence) in relief. When she appealed to for a small rise in the allowance, she was told by one of the Parish Guardians (administrators of funds designed to help the poor), a prosperous farmer called William Burden who lived at Kerscott, that she had a big boy (Sam's brother Tom) who should be put out to a farm to earn his own living.

Tom was all of nine years of age at the time …

At the period recollected by Sam Snell in his letter to Cecil Grimmett the old system of formally apprenticing to farmers poor boys and girls (often orphans or the offspring of large families who could not afford to feed their children) had become more or less extinct.

Nevertheless, Cecil Grimmett, writing in 1950, said there were still people living in the parish who had experienced something very little different to the old apprenticeships. Grimmett said: "Under this system, and less formal arrangements of later years, the majority of children had a very bad time, especially the girls who were made to do the heaviest work at a very young age, resulting in them becoming prematurely old.

"I know there are women living in Swimbridge today (1950), and not very old, who were sent out to work at nine years of age. Of course, it was cheap labour for the employer, whose only obligation was to board and feed the poor child."

In his reminiscences Sam Snell recalled that the standard farm wage at the turn of the nineteenth/twentieth centuries was about two shillings (10 pence) a day, but for a boy just leaving school the going rate was six pence (two and a half pence) a day, with work starting at 7am and continuing usually until 6pm, or at harvest time for as long as the light lasted.

The twenty-first century definition of poverty in

Cyril Tucker of Smalldon, with his back to the camera, watches his sheep go through the dip at Mill Court in 1935.

John Morrish, pictured with his wife Dorcas (née Leworthy), was foreman at Swimbridge tannery for more than fifty years until his death in 1911. A staunch Baptist and Liberal supporter, he was for some years a member of Swimbridge parish council.

Great Britain is the subject of much debate and Swimbridge parish church in 2015 has a poster in its porch advertising its willingness to accept items for a food bank. Hunger was certainly a very real concern for the poor of Swimbridge in the late nineteenth century and, for many families, well up to the time of World War Two.

Sam Snell's memoirs relate: "I remember many times coming home from school and saying mother, give me something to eat, I'm hungry. I can hear her saying, you don't know what it is to be hungry. My mother told me we were lucky, she could remember much harder times and more poverty."

After working at Tordown Farm for the tenant, George Geen, Sam eventually acquired the tenancy and the chance to be his own boss. He was succeeded at Tordown by his son Herbert, who in turn handed over the farm to his own son, George, and his wife Sheila.

Extreme poverty nevertheless bred resilience and the great majority of those struggling with minute incomes somehow managed to beat the odds and keep their families fed, clothed and respectable. As Sam Snell concluded: "I can never understand how poor old mother used to make such tasty dishes, out of little or nothing."

Food was certainly a major consideration for the cottagers of Swimbridge. Price apart, even obtaining supplies was no easy business. Sam Snell remembered: "I had to take two bushels of wheat every fortnight to Riverton Mill to get it ground into flour.

"If there had been a bad harvest the bread would stick to the roof of your mouth. In the years of a good harvest the home-made bread was very satisfactory. Old people used to say there was no substance in 'boughten bread'.

"We had home-made cheese and, of course, cider. Those who worked on farms were often given allowances of cider, and some were allocated small plots of ground on which they could grow potatoes and other vegetables to help feed their families.

"Most of the villagers kept a pig. The bacon used to be very fat. The shoulders of pork, hams and bacon used to be hung up to dry and kept for quite a long time when salted and packed."

Photographs from the period illustrate the great importance attached even by the poorest to respectability. Group photographs taken at Swimbridge School in the early 1900s show children who appear to be reasonably neat and tidy if not well dressed, even taking into consideration that a special effort would no doubt have been made on the day the photographer was due.

Family and individual portraits, usually taken again formal backgrounds at studios in Barnstaple, with the individuals wearing their 'best' or 'Sunday' clothes, also reveal a determination to appear in the best possible light.

Sam Snell's memoirs, as well as illustrating the tribulations of working class existence in the years immediately before and after the turn of the nineteenth/twentieth centuries, is also invaluable for providing a much more fleshed-out record of day-to-day life in Swimbridge than can be found in the pages of a directory.

The presence of boot and shoe makers in the village in the early years of the twentieth century has already been noted. Sam's memoirs explain that the older generation of village residents thought there was no substance in boots that came out of a shop in Barnstaple.

After the boots had been purchased from their makers, they were taken to the village blacksmiths for nailing and for the attachment of steel plates. An expensive item to replace, the boots had to be sufficiently robust to deal with conditions varying from the stony surfaces of a quarry, the thick mud of a pasture in winter and the slippery surface of the tanning shed – to say nothing of the need to be reasonably well-fitting and waterproof.

The Health and Safety regulations of the twenty-first century are often the butt of ironic humour, frequently with some justification. Throughout the nineteenth century and much of the twentieth century, safety was given a low priority and rules, when they existed, were often ignored.

Local newspapers carried many reports of horrendous accidents, frequently leading to deaths, and Swimbridge parish had its fair share, involving work in agriculture, industry and domestic service.

In May 1903 Charles Smith, a labourer, was killed at Swimbridge Newland as a result of being run over by a steam thresher, which was being towed by a traction engine. The inquest into his death heard that Smith's job entailed walking in front of the engine to warn people of its approach. He was also responsible for holding any restive horses which the machine might pass on the road.

The jurors were told that Smith might have attempted to climb on to the thresher for some reason, or might otherwise have become entangled in the machinery. It was suggested by the police that he may have been riding on the towing bar between the traction engine and the thresher.

Whatever the actual cause, his body was found underneath the thresher, with only his head visible. He had suffered what were described as 'shocking injuries', causing instantaneous death. A verdict of accidental death was recorded on Smith, who had no children, but left a 'crippled' wife.

Annie Smale (twenty-two) died following an incident involving a cow she was milking in a shippon at Hurscott Farm, where she had been employed for six years. The inquest into her death heard that the cow apparently kicked the bucket the young woman was using for her task. This frightened her so much that she had a heart attack, leading to a verdict of death by natural causes.

Sam Snell's future farming career was threatened when the axe he was using to chop wood slipped and he severed an artery in his arm. He was detained in the North Devon Infirmary but recovered to eventually take over as tenant at Tordown.

A fortunate escape was recorded at the tannery when William Sturgess, an employee of W. H. Smyth and Co had an apoplectic fit whilst in charge of a horse and cart. Only the quick thinking of tannery foreman John Morrish, fortunately on the scene at the time, saved the day.

Morrish seized the reins and saved the cart from being drawn over the stricken workman. It was reported at the time that the value of such modern day conveniences as the telephone and the motor car was evident, with the doctor being on the scene within twenty-five minutes of the seizure.

The impressive, heavily-bearded Morrish died in 1911, at which time it was stated that he had worked at the tannery for more than fifty years. As he was just sixty at the time of his death, he had started work as a ten-year-old – a not uncommon occurrence in the mid-nineteenth century.

A staunch Baptist and an ardent Liberal, he was much respected by the tannery owners, who closed the works on the day of his funeral.

Working inside a well-run middle-class domestic establishment also had its dangers. In 1908 an inquest was told that Alice Garman died whilst cleaning silver. She was using methylated spirits for the task and when she upset the container the spirits ignited and she was enveloped in flames.

Being 'in service', either as an inside servant – butler, footman, cook, lady's maid, housemaid, kitchen maid – or working outside as a gardener, game keeper, groom or forestry worker has been given a spurious glamour by the success of the television series *Downton Abbey*, where those working 'downstairs' appear to lead a life rather different than

Tannery general foreman Bert Liverton (standing right) watches Messrs Dinnicombe and Moore unload raw hides in the 1950s.

Domestic service still offered plenty of jobs, both indoors and outdoors, in the 1930s. Bill Holland, chauffeur and gardener to Mrs Harding-Nott, is pictured cutting the lawns at Tordown House, watched by his daughter Elizabeth (Betty).

Bill Holland's wife Nora was also employed by Mrs Harding-Nott and the family lived in one of the cottages (now a single dwelling) adjacent to Tordown House.

Reginald William Holland, pictured with his wife, was gardener at Dennington House between circa 1918 and the late 1930s, when the house was owned by Colonel Walter Rothney Battye.

Owen Dalling (right of picture) left the land in the 1950s to serve as an RAC motorcycle patrolman. He is pictured with a colleague at Mullacott Cross in 1954.

Significant social advance came in 1951 with the construction of 12 council homes at Archipark.

earlier accounts by people who actually experienced the mode of life.

Despite the long hours and drudgery – and the risk of accidents such as the one that cost the life of Alice Garman – there were advantages to service.

Employment was generally steady if the individual's work and behaviour was considered up to scratch, food was usually plentiful for live-in staff – in greater quantity and better quality than they would have had access to in their homes – promotion to the higher ranks brought responsibility and reward, and in many cases staff were comparatively well treated and recompensed by the standards of the time.

Without the opportunities offered by domestic service, the chances of employment for many village girls would have been slim, and the work and way of life was superior to the old system of apprenticing the offspring of the poor to farmers, where their treatment varied considerably.

The standards which girls who worked in service were expected to maintain often stood them – and their families – in good stead when they married. Many ordinary households benefited from higher standards of cleanliness, cookery and general housekeeping kept up by former servants when they acquired their own homes.

As the twentieth century progressed many factors combined to ease the lot of the ordinary working man and woman – the advent of council houses, the improvements carried out to existing cottage properties by private landlords and eventually the opportunity to buy homes.

Old age and occupational pensions, the advent of the NHS, more relaxed attitudes to learning and less corporal punishment at school, together with regular health checks for children and school meals, together with the material improvements to life first noticeable in the immediate post World War Two period made the second half of the century very different to the first few decades for the ordinary resident of Swimbridge.

The social changes in the village in the second half of the century can by plotted in the huge improvement in living standards, a process begun by the 1930s council housing built at High Cross, followed by Archipark in 1951.

New building in the village accelerated in later decades of the century with several housing projects – private at Orchard Close, Bestridge Meadow, and Hooda Close, and a mix of private and social housing at St Honorine de Fay Close and, in the present century, on Barnstaple Hill.

Mervyn Dalling's 1978 survey of villagers' jobs and occupations is also an excellent guide to social change.

From the very earliest part of the twentieth century Swimbridge residents sought employment in Barnstaple and the advent of bus services running

A good bus service allowed Swimbridge residents to work in Barnstaple. Rose Dalling, once one of the trio of carers for Miss Risdon of Endsleigh, worked in Barnstaple during the 1950s and 1960s, at Johnson Cleaners and later at Lee's, Photographers.

His findings also reflected the growing appeal of the parish as a place of residence for professional and business people. Mervyn's survey documented accountants, solicitors, an antique dealer, a pathologist, lecturers and teachers as residents, as well as a Member of Parliament – the late Jeremy Thorpe, who had a cottage home at Cobbaton.

In the earlier decades of the twentieth century, and certainly before the motor car became more widely available, professional and business people in all categories tended to live in the cities and towns where their work was situated (or at least in easily-accessible suburbs).

The vogue for working in town and living in the countryside grew considerably in the later years of the century and had a substantial effect on the make-up of the population of Swimbridge.

The village proved a magnet to many professional people – doctors, solicitors, senior local government officers, artists and potters and other creative roles, and even airline pilots and this continues to be the case at the present time.

Most people would agree that a wider social mix has proved beneficial to the village, despite the effect felt through factors such as house prices.

Swimbridge today has a reputation as something of a lively cultural centre and the obvious improvements in communal facilities such as the new park, the refurbished Jubilee Hall and the attractive stream-side garden have all benefitted from an injection into the population of enthusiastic new blood.

through the centre of the village greatly increased the opportunities to work in shops and offices in the market town.

Mervyn's survey revealed how widespread the range of occupations had become by the final quarter of the century, with a far larger number of people employed outside the village boundaries in retail and office jobs, factories and the building and allied trades.

The immediate post-war period saw great advances in the living standards of ordinary people in Swimbridge. In 1951 parish council member Miss E. M. Berry turned on the mains water supply for the village.

Chapter 3

A Village at Prayer

Swimbridge's churches and chapels

St James' church, pictured from Church Lane in the 1930s.

The early years of the twentieth century saw religious observance in Swimbridge at a peak.

With no fewer than six churches and chapels, all attracting substantial congregations to divine worship, and also making a highly significant contribution in the fields of education, social welfare and leisure provision, Christianity exerted a major influence on the life of the community.

In general members of the rival religious denominations represented in the parish – Anglican, Wesleyan Methodist and Baptist – rubbed along fairly well together, notwithstanding the nonconformists' strong opposition to alcohol in a village well supplied with licensed houses.

Occasionally however, strongly held beliefs, which often mirrored political differences, could prove divisive in everyday life. The noncomformists resented the fact that a proportion of the money raised by local taxation helped to support Church of England schools, and this resentment sometimes boiled over into direct conflict between Anglicans

and the other denominations.

The arrival of organised dissent in the village represented the first real challenge to an institution which had reigned supreme for almost a thousand years, originally in communion with the Roman Catholic Church and the Pope, and after the reformation of the sixteenth century, as the established Church of England, embodying the official state religion.

Christian worship in the area predated considerably the establishment of the first church at Birige, on the banks of the Venn Stream. In the era of Celtic saints and martyrs a young woman, Urith (Hieritha in Latin) is believed to have been born at East Stowford, on the southern fringe of what was to become Swimbridge parish.

She converted to Christianity and was martyred in the early eighth century – according to early legend her death came at the hands of haymakers, who beheaded her with a scythe, although later belief suggested that she was killed by invading Saxons or Vikings.

The tall and impressive tower of Chittlehampton parish church. The church is dedicated to St Hieritha, who is believed to have been martyred at East Stowford in what was to become Swimbridge parish.

Urith or Hieritha was declared a saint and her memory is commemorated in St Hieritha's church in the neighbouring village of Chittlehampton, which in medieval times was an important place of pilgrimage.

The earliest place of Christian worship to occupy the site of the present church of St James was probably constructed (almost certainly of wood) sometime in the eleventh century, to serve the settlement known then as Birige. Domesday records the existence of a chapel from the time of Edward the Confessor (1042-1066).

The death of Edward provoked an invasion by the Normans and Queen Matilda, wife of the new king, William I (or Conqueror), granted the manor of Birige to her chaplain, Sawin. The name of the village and parish, derived from Sawin's Birige, had by 1215 become Swinbrige, later evolving to Swymbridge and eventually to the modern Swimbridge.

From that date until 1866, the titles, glebe (Church-owned) lands and the patronage of the established Church in Swimbridge belonged to the Dean of Exeter Cathedral. After that date the Church lands and the tithes were transferred to the Bishop of Exeter.

The events and the individuals that over the years contributed to the power the churches and chapels wielded at the birth of the twentieth century, together with the emotions religious issues were capable of stirring among the inhabitants of the village and the wider parish, form a fascinating part of the Swimbridge story.

The Russell inheritance

The Church of England in the eighteenth century and in the early 1800s was not a vigorous institution. Protected by its status as the established Church, with the reigning monarch at its head, the Church was perhaps best described as being complacent. Some commentators went much further, with the state of the Diocese of Exeter in the early 1830s described by one source as 'miserable'.

There was a shortage of resident clergy in rural areas, with many livings held in plurality by a single clergyman. Although the stipends (salaries) of the individual churches were relatively small, when added together by a pluralist they could provide a more than comfortable income. Pluralist clergymen delegated much of their work to curates, and both services in church and pastoral care in the parishes often proved perfunctory.

The Rev. John Russell, perpetual curate of Swimbridge from 1832 to 1866 and vicar from 1866 to 1880, after parish status was awarded.

The position of a Church of England clergyman carried the status of a gentleman, was often regarded as a profession as opposed to a vocation, and was frequently occupied by the younger son of an aristocratic or gentry family.

It was into this world of religious affairs that the Rev. John Russell, 'Parson Jack' as he became universally known, was born in 1895, the eldest son of John Russell, rector of Iddesleigh in North Devon. The father was himself a hunting parson, a species by no means rare in the county, and his sons were involved in field sports from an early age.

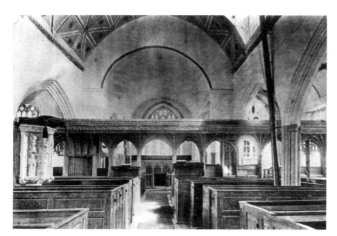

The east end of St James' church before the 1880 restoration.

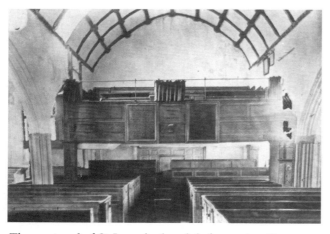

The west end of St James's church before restoration, showing the gallery where musicians would have played in the days before the introduction of organs to churches.

The future incumbent of Swimbridge was educated at Blundell's School in Tiverton, where he kept a scratch pack of hounds, anticipating his future life. He graduated from Oxford University in 1818, and was ordained deacon the same year and priest in 1819.

His first clerical post was a curacy at George

Nympton near South Molton, where he became friendly with the most controversial sporting parson of the era, the Rev. John Froude. Russell was proud of his connection with Froude, despite the older man's poor reputation. Parson Jack wrote: "I hunted as many days a week as my duties would allow with John Froude, the well-known vicar of Knowstone, *with whom I was then on very intimate terms* (author's italics)".

In 1826 Russell came into the orbit of Swimbridge, when he married money, in the form of Penelope Incledon Bury, daughter of Admiral Bury of Dennington House.

After a short period as his father's curate at Iddesleigh, he was presented in 1832 to the united chapelries of Swimbridge and Landkey, as perpetual curate. Swimbridge was not to become a parish in its own right, or Russell a vicar, until 1866, when its lands and patronage came into the hands of the Bishop of Exeter.

John Russell was a controversial character in his own time, and remains so today, dividing opinion among historians. Set against the criticism that he spent too much time (and money) hunting and socialising with his wealthy friends, is his well documented record as a conscientious minister of the Church.

Unlike many of his contemporaries who helped to give the Church of England a bad name (and who undoubtedly contributed to the rise of nonconformism), John Russell increased the number of services available in his churches at Swimbridge and Landkey.

The recorded statistics for baptisms, marriages and burials constitute an impressive rejoinder to claims that he neglected his flock in favour of following the hounds. In addition, Russell was said to be assiduous in visiting the sick and in attempting to help the practical, as well as the spiritual needs of villagers.

He preached many sermons in aid of charitable causes and is celebrated as a defender of the gypsy community in the area.

The Church of England, perhaps shocked out of its earlier complacency by the thousands of Methodist and Baptist chapels that sprang up across the country in the first half of the nineteenth century, was in mid-century beginning a renaissance, prompted by both its evangelical and high church wings.

Although Russell appears to have ploughed a furrow between the two extremes – conforming to the moderate churchmanship which saw its clergymen described as 'middle-stumpers – he certainly became increasingly active in the later years of his long incumbency at Swimbridge, which lasted for forty-eight years from his first presentation in 1832 to his departure for Black Torrington in 1880.

John Russell was the driving force behind church expansion in Swimbridge parish, overseeing the

In his later years the Rev. John Russell inspired the opening of chapels of ease in the remoter parts of Swimbridge parish. Pictured is the exterior of St Thomas, Travellers Rest or Cobbaton, in the south of the parish, which was opened in 1867.

A second chapel of ease, dedicated to The Holy Name, was opened at Gunn in the north of the parish in 1873.

The Rev. John Russell bequeathed to his successors not just a restored parish church and chapels of ease at Travellers Rest and Gunn but also a thriving congregation. Pictured is the Swimbridge choir, circa 1890, with the vicar, the Rev. Henry Harrison (with beard and stole, in the centre row) and, to his right, his curate.

opening of chapels of ease in the south of the parish, at Travellers Rest and in the northern section, at Gunn, as well as being the instigator of the extensive restoration of the parish church of St James. Russell's drive for expansion is described in more detail later in this chapter.

A photograph of the St James choir in 1890, ten years after Russell had left Swimbridge shows some 40 men and women – evidence of the strength of parish life he bequeathed to his successors.

On the debit side of the Russell balance sheet are a number of factors. There is some evidence that he could be quarrelsome, with a taste for seeking redress in the courts of law.

A dispute in the 1840s with Squire John Nott, of Bydown House, initially centred on issues surrounding the provision of relief for the poor of the area. Nott appears to have been enticed into ill-judged reactions to criticisms of his conduct made by Russell. Nott eventually came off much the worse in the quarrel between the two men.

Nott lost a libel action brought by Russell and had his reputation damaged by a criminal case in which he was accused of requiring witnesses to swear illegal oaths.

The squire, almost certainly an active Tory, held different views on politics and issues of religious doctrine than those espoused by Russell, whose supporters – an impressive line-up of local landowners, including the Duke of Bedford and the Fortescue and Chichester families – were at the time in question all Whigs or Liberals.

Despite the fact that John Russell emerged from the dispute as the undoubted victor, John Nott had his supporters in Swimbridge. In 1847 *The North Devon Journal*, carried a report giving a strong impression that he was regarded in many quarters locally as a benevolent man, only too willing to help the less fortunate villagers of Swimbridge.

During the previous months, the *Journal* said, Nott had 'exhibited great liberality during the severities of the last winter and dreariness of the spring'. Through his personal kindness, the newspaper added, 'the poor of his parish and neighbourhood were extremely relieved and many rescued from starvation who were ready to perish.'

A procession of 600 'old dames and maidens' had marched from Swimbridge churchyard to Bydown and presented a piece of plate to Nott, to express their thanks for his kindness. The marchers, who had endured a considerable climb via Kerscott Hill, were entertained to a lavish tea in Bydown House for their trouble.

It would probably be carrying cynicism too far to suggest that satisfying the wishes of the squire and the prospect of a lavish tea would have been enough to persuade the old dames and maidens to trudge to Bydown?

John Nott died childless in 1855 (the Bydown estate and his other land holdings passing to his sisters). His monument in Swimbridge church describes him as 'a humble minded Christian and the friend of his poorer brethren'.

He was buried in the family vault, with John Russell recording that this was the final burial to take place within the church.

There is a certain mystery about Nott's memorial in Swimbridge church (illustrated on page 27). This takes the form of an open book. On the right hand page is the inscription 'May our names, as his, be written in the book of life'. The claim has been made (and is believed by at least one former vicar) that an attempt was made at some stage to erase the words 'as his', purportedly to suggest that Nott's name did not deserve to appear in the book of life!

There is considerable natural discolouration of the monument above the scripts, and an alternative explanation could be that what has been presented as a spiteful attempt at erasure is simply an extension of a deterioration in the marble!

John Russell was also not slow to take action in court against parishioners who failed to pay him the money due for various parish matters.

The case for the prosecution against Russell was led in the twentieth century by the distinguished Devonian historian William George Hoskins, first met in the first chapter of this book, *A Village in Context*. Hoskins is still recognised today as the 'father' of the academic study of English local history.

The son of a baker, born at Cullompton, and the founder of the first English university department of local history, Hoskins was noted for always taking the side of the farm labourer, whom he believed had over the centuries been treated shamefully, not least by the 'gentlemen' clergy of the established Church.

In this context Hoskins, while praising work carried out on behalf of agricultural labourers by Canon Girdlestone of Halberton (a contemporary of Russell), took the opportunity to contrast Girdlestone with 'fox-hunting squarsons, Christian only in the sense that they had once been baptised'.

Hoskins, in another disparaging reference, referred to the 'futile Parson Jack Russell' and dismissed the Swimbridge clergyman as being 'notorious, even in a diocese (Exeter) where it was reckoned that 20 parsons kept packs of hounds.

"He (Russell) ran through £50,000 of his wife's money, and beggared and sold off the estates which had belonged to her family and which she had inherited."

Hoskins also quotes a well-known story from Russell's life, concerning an appeal made to him by Bishop Phillpotts of Exeter to give up the pack of hounds he maintained and stabled at Tordown House, which he rented for some years in the absence of a purpose-built clergy house in Swimbridge.

Richard Bury Russell, the son of the Rev. John and Penelope Russell. The already financially embarrassed 'Parson Jack' lost further money when the bank run by his son in Barnstaple collapsed.

Russell reportedly assured the Bishop that he would indeed give up ownership of the pack, and transfer this to his wife!

One can imagine that Russell's quick thinking response would raise a laugh around the dinner tables of his aristocratic friends in North Devon, and also at Sandringham, where he was the guest of The Prince of Wales, the future King Edward VII and preached a sermon in the local parish church.

Others might interpret it as a wholly cynical and disrespectful reply to his Bishop, a man to whom he owed loyalty and deference.

A further story recorded, among the many tales relating to 'Parson Jack', concerns an occasion when he was trying out a possible new curate by testing his abilities with a hunter. The potential curate remarked how bare of trees Russell's lands were. "Ah! said Russell. "The hounds eat' em".

W. G. Hoskins' overall conclusion in the case of John Russell was totally dismissive: "The day of such

The riding crop used by the Rev. John Russell formed part of an exhibition of Russell memorabilia to mark the centenary of his death. Also pictured are his chair, hunting horn, boots and spurs.

sporting ruffians is fortunately over for good", Hoskins said.

The author's conclusion is that, overall, the benefit of the doubt probably belongs to 'Parson Jack'. Hoskins' visceral dislike was essentially for hunting parsons and 'squarsons' – a mixture of squire and clergyman – in general. There is indeed plenty of evidence that many (perhaps most) did neglect the duties of their profession, an accusation of which John Russell appears largely innocent.

The evidence in Russell's individual case suggests that whilst some of his actions perhaps brought the Church of England into disrepute, he was essentially a good shepherd to his flock and a positive influence in Swimbridge parish.

It is not difficult to see how his passion for field sports would have helped to endear him to the local aristocracy and gentry. At a more modest social level, Russell's exploits in the hunting field and his reputation as a hearty 'man's man', as opposed to an over-pious moralistic clergyman, would no doubt have won him friends in many a North Devon farmhouse and public house tap room.

It is no surprise that most published accounts of Russell's life are essentially kind to the clergyman, although a brochure on sale in the parish church of St James acknowledges that his "qualities as a parish priest appear to be less well documented than his sporting ones".

The church where John Russell ministered for so many years became a focal point for visitors (and photographers) as early as the late nineteenth century. Although the association with Russell (and his grave in the churchyard) is obviously a prime motivation for many of the visitors, the church of St James is an attraction in its own right.

The fact that the church restoration was carried out in a generally sympathetic manner (not always the case in the Victorian era) is another major point in Parson Jack's favour.

After his forty-eight years in charge at Swimbridge John Russell moved in 1880 to a new living provided by one of his aristocratic supporters, Lord Poltimore. The stipend at Black Torrington was £300 a year, much higher than the value of the Swimbridge living.

The move to Black Torrington was probably unavoidable, at least in the light of W. G. Hoskins' claim that Russell was at the time in dire financial straits, partly caused by the bankruptcy of his son's bank (in which Parson Jack had been an investor) and partly by his extravagant lifestyle.

Russell returned to Swimbridge after his death in 1883, to be buried in the churchyard. It is believed that around 1,000 people attended the interment. His grave attracts many visitors to this day.

St James' is one of the Devon entries in *England's Thousand Best Churches*, by Simon Jenkins, former chairman of the National Trust and one of Britain's most prominent journalists.

Lest anyone should consider that a list of a thou-

A view of the west end of St James' church, Swimbridge in pristine condition, following restoration in the early 1880s.

The fifth birthday party of the Young Communicants Guild was held in the Old Schoolroom in February 1964. Pictured are, back row, l-r, Martin Sowden, Peter Cornelius, Roger Harris, Gillian Adams, Biddie Haddock and the Rev. John Read. Middle row, l-r, Wendy Howard, Pamela Hutchens, Linda Jeffrey, Philip Hutchens, Leslie Jeffrey and Richard Balment. Front row, Heather Chown, Josephine Dalling, Pat Moore, Wendy Knill, George Knill, Alan Mildon, Graham Elliott and Peter Down.

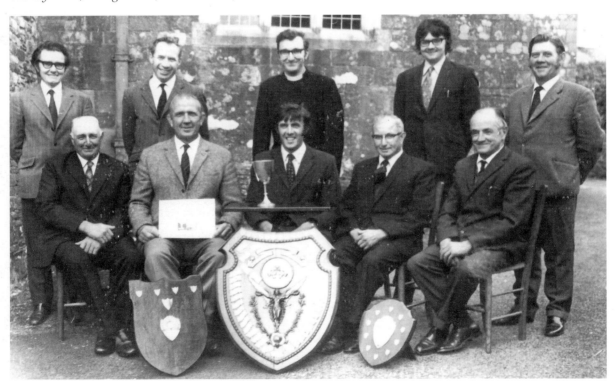

Swimbridge bell ringers swept all before them in the early 1970s, during the incumbency of the Rev. Richard Gilpin (1969-1973). Pictured l-r, back row, are D. Jewell, J. Conibeare, Rev. R. T. Gilpin, M. Sowden, A. McLeod. Front row, S. Bartlett, H. Jones, A. Bartlett (captain of the tower), J. Tose, H. Balment. S. Bartlett and H. Balment were churchwardens at the time.

Treasure house churches like Swimbridge need constant attention to maintain their splendour. The Rev. John Read inspects the state of the roofs of the chancel and north aisle in the 1960s.

Young people from the parish carry the cross to Hooda Hill on Good Friday, in a 1960s view.

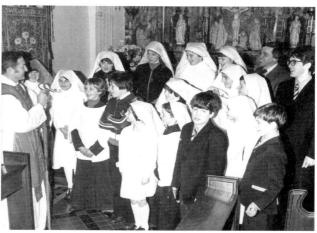

sand churches constitutes a fairly broad sweep, it is worth remembering that the Church of England maintains some 16,000 churches.

Jenkins selects 33 churches in Devon, but of these only nine are in North Devon. Of the county total, rated from one star to five star, only three exceed the three-star ranking achieved by Swimbridge. The church and its contents as seen today represent the various styles of architecture and ecclesiastical furnishing adopted as the building developed over the centuries, through successive enlargements, re-buildings and restorations.

The earliest part of the existing church is the four-teenth century tower and its leaded spire, which is nearly 90ft high. The nave, the body of the church, and the chancel, where the choir stalls and the altar are situated, reflecting the Perpendicular form of architecture, are believed to have been extensively rebuilt from earlier forms in the fifteenth and sixteenth centuries, and north and south aisles and chancel chapels were added in the same period.

The large-scale restoration carried out at the insti-gation of John Russell and superintended by the architect J. L. Pearson was carried out during the period 1879-82, being completed after Russell had left for Black Torrington. The church is renowned for the

The Rt Rev. Philip Pasterfield, Bishop of Crediton, talking to the candidates following their confirmation at St James' church in February 1979.

A presentation was made to Mrs R. Haddock in July 1983 to mark her retirement as secretary to Swimbridge parochial church council. Pictured l-r are Mrs Haddock, the Rev. Nigel Jackson-Stevens, and Mr Sid Bartlett and Mr Leonard Barker, churchwardens.

Parishioners gather by the side of the Venn Stream for the blessing of the seat placed by the bridge by the 'Over 60 Club' to mark the Silver Jubilee of HM Queen Elizabeth II, in 1977. The ceremony followed a special Silver Jubilee service in the parish church.

The parish church of St James attracted tourists in the late Victorian era. George Palmer visited in 1898 and took this photographic study of the covered font.

The parish church choir march with a new banner, bearing the earlier spelling of Swymbridge, and carried by Mr F W Tatham. The occasion is a choir festival in Barnstaple and the procession is seen in the High Street, passing the Guildhall.

Janet Balment first played the organ at St James's church in the 1960s and continues to enhance the musical life of the church in 2015.

Procession for the induction as vicar of the Rev. Eric Robotham, in 1950. Carrying the cross is Roy Dalling, followed by choir members D. Woolacott (facing camera) and D. Dennis, K. Ridd and J. Westcott, A. Yeo and M. Passmore, M. Dalling and A. Bartlett, J. Newton and R. Dennis, J. Shapland and H. Lee, and lay readers Messrs Parker and Upton.

quality of the wagon roofs in the nave and chancel.

The outstanding features of the interior of St James are the intricately-carved rood screen which extends for 44ft across the width of the nave and the aisles, and is 10ft high and the font, believed to have been assembled in the eighteenth century and consisting of a lead bowl contained in a cover which Pevsner described as mixture of sixteen century Renaissance and Gothic elements. The stone pulpit is Tudor, dating from around 1490.

Swimbridge has been served by many dedicated priests of the Church of England (and ministers and lay preachers of other denominations) since the days of Jack Russell. Apart from their qualities of pastoral care, many of the Anglican clergy men have entered fully into the day-to-day life of the village, playing cricket and occasionally sinking a pint in the pub.

It is a fair bet however that none of the other incumbents of St James', no matter how distinguished, will be remembered a century or more later or will have their names immortalised on the sign board of that same pub.

Nonconformism

There is nothing to suggest that the Rev. John Russell's attitude to nonconformism was anything other than tolerant during the forty-eight years during which he occupied the pulpit at Swimbridge church.

The same cannot be said of a predecessor as perpetual curate at St James', the Rev. Nicholas Dyer, the incumbent when the village's first Methodist chapel opened in 1816. Dyer, whose tenure at Swimbridge – forty-four years from 1787 to 1821 – was almost as long as Russell's, took stern measures against any of his congregation who were attracted by the teachings of John Wesley.

Wesley (1703-1791), an ordained Anglican clergyman who never ceased to regard himself as a member of the Church of England, toured the country on horseback, often preaching in the open air. His preaching centred upon the universality of God's grace for all, the effect of faith on character, and the possibility of perfection in love during this life. He organised the new converts locally and in a "Connexion" across the whole of Britain.

The first Methodist place of worship in Swimbridge, in Chapel Court, still exists. It was opened in 1816 and converted to a private dwelling when the new chapel was opened in 1898. In the picture are Mr Alf Cowley who purchased the property and his family.

He often faced organised hostility to his preaching, with Church of England clergymen outraged by his methods urging mobs to heckle his sermons and attempt to drown out his words by the use of hunting horns and other instruments.

Nicholas Dyer, in Swimbridge, appears to have adopted a more subtle approach, excluding a number of persons from the communion table at St James', because they were also in the habit of attending the Methodist chapel. He was eventually over-ruled by the Bishop of Exeter.

Swimbridge's first Methodist chapel, situated in Chapel Court, off the High Street, was opened in 1816, although the denomination had been active in the village for some years before that date, with the house of a Thomas Vickery and his wife Elizabeth licensed to be used for religious worship.

After Wesley's death Methodism splintered into several sections, not reunited into a single Methodist Church until the twentieth century. Swimbridge became associated with the Wesleyan Methodist cause, generally regarded as the more mainstream and respectable arm of the denomination.

At the other end of the spectrum were the Primitive Methodists whose adherents were less prosperous than their Wesleyan cousins, whilst the Bible Christian movement (founded at Shebbear in North Devon), and strong throughout Devon and Cornwall, also tended towards a more radical outlook than the Wesleyans.

Despite the aura of respectability that surrounded Wesleyans, many of whom prospered through the doctrines of hard work and self-sufficiency that were at the core of their beliefs, the folk memory of the Swimbridge society did include accounts of hardships and taunts.

In 1966, when the Methodist society celebrated its 150th anniversary, one of the church leaders, Mr Bill Clatworthy, wrote that the survival of the denomination for so long was due to "the courage and strength (of the founding fathers) to endure the scorn and derision of the populace."

Mr Clatworthy's remarks in 1966 about opposition to the early establishment of Methodism in Swimbridge were echoed at the 150th anniversary celebrations by the then Superintendent Minister of the Barnstaple Methodist Circuit, the Rev. R. Keith Parsons.

He said: "Our Swimbridge Methodist Society was founded at a time of moral and religious decadence, when the great mass of the people was still largely unlettered, and life was hard and uncertain.

"The Methodist preachers had to meet not only the irrational persecution that any community will raise against innovation, but often the planned opposition of the authorities, both civil and ecclesiastical. One did not, in those days, lightly join the Methodists. He who did so was open at once to all kinds of social pressures and petty persecution."

The Chapel Court building served the Swimbridge Methodists until the closing years of the nineteenth

The new chapel for the village's Wesleyan Methodists opened in 1898, on land given by the Duke of Bedford. It closed in 1990 and is now a private residence.

Methodist society members and friends at the opening of the new chapel in 1898.

A class for lay preachers at Swimbridge Methodist chapel. Pictured are, front row, l-r, Frank Morrish and Sidney Morrish, Middle row, l-r, William Buckingham, Cyril Tucker, William Dunn, the Rev. Meek, Walter Clatworthy and William Conibear. Back row, l-r, James Lock, Thomas Snell, W. Trute, George Seldon, Percy Tucker, not known.

George Lovering was the founder and first pastor of Swimbridge Baptist chapel.

Swimbridge Baptist chapel opened in 1837.

century. A new church was built, at a cost of £866 and 9 shillings, on land known as Cross Park, donated by Herbrand, the 11th Duke of Bedford, and opened on April 20 1898.

The Wesleyan Methodist reputation for self-help was certainly justified in the case of the new Swimbridge church. Members of the society, notably Mr Jeremiah Dunn, Mr William Mortimer, Mr John Tucker and Mr W. R. Shapland helped with the transport by horse and cart of stone for the building from Bydown Quarry, contributed by the quarry owner, Mr John Pengelly.

The old church in Chapel Court was sold to a Mr Alf Cowell for the princely sum of £100, as a private dwelling, a use which has continued to the present day.

The next denomination to arrive in Swimbridge was the Baptists, who opened a chapel in the village in 1837. The building, now a private residence, stands high above the main road on Barnstaple Hill, with the path to the door leading up a steep slope through the burial ground, to which relatives of those interred there still have the right of access.

The core of Baptist belief is the doctrine that baptism should be performed by total immersion and only for professing believers, as opposed to the practice of infant baptism.

The founder of Swimbridge Baptist church, George Lovering, was born in 1799 to a Church of England family at Chapelton, in Tawstock Parish. Throughout his youth and early manhood, he was considered worldly, enjoying field sports, but in 1833 underwent a conversion and professed his new-found faith by being baptised in the River Taw, at Chapelton.

He later began to preach in public and to organise meetings in a farmhouse at Swimbridge, before building the chapel on Barnstaple Hill, at his own expense.

George Lovering's foundation faltered for a while after his death in 1866, and during a period when the Swimbridge church was temporarily attached to one in South Molton, a service was held only once a month.

The fortunes of the church revived with the arrival on the scene of George Norman, who in 1870 moved to live at Dinnaton Barton in Swimbridge parish. Norman served as Pastor for the Swimbridge Baptists for half a century, until his death in 1920.

From this point until 1946, when the Swimbridge community decided to join with the Barnstaple Baptist church, there was no actual minister. The church celebrated its centenary in 1937 and its 150th anniversary in 1987, before dwindling congregations resulted in the final service being held in 1999.

With the influence of Methodism spreading in Swimbridge parish, Cobbaton Methodist chapel was opened in 1838, at a cost of £120, and was able to seat 150 people.

The Anglican response to the rise of nonconformism began in the south of the parish at Travellers Rest (Cobbaton) with the opening in 1867 of a chapel of ease, the church of Saint Thomas, with a nave and chancel and a small spire containing a single bell. The cost of the building was £850.

Cobbaton Wesleyan Methodist chapel, opened in 1838.

Although Travellers Rest church closed in 1976 for the inevitable conversion to a private dwelling, it again became licensed for weddings following the passing of new legislation. A newspaper article described how it was chosen, rather bizarrely, for a wedding venue by a couple who said that they wanted 'a church setting but not a religious ceremony'!

A further chapel of ease, this time to the north of Swimbridge village, was opened at Gunn in August 1873. The church of The Holy Name, was inaugurated by the Bishop of Exeter, Dr Temple, and cost £550. Gunn church continues to be used for worship to the present day and Mervyn Dalling enjoyed playing the organ there until his death.

The final flowering of church building in Swimbridge parish was the opening of Gunn Baptist chapel on April 7 1909, by Mr E. J. Soares, Liberal Member of Parliament for North Devon.

Prior to the opening of the chapel, Baptist mission services had been held in both the Gunn and Stone Cross areas of Swimbridge parish, accommodated in cottages, farmhouses and sometimes in the open air.

The Gothic-style building, in contrast to the cost of the Anglican churches at Travellers Rest and Gunn, respectively some forty and thirty-five years earlier, was constructed for the surprisingly small sum of £150.

Measuring just 35ft by 18ft, and able to accommodate 100 people, the chapel took barely two months to complete from the laying of the foundation stones.

Gunn Baptist chapel had a relatively short lifespan.

There was a recurrence of bad feeling between Swimbridge nonconformists and the established church in the early years of the twentieth century. All Church of England parishes hold a vestry meeting, usually in April and often immediately before the annual meeting of the parochial church council, to elect churchwardens for the coming year.

The meeting is open to people whose names are on the parish church's electoral roll (whether or not they actually live in the parish in question) and also to all people resident in the parish and whose names are on the register of local government electors.

This means that any resident of the parish and who is registered to vote, of any faith or none, can take part in the meeting.

In 1904 the Swimbridge vestry meeting was effectively taken over by a large number of nonconformists, who turned up unexpectedly and rejected the nominee for churchwarden nominated by the vicar and the church people – Mr F. R. Harding-Nott, of Tordown House, often referred to as Squire Nott and a member of the same extended family that had included John Nott of Bydown, the adversary of John Russell.

When the time for the 1905 vestry meeting came around, the church party was better prepared. The vicar, the Rev. Henry Harrison, had martialled his forces in expectation of another contested election.

Perhaps having made a point in 1904, the nonconformists failed on this occasion to show up. The local press asked the question, 'Where were the Dissenters?', claiming they had 'shown a white feather' and adding: "It was expected that the nonconformists would attend and nominate a church warden. Had they done so they would have been confronted by a large number of supporters of the church."

The vicar in his remarks said that the 'occurrence' at the previous year's vestry meeting was hoped by some to 'bring discredit on the church' and upon himself. The actual result, he added, was that the church people had rallied.

The Rev. Harrison went on to say that the church had experienced 'a very trying time' because of the nonconformists' action. "In future the church people do not intend to allow outsiders to interfere with the church's business."

Against a reported background of applause the vicar continued: "Church people do not interfere with the Baptists or the Wesleyans. We are capable of managing our own affairs without the assistance of outsiders."

In future, he declared, the appointment of churchwarden was to be by the vicar and his parishoners. He had a veto if he did not approve of the person selected.

The 1905 meeting duly elected Squire Harding Nott as churchwarden, a year after his initial nomination.

The press reports of the skirmish fail to record the actual reasons for the nonconformist invasion of the 1904 meeting. Whether it was a local issue, such as disapproval of Harding Nott, or the wider dissatisfaction of Methodists and Baptists at having to contribute towards the cost of Church of England schools is not made clear.

Local newspapers at the time were, however, carrying reports of North Devon ratepayers (including nonconformist clergymen) being prosecuted and having their belongings confiscated for withholding a proportion of their rates.

The influence of the various religious denominations, for a considerable portion of the twentieth century, extended far beyond simple church attendance on Sundays. Even in the last decade or so of the twentieth century, the churches of Swimbridge parish were extremely active. In 1988, Christmas in the village was the occasion for a veritable feast of services.

Four separate carol services were held on in the run-up to Christmas Day, two at St James' church (one for the village school), one at the Baptist church and one on The Square.

The parish church had a crib service on Christmas Eve, followed by Midnight Mass and, on Christmas Day itself, Holy Communion at 9 15am followed by family carols. Gunn church had a family communion service with carols on Christmas Day and there was a Christmas morning service at the Methodist church.

The strong connection between church membership and support for the Conservative cause, matched by nonconformist allegiance to the Liberal Party, endured well into the second half of the twentieth century and may well still be a factor.

Former Prime Minister Harold Wilson always insisted that the Labour Party in Britain owed more to Methodism than to (Karl) Marx. With Labour having only a minor role to play in North Devon politics, the nonconformist vote was still heavily in favour of the Liberals in the late 1970s.

The moral influence of nonconformism outflanked political considerations in 1979, when it is generally agreed that defections or abstentions on the part of Methodists and Baptists played a major role in the downfall of local MP Jeremy Thorpe.

Thorpe, educated at Eton and Trinity College, Oxford, and the son and grandson of Conservative MPs, was adopted as the Liberal candidate for North Devon in 1952 and three years later he halved the Conservative majority at the 1955 General Election.

Thorpe, a familiar and generally popular and respected figure in Swimbridge – he owned a constituency home in Cobbaton, which he retained long after he had ceased to be an MP – won North Devon at the 1959 election. He became Liberal leader in 1965.

Many constituents were deeply shocked when a former male model, Norman Scott, claimed that he and Thorpe had had a sexual relationship between 1961 and 1963, when homosexual acts were illegal in Britain.

In 1979, following newspaper revelations, Thorpe was forced to resign the Liberal leadership. Following police enquiries, Thorpe and three others were charged with conspiracy to murder Scott.

The trial was scheduled to take place a week before the general election of 1979, but Thorpe obtained a fortnight's delay in order to contest his North Devon seat at the election. Thorpe's majority at the previous general election in 1974 had been 6,721, and at that time he had won 48 per cent of the total vote, as opposed to the 36 per cent recorded by his Conservative opponent Tony Speller.

Fighting the 1979 poll against a background of the impending court case, Thorpe's share of the vote plummeted to 36 per cent and he conceded a majority of 8,473 to Speller.

Although the overall swing to the Conservatives, at an election which saw Margaret Thatcher become Prime Minister, obviously played a part in the result, it was widely felt that the allegations against Jeremy Thorpe had alienated the traditional, chapel-going elements which had always been at the core of his local support.

When the trial eventually took place, Thorpe and his fellow defendants were acquitted, with the judge, Mr Justice Cantley describing Norman Scott as "a crook, an accomplished liar, a fraud."

It was too late for Jeremy Thorpe, who effectively withdrew from public life, and suffered from Parkinson's Disease up and to his death in December 2015, only months after the death of his second wife, Marion.

Roman Catholicism

As a footnote to this chapter, it is worth noting that an additional and little known place of worship in Swimbridge parish existed for a while after the split between Henry VIII and the papacy.

The separation of the Church of England (or Anglican Church) from Rome begun by Henry in 1529 (and completed in 1537), brought England alongside the broad Reformation movement which had begun in Europe under Martin Luther in 1517.

Religious changes in the English national church proceeded more conservatively than elsewhere in Europe. Reformers in the Church of England alternated, for centuries, between sympathies for ancient Catholic tradition and more reformed principles, gradually developing into a tradition considered a middle way (via media) between the Roman Catholic and Protestant traditions – a situation which has lasted, broadly speaking, until the present day.

True Roman Catholicism, adhering to the older forms of worship and loyal to the Pope, endured in Swimbridge for some time due to the efforts of the Giffard family, which long adhered to the old faith.

The Giffards maintained a private chapel at their home at Accott Manor, although the actual dates

The old faith lingered for a while in Swimbridge parish after the Reformation. The Roman Catholic Giffard family owned Accott Manor and Mass was said in the building pictured .

when it was used for worship are not known. The building survived and has been restored by the current owners of Accott, Tom Oliver and Liz Pile.

The west country, in the immediate aftermath of Henry VIII 's split with Rome, clung to the old faith, with unsuccessful revolts in both Cornwall and Devon in support of the old faith.

Ironically, in later years, the West Country as a whole became identified with nonconformism.

The parish church of St James in Swimbridge has been identified for many years with Anglo-Catholicism and this endures, in a moderate form, to the present day. A rather strangely named website, *Ship of Fools*, uses 'mystery worshippers' to visit and rate Anglican churches.

The visitors to St James were very impressed by what they found at a Benefice Service, in which church members from Swimbridge, Gunn, Landkey and West Buckland (the other parishes in the united benefice) join together for worship.

The 'mystery worshipper' described the style of the service as being 'on the Anglo-Catholic side of centre', with a robed choir and procession around the church, as well as having an anthem sung by the choir between the readings.

The review also praised the friendliness of the congregation, described by the 'mystery worshipper' as being 'very welcoming and warm'.

Christian witness in twenty-first century Swimbridge is not confined to within the walls of the surviving churches of St James and The Holy Name at Gunn.

Each year since the 1960s a cross has been carried from the village to the top of Hooda Hill each Good Friday as witness to a Christian faith that has been part of village life for more than a thousand years.

Chapter 4

Village Learning
Swimbridge schools through the years

Swimbridge School is becoming accustomed to accolades. After generations of solid service to the community, valued highly in the locality but largely unrecognised beyond the immediate boundaries of the parish, the school now has a nationwide reputation for educational and pastoral excellence.

League tables published by *The Times* newspaper revealed Swimbridge to be the top primary school in the county of Devon and ranked it as the 30th best out of 17,000 schools in England.

It has come a long way since the early 1980s when, with just 33 pupils on the roll, Swimbridge featured on Devon County Council's published list of schools that might possibly have to close.

In the intervening thirty years the school, under the leadership of Garry Reed, believed to be the longest-serving headteacher in the country (he was appointed in 1981), has trebled its number of pupils and consistently attracted official praise for its all-round qualities.

The hillside school on the western edge of the village opened nearly 150 years ago, in 1866, designed to educate "children and adults, or children only, of the labouring, manufacturing and other poorer classes of the parish."

In 2015, a place at Swimbridge school is highly desirable, not only to parents living in the village itself, but to many, from all walks of life, living some distance outside the parish.

Classes were held in the Old Schoolroom, owned by and adjacent to St James' church, until the new school on Barnstaple Hill was completed in 1866.

Swimbridge School, with the main block virtually unchanged from the day it was built.

Garry Reed, pictured with Swimbridge School pupils in 1982. He found just 33 children on the roll when he arrived in 1981 and the school was threatened with closure. In 2015 there are some 115 pupils and the school has a national reputation for excellence.

The story of formal education in Swimbridge pre-dates the construction of the present school by more than a century.

A parochial school is believed to have been established in the 1700s, in the building still known as the Old Schoolroom, next to the parish church of St James.

The next step forward was made possible by William Russell, the 8th Duke of Bedford, a major landowner in the parish, who granted land to the vicar, the Rev. John Russell and churchwarden Thomas Yeo to build a school.

The building, the core of which still exists today, although with additions and alterations, was a local creation, with the architect, Alexander Lauder and the builders, Oliver & Son, both based in Barnstaple.

To mark the 125th anniversary of the school in 1991 Garry Reed, whose thirty-four years as head teacher now exceed the previous record tenure of William Shelley (thirty-three years from 1883 to 1916), helped by parents, teachers and pupils, published an excellent history of the school, largely drawn from the log books kept over the years.

Apart from records of attendance and other facts and figures, the book includes excerpts from the records touching on a number of subjects, from notable events over a century and a quarter, changes in teaching methods and in the subjects taught, discipline, and changes to the buildings on the site (the former residence of the head teacher is now part of the school itself).

Some remarkable anecdotes are included, particularly in respect of inspections of the school, a controversial issue throughout its history. In times past

Garry Reed, headteacher for thirty-four years at the time this book went to print, marked the 125th anniversary of the school in 1991 by publishing, with help from parents, teachers and pupils, an excellent history of the school, largely drawn from the log books kept over the years. Garry Reed was awarded the MBE in the 2015 Queen's Birthday Honours list.

inspectors, whether representing the government or the Diocese of Exeter (Swimbridge is a Voluntary Aided Church School) would travel to the village by train.

When they were expected, older boys would be posted on the top of Hooda hill, behind the school building. When they spotted a well-dressed passen-

Until Garry Reed became Swimbridge School's longest serving head, the record was held by William Shelley (thirty-three years from 1883 to 1916). Shelley, pictured here, kept scrapbooks of newspaper cuttings recording local and national events, from the first years of the twentieth century to his retirement in the middle of World War One.

An important part of the Swimbridge School team for many years. School crossing patrol warden Sid Scrivens of Station Hill is reckoned to have saved the lives of several children.

Swimbridge School pupils in 1916, the year William Shelley retired. The boys (20 of them), mostly wearing Eton collars, heavily outnumber the twelve girls, mostly in pinafore dresses, seen in the photograph.

The school recorded its highest number on roll, more than 140 pupils, when a large number of wartime evacuees had to be absorbed. Pictured is one of the evacuees, Berwick Coates, who in later years revisited the school to talk about his wartime experiences.

F. H. Drew, headmaster from 1921 to 1944, is pictured on the left of his pupils. The year the photograph was taken is unknown, but the shortage of girls noticeable in the 1916 shot has been rectified.

ger with a briefcase leaving the railway station, they would hurry down the hill to warn the staff of his approach.

Large families and the fact that Swimbridge took pupils up to the school leaving age (it increased progressively, reaching fourteen years in the 1930s) kept the numbers on roll at a sustainable level.

In 1896 the figure peaked at around 130 pupils, with the average being around 80 pupils in the inter-war years between 1916 and 1939.

The high water mark of attendance at Swimbridge school came in 1940, with the arrival of evacuees from bomb-threatened cities. The first batch numbered 47 and were renewed at intervals, with the total number of children on roll at one point exceeding 140.

Ray Liverton, a pupil at the school until transferring to Barnstaple Boys Grammar School, remembers considerable friction and fights between the local children and the evacuees. One evacuee certainly has mixed memories of the time.

Historian Berwick Coates, who taught at Park School in Barnstaple and is today the archivist at West Buckland School, spent his time as an evacuee at Hannaford Green. Looking back on the period in 2015 he recalled: "I was at Swimbridge School for eight months in 1941.

"For a city lad it was a different planet – primroses and violets in tall hedges, ringworm in a pupil's knee in class, and instead of shrapnel in the street in the morning, it was cow pats.

"I remember the broad accents too. I was particularly upset to hear the mangling of English when a classmate insisted on saying 'seed' instead of 'saw'. When I protested, she said, with remorseless logic: 'Well, I didn't saw 'im in 'aaf, did I?"

Mr Coates has visited the school on several occasions in recent times to talk about his experiences as

Berwick Coates today , historian, author, archivist at West Buckland School and former evacuee at Swimbridge School.

Swimbridge School pupils, both juniors and infants, in 1959. Infants teacher Bertha Chown is on the left and headmaster Douglas Harvey, appointed in 1957, is on the right of the group.

Teaching traditional skills in the 1960s – did the boys learn to sew too?

Painting, again in the 1960s, with a war scene chosen by the boy at the front. The library books in the backround are just as evocative as the view of the children.

Concentration. The toy gun in the background, no doubt waiting to be used at playtime, might be frowned upon today in some quarters.

How many children share their school playing field with ruminating cows (in the background, with a small linhay also visible)? The cricket club tea hut can also be seen at the top of the bank.

an evacuee and was 'comforted' when shown the register for 1941. "There I was – Berwick Coates. It was nice to be reassured that I had really existed."

Another part of Berwick Coates' recollections of 1941 relate to the primitive lifestyle that existed at the time in Swimbridge and many other rural areas – a great contrast to his home in London, at Wimbledon to be precise.

"A significant part of my education, of course, came from the cottage where I stayed at Hannaford Green. There was no electricity, no gas, no mains water, no metalled track to the door, and a pump at the bottom of the field.

"Oh – and a bucket out at the back."

Swimbridge School underwent major change in the years following the end of the 1939-45 war. The 1944 Education Act introduced by the wartime coalition government introduced two levels of schooling – primary schools for children up to the age of eleven and secondary schools for eleven-fifteen year olds.

The new provision took effect in Swimbridge in 1947 when the older pupils left to continue their education in Barnstaple or (later) at South Molton. In the case of Barnstaple there were the single sex secondary modern schools of the time or, if successful in the 11-plus examination, the similarly single sex grammar schools.

The first woman head at Swimbridge was Miss Rosemary Burgess, appointed in 1945. She oversaw the transfer of the older pupils – initially 15 travelled by bus to Barnstaple under the reorganisation – and was the first headteacher to have responsibility for what had become a primary school for infants and juniors.

In addition to Swimbridge and a much smaller parochial school at Travellers Rest (Cobbaton) which was open for forty-five years from 1876 to 1921, the parish has also been home to private educational establishments, generally of a specialised nature, at both Bydown and Dennington (described in the earlier chapter *A Village and its People*).

The private education sector has also over the years attracted parents from the parish, including at least one vicar whose daughters, in an early spirit of ecumenism, were educated at the Roman Catholic Marist Convent school in Barnstaple.

West Buckland School was founded in 1858 as the Devon County School, specifically to provide a public school education for the sons of farmers and the middle class. It was renamed West Buckland School in the winter of 1912/13.

During the 1950s it received increasing support from the Devon County Education authority and became a direct grant school. In 1976, when direct

Headteacher Ted Holmes (1962-1981) keeps a watchful eye on proceedings as some of his boy pupils try out the school's new swimming pool.

73

Left: *Rosemary Burgess, head teacher from 1945 to 1956, oversaw the transfer of older pupils to Barnstaple when, in 1947, Swimbridge became a primary rather than an all-age school.*

Below left: *Passes in the controversial 11+ examination were not particularly common in the early 1950s. Mervyn Dalling is pictured outside the home of his grandmother in Station Hill, proudly wearing his new uniform on his first day at Barnstaple Boys Grammar School.*

Below right: *Another proud educational achievement. Lindsey Cooper, a descendant of the Dunn and Thorne families of Swimbridge, pictured in the uniform of Barnstaple Girls Grammar School.*

A happy group of 25 junior pupils at Swimbridge School in the middle 1950s, before the retirement of Miss Rosemary Burgess (pictured far right on the back row), who left in 1956. Back row, l-r, Michael Snell, Chris Dennis, R. Peacock, unknown, Monty Bishop, D. Newland, Jeffrey Adams, Miss Burgess. Middle row, l-r, Alan Faulkner, Lorna Dalling, Carol Peacock, unknown, Christine Bartlett, Mary Palmer, unknown, Martin Sowden. Front row, l-r, Alan Mildon, Pat Balment, Mary Easterbrook, Kay Elliott, Colin Dalling, unknown, Jane Buckingham, Sally Hurley, Janet Balment and William Balment.

grants were abolished, it finally became a fully independent school.

One farmer's son who began his education at Swimbridge and was later sent to West Buckland became in later life an internationally famed horseman.

Albert Edwin Hill – Bertie as he was always known – was the son of Hubert Hill, who farmed at Birch in Swimbridge parish during the 1930s and 1940s. Born in 1927, he was a precocious equestrian, who first hunted with the Devon and Somerset Staghounds when he was four.

A year later he became a pupil at Swimbridge, riding his pony Joe the 3 miles to the village school. He stayed in the saddle when he transferred to West Buckland School, and often had to hustle to complete the longer cross-country journey on time. On occasions he had to run the gauntlet of outraged farmers and smallholders as he galloped through their farmyards, scattering hens, ducks and geese.

Bertie Hill left school at fifteen to help on the farm at Birch. Although still only a boy, he was given responsibility for his father's team of shire horses and

Former Swimbridge School pupil Bertie Hill, Olympic equestrian hero, seen in action at the Royal Windsor Horse Show.

the single furrow plough they pulled. At night during World War Two he patrolled Exmoor with the mounted section of the Home Guard, keeping a watch for German parachutists.

After the war, like so many farmers' sons (and

75

daughters) in and around Exmoor he became an amateur jockey in point-to-point racing. He went on to represent Britain in three-day eventing, winning a gold medal at the 1956 Olympic games in Stockholm, along with a host of other international trophies.

In the 1960s, Hill and his wife opened a riding school at Rapscott on Exmoor, where his son Tony and his wife Stephanie, a national hunter judge, still live. Bertie Hill trained a number of future international riders, including Princess Anne and Captain Mark Phillips, and is one of Swimbridge's School's most celebrated former pupils.

Another distinguished former pupil of Swimbridge School, winning renown in the world of academia, is Professor Richard Balment of the University of Manchester.

Another old boy of Swimbridge School, Richard Balment, receiving his doctorate at Sheffield University in 1975.

Professor Richard Balment in his laboratory at the University of Manchester.

After leaving Swimbridge School Richard attended Barnstaple Grammar School, then gained a place in higher education at the University of Sheffield, where he obtained a first class Bachelor of Science (BSc) degree in Zoology and a doctorate – a PhD in Renal Physiology – followed some years later by a Doctor of Science degree (DSc) in Comparative Endocrinology.

After working as a postdoctoral researcher at Sheffield he took up a lectureship post in Manchester. He progressed from lecturer to a personal professorial chair in Zoology. He was also Dean for International and Graduate Education at Manchester.

Richard worked in Manchester until his retirement in 2008, and also enjoyed short research appointments in overseas academic institutions, notably in France, Japan and Zimbabwe. In retirement he still holds an Emeritus Professorship in Zoology at Manchester.

One of his major research projects revolved around the flounder, a small edible flatfish that in its small body holds a wide variety of information relevant not just to purely academic research but also to the study of the mechanisms and problems of the human body.

Swimbridge School has had its share of headline-grabbing events over the years, varying from outbreaks of fire and the accidental deaths of pupils right up to the extensive media coverage of its pre-eminent position among Devon's primary schools.

Fire caused considerable damage on at least two occasions, in 1946 and again in 1979, and in March 1918 Roland Irwin, described as 'a late scholar' was killed outside the school premises by a traction engine.

No event recorded in the log books of Swimbridge School can match an occurrence at Travellers Rest School in the first decade of the twentieth century, which was hailed in the local media as 'Swimbridge sensation!'

Travellers Rest School, Cobbaton, opened just ten years after the larger school at Swimbridge. It was built at a reported cost of £300, and designed to accommodate up to 40 pupils, drawn from the hamlets and scattered farms in the southern part of the parish.

The simple rectangular building, constructed of rough-coursed stone rubble with ashlar facings, was saved from bland anonymity by its embellishments, notably a tall chimney stack of chequered stone, a distinctive timbered porch and a bellcote – a turret or framework located on the gable at the east end of the school, housing a single bell.

In August 1876 the Swimbridge headteacher, Walter Edward Turner, who had previously taught at Weare Giffard, travelled through the narrow lanes to Travellers Rest, to ring the bell and receive the first pupils.

Travellers Rest School, opened in 1876 at a cost of £300 and closed in 1921 due to insufficient pupils on the roll.

The number of pupils on the roll usually hovered just below the school's official capacity. In 1878, when the school mistress was a Miss M. Huxtable, the average attendance was 30 children.

In 1902, by which time one Robert Stephens had taken charge, the figure was 38, falling four years later to an average of 33 pupils. William Shelley at Swimbridge noted on several occasions that attendances at the Travellers Rest School were causing concern.

During the middle years of the first decade of the twentieth century, the school seems to have struck a particularly difficult patch, with the annual reports of HM Inspectorate effectively damning the establishment with faint praise.

Training for work in the classroom had been tinged with controversy in the late nineteenth century, when the progressive extension of free and compulsory elementary education led to a demand for teachers which it proved difficult to satisfy. The shortage of qualified teachers was met by the employment of 'uncertificated' teachers – those without a qualification from a recognised training college – and also pupil teachers, who effectively worked their way through the later stages of their own education by assisting in the classroom.

Robert Stephens, who in 1908 was nearing his sixtieth birthday, was a 'certificated' teacher, possessing a formal teaching qualification or certificate. Nevertheless, standards at the school during his tenure were subject to regular criticism.

Stephens' work at Cobbaton was, in theory at least, supervised on a regular basis by the school managers. These were local worthies who were required to visit the school, on at least a monthly basis, and inspect both the administration of the establishment and the work being undertaken by the pupils.

The school log books record that the most frequent visitors were the Rev. Henry Harrison, vicar of Swimbridge from 1899 to 1911, and F. R. Harding-Nott, of Tordown House, a member of a branch of the landowning Nott family, who was generally referred to by local residents as 'Squire Nott'.

In addition to the activities of the managers, Travellers Rest School was subject to annual inspections by HM Inspectorate of Education. In successive annual reports inspectors described the pupils at Cobbaton as being 'in good order and are fairly well taught'. The syllabus and records of the work undertaken by the pupils needed, according to the inspectorate's report, to be 'more fully and systematically kept'.

Twelve months after these comments were recorded, a further report found that although discipline in the school was 'satisfactory' and the instruction 'fairly accurate', the teaching was considered to be 'of too mechanical a character' and 'in some ways unmethodical'.

The inspectorate summed up the school in the following way: "The defects reported have been noticed in previous reports and it is expected that a determined effort will be made to bring about improvement in the coming year."

Events in 1907 were to reveal that Robert Stephens was burdened with problems in his home life as well as at school. During the summer of that year he was to become one of the leading figures in one of the most sensational events in the modern history of Swimbridge parish.

The lifestyle of the Stephens' household at Cobbaton was somewhat different to that enjoyed by William Shelley and his wife Alice at Swimbridge. The Shelleys, who had two children, enjoyed what appears to have been a rich and fulfilling cultural life.

The couple were fond of concerts and plays, they organised village entertainments, and generally played the sort of leading role in local society to be expected of professional members of the community.

Stephens, who had been born in Cheltenham, had at some stage lived in the village of Dacre, near Harrogate in North Yorkshire, where his wife and his two eldest surviving children were born. By 1901, when the family was established in Cobbaton, there were nine children between the ages of nineteen and three to feed and clothe on a relatively small salary.

In July 1907 the second child of the family, Mary Elizabeth, who had been born in Yorkshire and who until February of that year had worked in domestic service, had returned to live at home. One Monday morning, whilst her father was teaching in the nearby school, she gave birth to a male child, full-term, fully developed, of good proportions and weight.

Evidence given to the subsequent inquest by Mary's mother, Jane Stephens, suggested that no one had been aware of her daughter's pregnancy, and no preparations had been made for a birth. Jane Stephens had only been aware of the actual circumstances when she heard Mary call out and, going into the bedroom, had discovered the child lying on the bed beside her daughter.

The inquest was told that it was their task to consider whether the child was born alive and whether it had met its subsequent death by natural causes or foul means.

The jury was told that on the day after the birth Mary's mother and her brother William, who was at that time unemployed and also living at home, put the body of the child in a plain wooden box and took it to the cemetery at Barnstaple, requesting that it should be buried.

The cemetery keeper told them that the body could not be interred without a certificate from a doctor or the coroner.

Mrs Stephens and William then went to the surgery of a doctor living nearby, to request a certificate, stating that the child had been stillborn. The doctor informed the coroner, and a police constable was sent to take charge of the child's body.

When Mrs Stephens took the witness stand, she told the coroner and the jury that on being questioned her daughter had said that she had been raped at Venn, by a 'beastly old man, dressed in brown with a box hat'.

Mrs Stephens denied that either she or her husband had any knowledge of symptoms of preg-

nancy in her daughter. Her daughter had been unwell since returning from service but when her father had questioned her about her sickness she had denied that it was caused by pregnancy.

Mary Stephens had taken to her bed on the Friday before the birth had occurred on the Monday, but the parents had still not linked her biliousness and other symptoms of illness to pregnancy.

The mother added that on going into her daughter's bedroom on the day of the birth.and discovering the baby on the bed, she had heard no cries or discovered any evidence of breathing from the child.

Her daughter had told her that the baby boy was dead. No attempt had been made to nurse the child, no midwife or doctor was called, and the body was simply placed in the box.

When asked why the body was taken to the cemetery in Barnstaple, with no attempt to have it buried in Cobbaton churchyard, Mrs Stephens replied: "We wanted to keep it quiet."

In later evidence Mrs Stephens said the first her husband had known of the birth was when he came in from teaching in the school. He was surprised, as he had no idea that his daughter was pregnant.

The inquest was adjourned until 1 August 1907, when at the end of the prolonged proceedings the jury found that the child had died on 8 July, but that

Elsie Stephens (on the left of the back row in the photograph) taught at Travellers Rest until the school closed in 1921 and later at Umberleigh. In 1907 her father, the then headteacher at Travellers Rest and other family members were involved in a major sensation described in this chapter.

Cross-bearer Richard Balment heads the procession from Swimbridge School to St James' church for the school's centenary service. Pictured at the rear of the procession is headteacher Mr Ted Holmes with his wife Joyce on the right of the children.

there was no evidence to show how it had come by its death.

The jurymen further found, on the basis of the medical evidence, that if the child had received proper attention at birth it would have lived. They severely censured the mother of the child and her parents for their behaviour.

The coroner went further than the members of the jury. Calling Mr and Mrs Stephens before him he said that Mary Stephens had told the court what he could only describe as 'a concoction of lies'.

With regard to the 'extraordinary story' of the man at Venn, he did not believe a single person in the room, including Mary Stephens herself, believed one word of the tale.

The coroner went on to say that he was unable to believe that Mrs Stephens, the mother of nine children, had no idea of her daughter's condition prior to the birth.

The medical evidence indicated that, although the child was probably still alive after it had been born, it was not possible to carry the case far enough to place Mr and Mrs Stephens and their daughter in what he described as 'a most awkward position'.

The coroner concluded that the trio had 'escaped very narrowly being indicted by the jury for the wilful murder of the child; they had only missed it by the skin of their teeth."

Perhaps surprisingly given the fact that the coroner largely disbelieved the evidence given by both Robert Stephens and his wife (who also sometimes taught in the school), the couple kept their jobs.

Some months later, however, the problems at the school came to a head, apparently following an inspection not, on this occasion, by HM Inspectorate, but by the Church of England Diocese of Exeter.

Not just Stephens, but the school managers as well, were criticised. No manager had attended at the school for some months and the registers had not been signed.

Did they stay away because of distaste at what had occurred at the school house?

On 22 May 1908, there was a laconic entry in the school log book – 'resigned duties', signed R. Stephens. When a new head was appointed, she made damning comments on the former regime.

There is some evidence to suggest that Mary Stephens later married a soldier and returned to Yorkshire, where she had a further child.

Jane Stephens, her mother, died in 1921, at the age of sixty-four, whilst Robert Stephens lived to the age of ninety, dying in 1938.

Although Robert Stephens had resigned his post as head teacher at Cobbaton in 1908, that was not the end of his family's connections with the school.

Another daughter, Elsie, just thirteen years of age at the time of the scandal, taught at Cobbaton before the school's closure in 1921, and later at Umberleigh. Elsie Stevens is remembered as a very conscientious teacher, who walked daily from her home at Travellers Rest to Umberleigh and back.

She never married and continued to live in Cobbaton until her death in 1973.

Travellers Rest School, which stood empty for many years, has survived with its main features unchanged and in 2014 was being restored as a private residence.

Swimbridge School, for all the ups and downs of pupil numbers, restricted accommodation, fires and the odd newsworthy occurrence, managed to avoid headlines of the less savoury kind.

One small official excursion made by pupils in the mid-1960s would nevertheless probably raise eyebrows fifty years later in 2015.

On 18 January 1965 the entire school walked down the hill to the Jack Russell to see a meet of the Dulverton West Foxhounds.

Chapter 5

A Village at Work

Swimbridge's agriculture and industry

Directory listings for Swimbridge throughout the twentieth century were dominated by long lists of farmers (both men and women) and those following trades directly linked to the parish's agricultural economy – smallholders, market gardeners, farm bailiffs and overseers, contractors, dairymen, water millers, blacksmiths, saddlers, wheelwrights and even professional rabbit catchers (as opposed to those simply seeking something tasty for the pot).

In the middle years of the century, taking in World War Two and the austerity period of the late 1940s, when the nation's ability to produce its own food was of paramount importance (and when agriculture as an industry was valued to a much greater extent than it is today) there were no fewer than 46 farmers working the land within the boundaries of Swimbridge parish.

Twentieth century Swimbridge was primarily an agricultural community, in a district and a county where farming and its associated activities dominated to a far greater degree than is the case in the first decades of the new millennium.

At the same time Swimbridge possessed an industrial base much more extensive and important than that experienced by most rural communities of similar size, not only in Devon but also throughout the country.

If the fertile land surrounding the village fostered successful agriculture, the parish was also rich in resources which encouraged industrial development. Throughout the Victorian era the discovery of valuable minerals below the green hillsides, the ready availability of water, and the steadily improving communications, notably the opening of the Taunton to Barnstaple railway line in 1873, provided the impetus for Swimbridge to develop both extractive and manufacturing industries to supplement its agricultural wealth.

In the 1830s, at a difficult time for farming, the traditional rural occupation of leather tanning completed a gradual transition from what was essentially a cottage pursuit into a mechanised industry, helped by the development of steam power.

For generations North Devon farmers had

Swimbridge for much of the twentieth century was a village of contrasts. The tannery pictured after closure and decaying constituted a considerable industrial site.

From Station Hill billowing black smoke from the tannery obscured the view of the hillsides to the south of the village.

Contractor and haulier Jim Yeo with a team, pictured on Swimbridge Square.

A stone's throw from the tannery and its smoking chimney cattle meandered across The Square to be milked at dairies in the village.

Oblivious to the smoke of the tannery George Richards of Mill Court Farm is pictured in July 1956 carrying hay on the Long Moor, with his cart horse Violet. The Richards family stayed loyal to the use of horses for longer than any other local farmers.

quarried the stone outcropping on their land in order to extend their houses and build barns, and there was a demand for lime for use as a fertiliser. At much the same time as tanning became viable on a large scale, the demand for minerals and ores also progressed from individual enterprise to full commercial exploitation.

Although the agricultural depression of the period prompted many farming families to leave the land – many members of the extensive Yeo family from Swimbridge emigrated to Australia, New Zealand and Canada – the rising industrial activities provided increased employment possibilities for the labouring class.

From early Victorian times to a point well into the second half of the twentieth century, agriculture and industry co-existed in the village and parish.

Co-existence is an important phrase. Throughout the period under review many employers had interests in both agriculture and industry, and workers in both the tannery and the quarries were able to switch (or be switched) between the two, dependent upon the seasons and the state of the economy.

Industry

Britain's industrial revolution was based upon the nation's early lead in the development of steam power. Harnessing steam to industry is generally regarded as a Cornish as opposed to a Devonian achievement, with its early use in the tin mines of the county on the far side of the Tamar.

Yet steam began to play a part in Swimbridge life in the earliest years of Queen Victoria's reign, when pack animals and sleds were still as common on North Devon's farms and roads as wheeled vehicles.

Housewives trying to avoid black smoke from the tannery also had to be wary of blasting from the deep scar of Hooda Quarry. Like the tannery, the quarry, seen here in 1948, was right in the heart of the village and continued to operate for some years after World War Two.

Stationery steam engines for industrial use arrived in the parish, initially to power the tannery and later to help transport limestone, more than 40 years before the Devon and Somerset Railway brought locomotives to the village.

Marsh Barton Farm, where the land lies along the Venn Stream to the south west of Swimbridge, was the location of a limestone mine or quarry used to feed lime kilns (still visible today) owned by farmer William Hartnoll.

What made Marsh stand out from other similar operations both on the North Devon coast, where coal for firing was brought by sea from South Wales, and in inland areas of the district, was the fact that the stone was transported to the kilns from the point of extraction by wagons running on an inclined plane, hauled by means of steam power.

With safety regarded as secondary to productivity, accidents were a fact of life in the extractive and mineral processing sector. At Marsh in 1856, a sixteen-year-old boy named Kingdon, employed to tip the wagon containing the stone on arrival at the kilns, was the victim of a fatal accident. The steam engine was put in motion in order to wind up some slack chain but revolved too often and caused the employee to be crushed between the wagon and the machinery.

An inquest was told that his head and neck 'received a dreadful crush, causing his death'. A verdict of accidental death was recorded, with the coroner stating that no fault was attributable to anyone.

Production of lime on an industrial scale was also carried out at Bestridge, close to the centre of Swimbridge village.

Advertisements which appeared in the local press in 1876 for the lease of Bestridge lime quarry and associated works, together with a large amount of machinery and other equipment, give a good idea of the scale of the operation.

The items listed for sale together with the lease of the site included what were described as 'large and powerful' water wheels, tramway rails, tramway wagons of both iron and wooden construction, and a complete range of tools and equipment for a black-smith's shop.

The prize item in the auction list was a 12 horse power portable steam engine, described by the sellers as being 'very costly'. The engine, described as being in working order, had been manufactured by Clayton and Shuttleworth of Lincoln, a company which had built the first engine of its kind in 1845.

Bestridge quarry had also utilised more traditional horsepower; two draught horses, said to be 'useful and powerful' were also included in the sale.

Lime was a valuable commodity in North Devon, where the nature of the soils made necessary its extensive use as a fertiliser. Speculators during the 1800s and in the early years of the twentieth century searched extensively in Swimbridge parish for other valuable minerals, although with limited success.

An early edition of the Ordnance Survey showed a copper mine at Hannaford and mining for silver was carried out at East Combe and in a field opposite to Newland House at Swimbridge Newland.

Investors in the latter project reportedly included the Rev. John Russell, no doubt attempting to repair the virtually constant hole in his finances caused by his lifestyle. In this instance, it would seem that his investment failed to pay dividends.

As in the case of the sixteen-year-old boy killed by machinery at Marsh, the Hannaford mine suffered fatalities. A seventeen-year-old boy ventured down the shaft in order to discover its state after heavy rains had halted mining operations. When the boy did not reappear at the time expected his father and a cousin went down the shaft to look for him.

All three became the victims of foul air in the mine. Their bodies were eventually located and brought to the surface by means of grappling irons.

The East Combe mine was sunk in the hope of extracting both silver and lead, after what was described as 'native silver ore, of a very rich quality' had been discovered. The mine flooded, due to lack of power from what had proved to be an inadequate water wheel. There were plans to install a steam engine to provide sufficient pumping power but the necessary additional capital could not be raised.

Despite the repeated problems with flooding, get-rich-quick speculators were still looking for silver in the summer of 1907, when a find was reported on land at Newtown Farm.

The quarrying of limestone for road making and other construction purposes was less romantic but much more practical than the abortive attempts to mine silver in viable quantities.

Productive quarries at Bydown and at Hooda, in the centre of Swimbridge village, were worked for many years. Production continued at Hooda until the 1950s and Ray Liverton remembers how the foreman would walk around the village with a whistle to give notice of imminent blasting.

Tanning leather was a less dangerous occupation than mining and quarrying, although a dirty and smelly trade. People who grew up in Swimbridge as late as the 1950s have vivid recollections of the pungent odours coming from the raw hides as they were carried by lorry from the railway station to the tannery.

Leather was produced in the village for hundreds of years, from at least the sixteenth century right up to the final demise of the industry in the village in the mid-twentieth century.

Prior to the industrial revolution tanning was essentially a cottage industry, with small tanneries scattered around the North Devon countryside, using local hides and other materials.

There are occasional mentions of tanning in local records, including the burial of a tanner in Swimbridge churchyard as far back as 1580, and a report in 1773 of a tanner named Upham being robbed when returning home from South Molton market.

The process became industrialised in the Victorian era, when the substantial site off Hannaford Lane, by the side of the Venn Stream, where many of the buildings still exist, first came into being.

From the creation of the tannery, around 1831, to its closure in 1965, apart from a brief period during and following the 1914-18 war, the business was in the hands of just two families, the Smyths and the Fulfords.

The first proprietors were the Smyths, who worked the enterprise as a traditional bark mill. Steam power was introduced to the process by 1863 and the site continued to be developed by the Smyths, for much of the time working in concert with the Rackfield Tannery in Barnstaple, which the family also owned.

This photograph taken from Hannaford Lane shows how central a position the tannery occupied in the village.

Tanning in Swimbridge remained largely viable at a time when the industry as a whole experienced frequent slumps in trade. The Smyth's business, which at a peak employed some 40 men, was able to make better leather than its competitors, due largely to a slightly acid and iron-free water supply.

A second favourable factor was the fact that that the Smyths were able to combine their tanning activities with agriculture. Tanning in Swimbridge, at least during the time the activity was controlled by the Smyths, was largely a seasonal operation.

Stocks of leather would have been built up during the slack season on the farms, with tannery labour being switched to work on the land during the busy times for agriculture – a rotational system which enabled the tanning business to survive when similar companies in Britain went to the wall.

Even so, the Swimbridge tannery experienced a crisis in 1911, when the high prices being charged for the raw hides which constituted the prime material used in the business, combined with poor sales, led to the announcement of a gradual run down in activity, with a view to eventual closure once the existing stock of materials had been processed.

The potentially serious blow to employment in the village sparked a considerable political row. The months between early 1910 and mid-1911 saw intense political activity in North Devon. One of the major issues dividing the Liberal and Unionist (Conservative) Parties was the question of free trade and, in particular, the effect this policy was having on the tanning industry.

There were two General Elections in 1910, one in January and one in December.

An election meeting held in Swimbridge during the first campaign, on behalf of the Liberal sitting member for Barnstaple, Ernest Soares, brought the difficulties facing the village tannery into the open.

The meeting saw a bitter exchange between Soares and the tannery owner, W. H. Smyth, who criticised Soares for declaring that the tanning trade was 'prosperous'.

On the contrary, claimed Smyth, the industry was in difficulty both nationally and locally, with several tanneries having closed and many others working on a short time basis only. Smyth blamed the free trade policy of the Liberal party for encouraging the import of cheap foreign leather goods.

The tannery owner added: "Under the present conditions of unfair imports of foreign leather, with no possible retaliation, I see no chance of any increase of imports of hides."

The election produced a hung parliament, with the Liberals, who won the largest number of seats, forming a government under their leader Herbert Asquith.

Ernest Soares, first elected for the constituency in 1900, was again returned for Barnstaple. His major-

The tannery struggled for work in the years immediately before World War One and its plight became a political issue in 1911. Barnstaple MP Sir Ernest Soares left and his successor Sir Godfrey Baring were Liberals and free traders. The tannery owners said free trade was wrecking their business.

ity was considerably reduced, from 2,045 votes at the previous General Election in 1906, to 882.

A couple of months later, Asquith appointed Soares as a government whip. Under the Parliamentary Rules of the day, Soares had to resign and face the electorate at a by-election. Despite their progress at the recent general election, the Unionists decided not to oppose his candidacy, in view of the uncertainty of the national political situation and the likelihood, in the light of the hung parliament, of another general election.

Soares was duly returned unopposed and when the second General Election of 1910 was held, in December of that year, he increased his majority by ten votes!

There was some speculation as to whether or not the tannery workers of Swimbridge and Barnstaple, all nominally Liberal voters, had continued to support Soares in the light of the claim that free trade was a threat to their continued livelihood.

Later in the year, due to ill health, Soares resigned both his post as a whip and his seat in parliament. The constituency Liberal party chose as its candidate at the resulting by-election another devoted free trader, Sir Godfrey Baring, who had previously been a Member of Parliament for the Isle of Wight.

W. H. Smyth, who had by now announced the planned closure of the Swimbridge Tannery, took the opportunity to return to the attack.

"Ernest Soares, into whose shoes Sir Godfrey Baring now desires to step, was clearly told what was happening (to the Swimbridge Tannery) in the heart of his constituency but he and the members of the radical party have not lifted a little finger to help the British working man to overcome the serious disadvantage under which he labours by reason of the unfair treatment accorded to the foreigner at his expense.

Swimbridge tannery workforce in 1911. In the centre of the front row is the foreman, John Morrish, with hat and beard.

"The result is that this particular tannery is to be added to the long list of those which have been forced to put the shutters up, and between 30 and 40 men will find themselves out of work.

"This is another instance of how our once flourishing industries are coming to grief through the unchecked and unfair competition of the foreigner, made so easy under what Sir Godfrey Baring describes as 'the blessings' of free trade."

Despite the best efforts of W. H. Smyth and the local Unionists, Baring had a comfortable victory when the 1911 by-election took place, pushing the Liberal majority back over the 2,000 vote mark.

Nevertheless, Smyth's pessimism proved justified when the tannery **was** forced to close its doors soon after the political dispute.

The doors of the works were closed for some five years, although the hardship in the village was reduced to some degree by the shortage of labour caused by the outbreak of the 1914-18 war.

The war was the direct cause of the tannery being re-opened. The demand from the armed forces for leather grew considerably as the conflict dragged on and towards the end of 1916 it was announced that the moribund tannery had been bought by the British Electric Tanning Syndicate Ltd, from Langport in Somerset.

The British Electric company was expanding its operations, having already agreed to resuscitate another closed site, the Yatton Tanneries near Bristol. It announced that the Swimbridge tannery would be re-equipped with modern machinery which would be used to produce leather made on the latest scientific lines, of good quality and moderate price.

Operations at the reopened Swimbridge site began again early in 1917 and the resuscitated industry was to remain part of the village's economic and employment base for almost another four decades.

The Fulford family took over the tannery in 1921, restructuring the business to produce exclusively sole leather, utilising modern mixed tannage and using chemicals rather than oak bark. Traces of the old raw materials lingered in the older parts of the tannery for many years.

The first managing director of the new company was Horace Fulford who, like his predecessors the Smyths was to play a significant role in the local community, including playing cricket for the village team.

His son John, who was in control of the business at the time of the tannery closure in 1965, recalled the early days of his family's control.

"My father found the factory poorly equipped and the workmen far more skilled in farming than in tanning. He might well have despaired of ever turning a neglected works with untrained labour into a modern production unit.

"However, there were buildings and inside the buildings there were pits, and from such bare essentials he built, slowly but surely, until he had a factory which could produce leather according to modern principles."

Any doubts Horace Fulford and his brother, A. A. Fulford, who was also a working director of the firm, might have felt about the local workforce, soon disappeared.

John Fulford later recalled: "If there were misgivings about the training of suitable labour they were not borne out by events; from the staff which he recruited in those early days were drawn the foremen and responsible personnel of a later era.

"Perhaps, after all, the native occupation of farming is as good a background for a tanner of sole leather as any. The tanner begins where the farmer finishes, and both are pursuits in which patience is the supreme virtue, where coaxing brings rewards but hurried methods fail."

During its peak between the end of the 1914-18 War and the middle of the twentieth century, the tannery blended modern machinery and techniques with a traditional working layout.

Power from the national grid reached the tannery in 1937, replacing steam and an earlier system by which electricity for illumination was supplied by a water wheel. The disposal of waste liquors continued to be a problem. The village sewers were not capable of accepting trade effluents and it was necessary to discharge these into the Venn Stream – an unsatisfactory state of affairs.

That such a disposal method would eventually be prohibited was foreseen by John Fulford as early as 1953, when he predicted that tanners would be unlikely to meet the high standard of effluent disposal likely to be insisted upon in the future by the new river authorities which were being established at the time.

By the time of final closure of the tannery in 1965, John Fulford employed some 20 staff. The tannery site, and some of the buildings, were adapted for light industrial purposes, including a brewery which operated from 1981 to 1983.

Memories of the tannery are still very much alive in Swimbridge today. The author's maternal great-grandfather, John Morrish, was foreman at the turn of the nineteenth/twentieth centuries and his paternal grandfather, Charlie Dalling, was also employed by the Smyths for a time.

Ray Liverton's father Bert was employed at the tannery for most of his working life. Ray explained: "Dad had a good working relationship with the Fulford family who took over the tannery from the Smyths, and was made general foreman just before

World War Two broke out.

"My father was in charge of the tanning pits on the ground floor of the two-storey sheds (now demolished). The drying room was on the first floor, where the foreman in charge in later years was Bill Clatworthy.

Bert Liverton (left) and Ern Cox in the dark, dank conditions of the tanning shed.

Working in the tannery offered some of the benefits as well as the drawbacks of industry, including long-service awards. Victor Smart (far left) receives a long service award from general foreman Bert Liverton. Watching are l-r, Ernest Cox (part hidden), Scott Pearson, Ken Dennis and Bill Folland.

"Dad volunteered for the RAF at the start of World War Two but the tannery would not release him. Horace Fulford had already lost his son John to the forces and he argued that my father was the only man apart from himself who understood all the tanning processes.

"With the tannery dedicated to exclusively turning out leather for Army boots throughout the war, Horace Fulford insisted that Dad's job was essential war work – and he won the argument!"

Since closure in 1965 the surviving buildings on the tannery site have been used for a variety of light industrial purposes.

Swimbridge Brewery produced specialised bottled ales, such as the one shown, which commemorated a hundred years since Parson Jack Russell's death and illustrated on its label his original terrier, Trump.

This view from Hooda shows the tannery site partially cleared, with the demolition of the long three-storey wooden shed, pictured in a derelict state in the first photograph in this chapter.

Part of the tannery was utilised for a while by experienced brewer Jeffrey Patton to produce Swimbridge Best Bitter and other high quality ales, using only the best ingredients and production methods.

The most appetising product to come out of the old tannery was undoubtedly the beer produced by Jeffrey Patton in the 1980s. Today there are hundreds of what are termed micro-breweries in Britain, producing thousands of different varieties of draught and bottled beers.

Swimbridge Brewery was among the first batch of independent breweries and in 1981 Jeffrey Patton and his assistant Richard Maisonpierre were turning out 30 barrels a week – with 36 gallons in each barrel. The brewery's main product was Swimbridge Bitter, a real ale, made from pure ingredients and designed to be served by gravity, hand or electric pump, without the aid of gas.

The enterprise was greeted with enthusiasm by lovers of real ale. At the time Jeffrey Patton told *North Devon Journal* reporter Richard Howe: "People are going mad for it. I don't blame them. I won't drink keg beer myself and a lot of people are deciding they have had enough of beer produced by accountants in big companies."

Sadly, the brewery had only a short lifespan.

Yarnacott was typical of the hamlets in Swimbridge parish, having a cluster of farmhouses close together. The house with a gabled porch in the left hand foreground is Yeocot, the last of the Yeo family homes, now part of Swimbridge Nursing Home.

Agriculture

Throughout much of the twentieth century it was difficult to walk across The Square in Swimbridge without having to step around the liquid by-products of the milking herds which were daily driven through the village.

During the first half of the century, Swimbridge was much more recognisably the centre of an agricultural community than it is today.

Kelly's directories from the earliest years of the century to the immediate post-World War Two period show a fairly consistent number of residents of the parish – varying between 40 and 50 – describing themselves as farmers, smallholders, or dairymen.

In 1978 Mervyn Dalling took the electoral register for the parish and inked in the trades, occupations and professions of every individual voter. This invaluable and fascinating document reveals that those describing their occupation as farmer or some directly allied trade had fallen by nearly half in little more than thirty-five years.

Making hay at Dennington Barton in the 1920s. Mr Arthur Elworthy is on the cart and a Mr Butcher, who lived at Dennington Lodge, is on the left with the pitchfork.

Cutting oats in 1934 at Tordown Farm. The right-handed binder is being operated by Herbert Snell and his brother Walter.

Those three and a half decades had seen immense social change in the agricultural sector, with a general drift from the land and the sale of farmhouses to be used as homes by non-farming families, with the attached land either rented out or amalgamated into other and larger holdings.

In terms of both arable production and the raising of livestock, widespread mechanisation, improved fertilisation, and modern marketing methods had combined to encourage much larger agricultural units.

Mervyn's survey also faithfully reflected the fact that modern farming was also much less labour intensive. Only one man on the electoral register was marked as being a farm worker. He was joined by an agricultural engineer, an agricultural contractor and an estate worker – figures almost lost among almost ten times as many factory workers.

Add another thirty-five years or so – taking a snapshot of Swimbridge in the second decade of the twenty-first century – and the number of residents of the parish earning a living from agriculture has once again declined.

Few men are better qualified to reflect on the factors that have influenced local agriculture over the past century or so than John Bartlett of Sandyke. His family has farmed in the parish for more than a century (and was established in the Clovelly area of North Devon for generations before moving to Swimbridge).

John's experience embraces not just practical farming but also the modern bureaucratic aspects of an industry that now demands much more from the farmer in terms of administration and regulation. Having grown up on a farm in the parish, he worked for the then Ministry of Agriculture, Fisheries and Food (MAFF) in Lancashire before returning to Swimbridge and buying first Sandyke and later the lands which had previously been part of Accott Manor.

"The number of individual farms in Swimbridge parish increased at the end of the nineteenth century, when the large landowners started to dispose of their holdings," John explains. "Local people were able to rent or on occasions buy enough acreage to make farming viable, although in reality the farms were generally small, mixed, and not very intensive.

"The farmers kept a few sheep, a few cattle and their holdings were entirely self-sufficient. All the feed needed for the stock was produced on the farm, with nothing bought in, and the only cash-type crops were mainly for the family's consumption – potatoes, Swedes etc.

"Land in the parish was (and is to this day) based on naturally acidic shale-based soils, and the addition of lime as a fertiliser was essential. Oats, which would grow on acidic soil, and which cattle and sheep can digest whole, as opposed to grain which has to be milled, would have been a popular crop.

"As far as livestock was concerned, in the early

The Bartletts are still at the heart of Swimbridge's farming community. Pictured left is John, of Sandyke Farm and Bert, of Coombe. In the centre is John's son James. Bert is a vintage tractor enthusiast and is seen with one of his vehicles.

Ernie Mogridge of Smalldon Farm is at work in 1956 with the Richards' family's horse Madam, which has sadly had its head cut off by the photographer. Long Meadow is next to the Link Road (formerly the Taunton-Barnstaple railway line) and Yeoland House can be seen in the background.

Dairy classes were held in the Old Schoolroom in the 1920s.

Above: *Derelict machinery at Riverton Mill.*

Left: *The 18ft water wheel at Mill Court, pictured in 1936.*

Below left: *Riverton Mill, restored in the 1970s.*

Below right: *The certificate presented to Albert Westaway of Coombe Farm for his work in chairing the local War Agriculture Committee from 1939-45.*

On Behalf of His Majesty's Government I wish to thank you for the service you have rendered to the nation during the war. The task of British agriculture, an arduous, indeed a vital one, was to keep the nation fed. With your help it has been done.

W.A.E.C's by their care and consideration, secured the willing co-operation of the farming community, and have, by their energy and example, raised the production of our farms to a new high level.

I am confident you will always be proud of having played so important a part in the contribution which British agriculture has made to our Victory.

Minister of Agriculture and Fisheries, 8th May 1945.

To Mr. A. K. Westaway
Coombe, Swimbridge
Barnstaple.

years of the twentieth century people would have kept the traditional shorthorn cattle and Devon close-wool sheep, which thrived on feed of a lesser quality.

"The concept of self-sufficiency extended to every farmer with cattle keeping his own bull and, unlike today's extensive use of contractors, the work of the farm would have been carried out by the farmer, his sons and farm labourers, with extra help brought in at harvest and other busy times."

Farms became bigger and more mechanised as the century progressed. The forerunner to mechanised farming locally had been the first reaping machine in the district, introduced to the parish in the 1870s, by John Squire at Accott. The machine aroused huge interest, with a large crowd assembling near Sandick Cross to see its capabilities demonstrated. Although the spectators were drawn by curiosity John Squire and his son, also John, were taking no chances with their revolutionary acquisition.

Mechanisation, whether on the land or, at an earlier stage in the textile and other industries, had led to fears of unemployment and, fearing sabotage, the Squires locked the reaping machine securely in a barn at Accott. Tractors appeared in increasing numbers in the years between the twentieth century's two world wars – John's father, Sid Bartlett, acquired his first machine about 1930.

It was becoming harder and harder to make a living from the old traditional methods, off a small acreage, with limited numbers of livestock. Innovations such as the introduction of the Milk Marketing Board in 1933 accelerated the process of growth in the size of holdings, making possible increased sales of milk and subsequently to larger dairy herds.

Regulation in the industry increased as the years passed, and was particularly stringent during and immediately after World War Two, when a much higher level of food production became essential to Britain's survival.

John Bartlett's grandfather, Albert Westaway, had been a regular soldier, reaching the rank of sergeant in the North Devon Yeomanry, before leaving the Army in 1912 to rent Combe Farm, – the home today of John's brother Bert. During World War Two the government established War Agriculture Committees, on a parish basis, and Albert Westaway was appointed to take charge of the Swimbridge body. His job entailed ensuring that the farmers in the parish were growing the crops demanded by the needs of a wartime economy.

John Bartlett said: "It was a difficult position, and it seems a strange relationship, with one farmer telling others what to do. But my grandfather was well respected in Swimbridge and had the authority, perhaps because of his Army experience, to make a success of the job."

After the war the grip established by the govern-

Henry and Seymour Hammett, of Swimbridge Newland, were rabbit catchers. Rabbits for the pot were a desirable commodity, especially during World War Two.

ment was to a certain degree maintained, especially with the introduction of subsidies, which today include the single farm payment payable to anyone involved in agriculture. Britain's membership of the European Economic Community and later the European Union also increased the amount of regulation.

"The farming business obviously changed radically over the course of the twentieth century. Swimbridge today is still primarily an agricultural community, although there are far fewer individual farms, and the economic and environmental pressures on surviving farmers are intense," John Bartlett added.

The day-to-day evidence of farming in the very centre of Swimbridge village was present until well into the second half of the twentieth century.

Mill Court, where the farmhouse and the former mill are now private residences, was the last working farm in the village itself. The Richards family farmed

Barnstaple livestock market was still busy in the 1970s. Auctioneer Geoffrey Clapp is seen selling sheep. Farmer Sid Bartlett of Swimbridge, a renowned sheep expert, is pictured right, in the trilby with a feather in the brim.

A break from the hard toil of a harvest field at Mill Court Farm in 1953. George Trute of Chapel Court sits on a horse held by Fred Richards and Peter Vellacott of Church Lane is astride a horse held by Florence Richards.

in a very traditional manner and were also perhaps the last farmers in the parish to make extensive use of working horses.

Town Tenement, on the main road through the village, housed the Smale family dairying business, which also rented the Glebelands and land off Road Lane for grazing.

Pitt Farm (also known as Smalldon or Smoldon) was farmed in the mid-twentieth century by Percy Tucker, whose land ran as far north of the village as the railway line. He also worked land on Kerscott Hill, near the former Methodist chapel.

Bestridge was centred around the pond and the old lime kilns, close to where the housing developments of Orchard Close and Bestridge Meadow now stand.

The Dunn family, with farming roots in Swimbridge extending back into the nineteenth century, at one time owned the post office and stores and ran a dairy business from the premises. The family's land holdings in the village included the site of the houses at Archipark.

The Balment family from Yarnacott also had land in Swimbridge itself, off Hannaford Lane, whilst Marsh Farm occupied the western fringes of the village.

At the time of writing there are three dairy farms in Swimbridge; John Bartlett's herd of Holstein Friesans at Sandyke, the Elworthy family's herd on the other side of the valley, at Bickle and the Jackson family's herd at Higher Kerscott. This latter holding has been extensively developed, with new buildings, designed for an increase of the family's herd to 200 cattle.

Any cereals grown in the parish continue to be exclusively for the farms' own uses, rather than constituting cash crops.

Other present-day farms in the parish – there are around a dozen operating in Swimbridge today – continue to pursue a fairly traditional course, either mixing beef cattle and sheep or running sheep alone.

Despite the difficulties that continue to confront British agriculture the future for farming in Swimbridge looks pretty bright. In the case of both the Bartlett and Elworthy families sons and grandsons offer hope for the future.

Owen Dalling is seen on top of a heavily-piled loose load at Town Tenement.

Indiwell farmhouse smoulders after the major fire that reduced the building to a shell in 1913.

Chapter 6

A Village at Play

Swimbridge relaxes

It may be a cliché, but there is a lot of truth in the old saying that all work and no play makes Jack (and Jill) a dull boy (or girl).

Despite the hard manual labour that was the lot of most village people for much of the twentieth century, with long hours spent on the land, in the tannery sheds or in the local quarries, Swimbridge people have always found time for pleasure.

Mervyn Dalling's photographic collection is rich in illustrations of villagers enjoying themselves. For more than a century cameras, amateur and professional, have captured pleasure seekers at carnivals, revels, fetes, dances, film shows, plays and concerts, held in the school or at the Jubilee Hall.

The collection illustrates the competitive side of a village at play, recording gymkhanas, sports days and sheep shearing competitions. Preserved for posterity are village cricket and football teams, trophy-winning bell ringers, successful skittles and darts players and members of local hunts meeting on The Square.

Healthy appetites meant that dinners, lunches, tea parties and Sunday School treats with plenty of buns and fizzy drinks are depicted.

There is a fascinating record of outings – originally by open-topped charabancs – organised by village groups such as the British Legion, the Young Communicants Guild from the parish church, the Youth Club, Womens' Institute, the Mothers Union,

The start of the wheelbarrow race at Swimbridge Fête in 1914, with the village policeman firmly in control. The 'drivers' were blindfolded!

Photographs taken in the weeks leading up to World War One have a special poignancy. The sheep shearing contest and sports organised by the National Deposit Friendly Society – the 'Club' – at Swimbridge in the early summer of 1914 was attended by many whose lives would be affected by the conflict, including sisters Elsie, Katie and Marjorie Symons of Marsh Farm, seen in the back row of spectators to the left of the picture.

Maypole dancers in the Vicarage field circa 1925. Front row, l-r, Evelyn Balment, unknown, Anna Burgess, Phyllis Westaway, Grace Trute, Rose Dalling, Ena Leworthy, Elizabeth Pickard, Emma Holland and Amy Yeo. Most of the rather sheepish looking boys have not been identified.

the choir of St James, and the United Womens Own from the Wesleyan Methodist Chapel.

Desinations varied from local seaside resorts to much farther afield as the century progressed.

Mervyn's own camera recorded many events in the later years of the twentieth century. Boxing Day wheelbarrow races and tussles across the Venn Stream, events to mark HM Queen Elizabeth II's Silver, Golden and Diamond Jubilees, and many memorable nights in the Jack Russell.

Despite the appearance of wireless sets, televisions, and the latest twenty-first century electronic gadgets, Swimbridge retains a reputation as a village which knows how to enjoy itself and how to celebrate an event.

Revels and reviews

In the first decade of the twentieth century, organised entertainments were relatively few and far between, mostly staged by the school and churches for the children of the parish. Treats of all kinds survived even during the grim years of World War One, with villagers determined that their children should not be deprived.

The travelling showman, walking from village to village to provide a rare out-of-the-way spectacle was still to be found in North Devon in the years before the Great War and for some time after. Elsie Symons, a daughter of the farming family at Marsh, on the western edge of the village, later recalled that as a small girl she saw a man with a dancing bear silhouetted against the skyline on Hooda Hill.

Barnstaple Fair was eagerly awaited each

September by the village children not just for the possibility of being taken to town to enjoy the rides and fairings, but also for the free show provided when the wagons and living vans of the show people moved at a snail's pace up Barnstaple Hill, past the school, hauled by steam traction engines.

At the end of the fair the spectacle was repeated, but this time it was the even more demanding slope of Kerscott Hill that had to be surmounted, with the traction engines topping up their water supply from the stream before attempting the ascent.

Headmaster William Shelley organised many concerts and reviews in the school, which was the

The school was frequently the venue for musical and dramatic productions before the opening of the Jubilee Hall. The title of the show pictured here is not known, but the dancers can be identified. Standing, l-r, are Ena Burgess, Hannah Holland, Doris Trute, Daisy Butcher, Margaret Leworthy, Nellie Tucker, Vera Gould. Kneeling in the second row are Olive Cox and Kate Tucker, with Vera Yeo and Hilda Trute at the front.

largest public building available until the opening of the Jubilee Hall in 1938. Shelley, an enthusiastic performer himself, formed the Swimbridge Winter Concert Society, which brightened many a dark winter evening.

A programme for a review in 1905 featured songs, sketches, a cornet solo, pianoforte solo, and a sketch by the Strolling Players. Like so many later social events, it was staged not just for entertainment but to aid local charities and institutions, in this instance the North Devon Infirmary.

Although carnivals, with their street parades and the crowning of a queen for the day are a modern innovation, Swimbridge Revel dates back for centuries, probably first being held soon after the original establishment of a church by the Venn Stream in the twelfth century.

The word 'revel' shares a Latin origin with 'rebel', and the early revels were no doubt seen by the villagers as a rare opportunity to let their hair down and run riot for a few hours, forgetting the tedium of their daily lives.

Revel is specifically a West Country word, with a similar meaning to the 'feasts', the 'wakes' and the 'mops' of the Midlands and North Country. Revels were often held in conjunction with 'Church Ales', when strong ale would be brewed by the parish to help the merrymaking along.

Before the Reformation and King Henry VIII's

Members of Swimbridge and Landkey British Legion on their annual outing (destination unknown) in the late 1940s. Pictured in the back row are, l-r, Sid Facey, Ken Dennis, Albert Facey, Hilda Hurley, Cyril Holland, Harry Berry and Tom Holland. In the second row, l-r, are Bill Mearles, and Reg Hurley. At the front is Ron Elliott.

break with Rome, the Catholic Church had a virtual monopoly on the brewing of ale. The ales used for village festivals were often brewed in church houses, the medieval equivalent of modern church halls.

The best example in North Devon of a former church house, where ale was brewed, still stands within the boundaries of Parracombe church, although it is now a private dwelling.

World War Two and the following austerity did not prevent families from enjoying the traditional pleasures of North Devon beaches. Mrs Mary Yeo (left) of Tordown Farm and Mrs Nora Holland of Tordown Cottages enjoy the comfort of deckchairs. Sitting on the sand, l-r, are Patricia Holland, George Snell, Diana Dalling, Leonora Snell and Betty Holland.

A Liberal fête at Bestridge in the late 1950s. North Devon MP Jeremy Thorpe is pictured second from the left.

A cake stall is a big attraction at a Bestridge fête, again in the late 1950s. Not all of the fête-goers can be identified but the two girls at the front are Valerie Crook and Brenda Huxtable, with schoolteacher Bertha Chown and Mrs Audrey Crook standing behind them.

The 1978 Swimbridge Revel featured a Jack Russell terrier show.

A parish was not required to have a church house, as the nave of the church itself could function as a secular meeting-place for medieval parishioners, as well as a religious one. The modern practice of having concerts, talks, coffee mornings and craft fairs, and serving tea, coffee and, on occasions, wine, in church is not a new departure, but simply a return to the practices of the past.

Revels in former years were the occasion for boisterous and noisy behaviour, with dancing, sports and a heavy consumption of ale. Not surprisingly there were several attempts to ban the events, with Devon justices in 1600 pledging to suppress both church ales and revels. Later in the seventeenth century, during the rule of the Puritan dictator Oliver Cromwell, revels were actually banned by law, as being 'improper and unseemly' behaviour.

In 1660 when the monarchy returned in the person of King Charles II, merry making and feasting was once again permitted, with revels continuing to be an excuse for drunkenness. As late as the nineteenth century the churchwardens at Swimbridge were heavily criticised for failing to keep proper control of the imbibing.

The rebel tradition of the revel endured in a mild form until at least the middle of the nineteenth century. In Swimbridge, on the second day of the Revel, the village was designated as a 'borough' by the residents, who staged a 'municipal election' to choose a mayor, town clerk, and aldermen.

Swimbridge Revel was held on (or as near as possible to) 25 July, the feast day of the patron saint of the parish, St James. In 1985 the patronal and dedication festival began on the Wednesday (July 24) with evensong and continued the next day, St James' day, with a celebration of the Eucharist.

On the Saturday of the same week the social side of the Revel was held in the extensive grounds of the old Vicarage, off Barnstaple Hill, with the proceeds going to the church, the school and local charities. The evening event, more sober and decorous than on occasions in the past, featured dancing by children from the school, a family pet show, a barbecue, pony rides and sideshows.

The 1985 event was the last to be held before the Vicarage was sold by the Church and the following year the Revel moved to the grounds of the Jubilee Hall. It was later held in Bestridge Meadow, before the land was used for housing.

The traditional meal for Swimbridge Revel was roast duck, green peas, mazzard pie and cream. Mazzards were a species of black cherries, with two main varieties, Dunns and Little Blacks. They retained their flavour when cooked but stained the fingers, the stain taking several days to disappear.

The orchards where the cherries were grown, now disappeared from Swimbridge, were known as 'Mazzard Greens'. They were a natural target for

The finish of the egg and spoon race at the 1977 Queen's Silver Jubilee sports day.

Right: Michael Chapman, son of the then landlord of the Jack Russell, with his Silver Jubilee Mug, as presented to all Swimbridge children in 1977.

Below: Swimbridge Carnival 1951. Carnival Queen Betty Yeo (centre) is pictured with attendants Jean Dennis (left) and Gladys Hancock. The crown bearer at the front of the picture is Jane Buckingham.

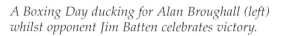

A Boxing Day ducking for Alan Broughall (left) whilst opponent Jim Batten celebrates victory.

Above: *Fancy dress at the 1951 carnival. Colin (left) and Mervyn Dalling as farmworkers, with their model tractor and trailor.*

Above right: *The 1966 Carnival Queen Josephine Dalling is crowned by her predecessor, Doreen Wheaton, outside the Jubilee Hall. The attendants are (left) Vera Cox and Pamela Hosegood.*

Below: *The 1966 carnival had to contend with wet weather. The mounted marshall, Major M. D. Murphy of Dennington House, leads the parade away from the railway station, ahead of South Molton Town Band.*

Above: *Fancy dress at the 1966 carnival. Simon Scarecrow, alias Peter Petherick.*

Left: *Lighting designer Dave Bryant, who lived at the former Indiwell Farm, Swimbridge, designed and executed a spectacular night time walk in August 2002. Crowds estimated at between seven and ten thousand people crowded into Swimbridge for the event.*

birds, and in earlier times men were employed to shoot and scare the feathered raiders. Swimbridge's neighbouring village, Landkey, planted a new Mazzard Green to mark the millennium.

The final Swimbridge Revel was held in the mid-1990s, although there was a later, unsuccessful attempt at a revival.

Swimbridge Carnival flourished in the immediate post-war years, disappeared from the village calendar of events and then was revived in 1965 by the Jubilee Hall Entertainments Committee, in aid of a fund to provide an extension to the hall. The event, featuring Miss Doreen Tucker as Swimbridge's first Carnival Queen for some years, made a profit of £104 and encouraged the organisers to repeat the event in 1966.

The 1966 queen, 15-year-old Miss Josephine Dalling, was crowned at the Jubilee Hall before, with her attendants, joining the street parade which assembled by the railway station.

After the judging of the various fancy dress classes and the floats, and despite what the local press described as 'a steady downpour' the procession, with a police escort and headed by a mounted marshall, Major M. D. Murphy from Dennington House, and the South Molton Town Band, passed down Station Hill, continuing along the main road in the direction of South Molton as far as the Coach and Horses pub (still trading in those days).

The route of the parade then took in High Street and Church Lane before rejoining the main road, ending at The Square. A dance was held in the Jubilee Hall in the evening, with the music provided by the All Stars Dance Band, who charged £13 (including travelling expenses) for playing for four hours.

Other major village events during the second half of the twentieth century included celebrations for the coronation of Her Majesty Queen Elizabeth II in 1953, and subsequently for her Silver, Gold and Diamond Jubilees. These festivities included the usual teas and commemorative mugs for the children, but Swimbridge, surrounded by hills, was able to add its own special touch by lighting beacons and bonfires.

Another royal event to be commemorated was the wedding of Prince Charles to Lady Diana Spencer in July 1981. Following the usual teas, children from the village were presented with Crown coins and there was a bonfire, with hot dogs, in the Vicarage garden.

The village in recent years has earned its widespread reputation for organising successful events, in particular to support the campaign for leisure facilities run by SNAP (Swimbridge Needs A Park) and, most recently, the fund-raising for the re-development of the Jubilee Hall.

The spirit of enterprise was very evident in the first years after the millennium, when lighting designer Dave Bryant, who lived at the former Indiwell Farm, situated in the valley below the main road to South Molton, below Kerscott Hill, designed and executed a spectacular night time walk in August 2002.

The hugely-talented Bryant had sold his London-based company Midnight Design and returned to his West Country roots to continue his struggle with cancer. Despite being diagnosed with a brain tumour, which affected his hearing and eyesight, he was determined that his creativity would continue.

Part of Bryant's inspiration for staging the Swimbridge Light Walk was the lifting of the restrictions imposed during the 2001 outbreak of foot and mouth disease. He wanted to get people back into the countryside.

Crowds estimated at between seven and ten thousand people crowded into Swimbridge for the 4½ mile walk in aid of the North Devon Hospice, following a trail of 10,000 lights through the hills surrounding the village, augmented by five large illuminated figures built with fire and light.

The largest and most elaborate figure, 'The Angel of the South' combined more than 700 flaming torches with state-of-the-art lighting technology. The lighting effects were accompanied by an appropriate soundscape.

Bryant repeated his Lightquest success in 2003, with an event entitled Dreamwalk, staged in the grounds of Lord and Lady Arran's home at Castle Hill, within the Fortescue Estate at Filleigh. Before his untimely death in 2007, at the hospice for which he had raised funds, he had planned another lighting spectacular in The Valley of Rocks at Lynton. Sadly, this had to be postponed because of another outbreak of foot and mouth, in south east England.

The hugely-talented Dave Bryant sold his London-based company Midnight Design and returned to his West Country roots to continue his ultimately unsuccessful struggle with illness.

Swimbridge's cricket pitch was situated in the field below the village school and the pupils took advantage of its proximity to play their own games on the rough bank which led down to the carefully-prepared square. In the background, by the hedge, are the two huts which provided changing and tea facilities for the village team. Scores were hung on the left-hand hut when matches were in progress.

Sport in Swimbridge

Sport prospered as never before in post-World War Two Britain, as a population starved of entertainment during the grim years of hostilities determined to make up for lost time.

North Devon was no exception to the national trend. Football boomed as never before in the area, with crowds of up to 5,000 watching Barnstaple Town and Bideford in league and cup action. Older villagers remember that post-war Swimbridge on occasions filled a coach for the 100-mile trip to watch the Exeter Falcons speedway team ride at the County Ground, when that sport was enjoying its golden age of popularity.

Sport in the villages also rode the crest of the wave of post-war enthusiasm and Swimbridge had thriving football and cricket teams.

Although both sports had been played in the village in earlier times, with cricket remembered on a field at the end of what was to become the lane leading down to Archipark, and also on land near to the present Hooda Close, accessed from Road Lane, the late 1940s and early 1950s represented a golden era.

The football team in particular enjoyed great success on the field, winning no fewer than three trophies in the 1951-52 campaign, but was unable to maintain the momentum, largely because of losing players to other sides, and the Swimbridge name disappeared from the North Devon League tables within a couple of seasons of the club's triumphs.

Cricket flourished for considerably longer, but the ground, opposite the village school, became unavail-

Swimbridge Cricket Club, pictured in 1948. Left to right, back row, C. Sowden, R. Elliott, A. Fulford, W. Folland, K. Dennis, S. Facey, A. Dennis, T. Buckingham, Owen Dalling (umpire). Front, L. Dennis, D. Holland, P. Dennis and Henry Smale.

able and the club folded. What was arguably the peak of cricket's popularity in Swimbridge, with the club on one memorable occasion able to field two sides with a full 22 players, coincided with the triple trophy success of the football team in 1951.

Early in the season it was discovered that the cricket club had arranged two matches for the same Saturday afternoon, an away fixture in Barnstaple against Raleigh B and a home game against Pilton.

After some hard work on the part of the Swimbridge secretary two teams were raised – no mean feat for a small village club – and both matches took place. The secretary came in for considerable praise for his efforts, but the available talent had been stretched a little too thinly, and both Swimbridge sides were defeated.

The cricket club had overcome considerable odds

just to play the game in the village. The square was at the foot of a considerable slope and the facilities were fairly spartan, consisting of a small dressing room and a tea hut. Like on many rural cricket fields, cattle were grazed on the ground, adding to the hazards of batting without a sight screen.

Cricket certainly brought the village together for a couple of decades or so following the end of World War Two.

The regular team at the time of the double fixture booking included the vicar, the Rev. Eric Robotham and the tannery owner John Fulford, together with a line-up drawn mainly from local men.

A previous vicar, the Rev H. J. A. Rusbridger, also played cricket, helping to keep the sport alive during the darkest days of the war. In late August, as the Battle of Britain was raging over the skies of the south eastern counties, Swimbridge travelled to Bratton Fleming, beating their opponents by five wickets.

The vicar was the team's outstanding performer, scoring 55 not out and taking one wicket for just four runs as Bratton were skittled out for just 38. L. Dennis took four wickets for nine runs and A. Sturgess three for six.

The English historian G. M. Trevelyan famously remarked of the circumstances leading to the 1789 revolution in France that if "the French nobility had been capable of playing cricket with their peasants, their chateaux would never have been burnt."

The fact that Swimbridge lies in a deep valley has always meant that land suitable for the playing of team games was at a premium.

Both before and after World War Two Swimbridge Cricket Club played its home matches on the Vicarage Field, opposite the school. Facilities were primitive, especially at first.

The wickets were cut using a push lawnmower and the area of the square was fenced off with hurdles between matches to prevent the incursion of the cows which grazed the field. The outfield was unfenced and needed to be carefully inspected and cleared before the umpires and and the teams took the field!

A couple of planks were fixed into the bank above the playing area for use by spectators but initially there were no facilities apart from that, except for a cattle shed in the top corner of the field which provided a little privacy for changing.

Teas, an essential part of any cricket match even today, were served, although the methods employed initially would have raised eyebrows at Lords or Trent Bridge. Two of the hurdles normally used to protect the square were hammered into the ground with a wide plank placed on top to form a table.

Water for tea was brought to the ground in buckets and boiled on a primus stove. A rudimentary scoreboard was made from wood, with nails to hold numbers painted on tin, showing the total score, the number of wickets that had fallen and the score made by the last man.

The board was mounted on a piece of piping, which itself slotted into another pipe which had been driven into the ground.

Mervyn Dalling was the secretary of the cricket club and scorer in 1957 (his father Owen often acted as umpire) and later recalled: "It was all very home-made, but perfectly adequate. Given the facilities it was surprising just how much local skill existed.

"A lot of enjoyment was had in those days even though, if the match went on for longer than expected, the cows would arrive back in the field after milking. It was not unknown for a fielder to step in a cow pat, or to dive into one when taking a catch.

"Both the cricket and football clubs did a lot to foster community spirit in the village."

From time to time improvements were made to the cricket field. By 1948 a shed had been bought and erected to act as a changing room and, with the front opened up, as a tea hut. A larger hut was later provided for changing and the club also acquired the front roller from an old steamroller. When fitted with a wooden frame, it required most of the team to pull it up and down the pitch.

At the time of writing several members of Swimbridge Cricket Club are still living in the village, including, Sid Facey, Denzil Holland and Alan Mildon, who was the scorer in later years and whose father, Charles, also umpired.

Sid Facey remembers vividly an occasion when he was due to bat first wicket down. Thinking he had plenty of time, he lit a cigarette, stuffing his box of matches into his cricket flannels. He had no time to take them out of his pocket when a wicket fell and he had to go to the wicket.

He had to face a particularly aggressive fast bowler who eventually struck Sid on the thigh, causing the matches to explode into flames!

Swimbridge's fixture list over the years included matches against neighbouring villages, including Filleigh, North Molton, High Bickington, Goodleigh, and Marwood, and works teams such as Rawle Gammon and Baker and Yelland Power Station.

Some matches meant longer trips, with an annual match away at Dawlish, and the village side also enjoyed a much coveted fixture away against Lynton, in the spectacular Valley of the Rocks ground.

Turning to football, Swimbridge has a secure place in the history of the North Devon League, although the initial involvement of the village in the competition was wholly negative.

When the *North Devon Journal* carried an advertisement in February 1904 calling for teams to enter a new football competition, Swimbridge was among the eight clubs to respond, along with teams from much bigger centres such as Bideford, South Molton

Swimbridge's B team in 1951-52, probably photographed at Barnstaple Town's Mill Road ground. Back row, l-r, Ron Dennis, Eddie Dennis, Tony Chalk, D. Lake, David Dunn, K. Moss, B. Payne (linesman). Front row, l-r, C. Snow, David Dennis, Ken Dennis, Henry Smale and Denzil Holland.

and Ilfracombe – all still active in the same competition 111 years later.

Reporting the foundation of the league, an item on its excellent modern-day website records, quite simply, that: 'it appears Swimbridge did not start the season.' The assumption must be that a football club must have either been in existence in Swimbridge prior to the founding of the league, or that the delegates from the village who attended the initial league meetings must have been confident that they could form a team before the start of the 1904-1905 campaign.

More than 40 football seasons were to pass before Swimbridge took its place in the North Devon Football League.

The club made its belated bow in the 1948-49 season, with the team finishing sixteenth out of seventeen sides in the league's Division Three, playing 32 matches, of which four were won, five drawn and 23 lost.

The division in the late 1940s and early 1950s was remarkable for the number of very small communities able to field a team, at a time before the drift away from the land had greatly reduced the numbers of eligible young men in the rural areas. The only team below Swimbridge in the league table was Brayford, whilst neighbouring Filleigh finished one place higher. Other teams from tiny communities included Kentisbury and Alverdiscott.

The 1949-50 season saw the quite large Division Three split into two sections, North and South. Swimbridge was placed in the South section and enjoyed a greatly improved season, finishing third behind champions Landkey and runners-up Chittlehampton.

More progress was made in 1950-51, with Swimbridge finishing as runners-up to Chittle-hampton. Another side providing a local derby,

Chittlehamholt, suffered a disastrous campaign, losing all 12 of its matches and conceding 90 goals while scoring just seven in return.

In the team's fourth season, 1951-52, Swimbridge finally hit the jackpot. The club fielded two teams during the campaign, A and B, and the A team won the championship of North Devon League Division Three South. The B team competed in Division Three North, finishing seventh.

In addition to the league success, the club won no fewer than three cups – the North Devon League Cup (Third Division), the Braunton Cup, and the South Molton YMCA Cup. The YMCA trophy, with the Swimbridge victory recorded on the plinth, spent much of 2014 on display in the Jack Russell pub. The trophy was held at the time by Landkey Town, whose headquarters today is at the Jack Russell.

Landlord Paul Darch was happy to allow Sid Facey, a member of the 1951 Swimbridge side, to be photographed with the trophy and recall memories of village football more than sixty years ago.

After the 1951-52 season of triumph, Swimbridge returned to fielding just one team for the following season. As the A team had finished top of its division in the previous campaign, Swimbridge was elevated to the North Devon League Division Two (or Junior Division, as it was known at the time).

Swimbridge finished a creditable fifth, against much stronger opposition than had been the case in previous seasons. Yet despite this, the club folded at the end of the season, after an existence of just five league campaigns.

The guiding light behind the team was Dennis Smith, who lived at Bydown and died in 1976. The team played on a level field at Bydown (about 100 yards from Bydown House). The field was owned by the Shapland family of Kerscott.

Changing facilities were provided at the Old Schoolroom, with the teams facing quite a long walk before and after the match, although team member Ken Dennis of Station Hill remembered some use also being made of a cart linhay nearer the actual pitch.

Swimbridge Football Club in its original post-war form was short-lived and the cricket club also eventually folded.

Things took a turn for the better again in 1984, when at a meeting in the Jack Russell on Leap Year Day (February 29) enthusiasts for both sports formed the Swimbridge Sports and Cricket Club. Former pub landlord Tom Snell was made president, with Mervyn Dalling as vice-president.

One of the new club's constant themes was the need for a new playing field in the village, with provision for both cricket and football – something which, thirty years later (in 2015) at least has a chance of becoming reality.

In the 1980s the cricket branch of the club sought various grounds, including use of the facilities at

West Buckland School and nearer home considered land at Crossways Caravan Park (which proved to be too narrow) and at Dennington House, then in educational use, where the former pitch needed re-turfing.

Some fixtures were fulfilled at West Buckland School, with the club's accounts showing a figure of £40 for pitch fees in the financial year ending in March 1986.

From a football point of view, the name of Swimbridge had re-appeared in the North Devon League fixture list for the 1988-89 season. The team played at Rock Park in Barnstaple, no suitable ground being available in the village. The club played for 16 seasons, mostly in the league's Intermediate divisions three, two and one, with a single campaign in the senior division.

Occasional matches were played in the later years of the last century between a Jack Russell team and Filleigh, on a pitch close to Filleigh church.

Whether the provision of the new park in Swimbridge will eventually lead to the formation of new football and cricket teams, remains to be seen. The park is designed to be also used for sport by the village school, which in the past made use of the old cricket field, conveniently situated just across the road.

Other organised sport in Swimbridge has generally been of the indoor variety, with successful skittles and darts team based at the Jack Russell, where both pastimes flourish still.

In the years leading up to World War One, competitive rifle shooting was encouraged, something covered in Chapter Eight, *A Village at War*.

It would be impossible to write about sport, even in the twentieth century, without a mention of hunting. The very fact that Swimbridge was for nearly half a century the home of the Rev. John Russell, 'Parson Jack' has ensured that the name of the village has an honoured place in the history of the sport, which today is still the most popular and avidly followed sporting activity (with shooting a fairly close runner-up) on Exmoor and the surrounding countryside.

The parish was at one point also the location of kennels, with Russell keeping a pack of hounds at Tordown House, where he lived for a time.

A stag was taken at Swimbridge in 1913 by Sir John Amory's hounds. It entered the village from Bydown, ran to Bestridge, entered the churchyard

Crowds gather to watch a meet on The Square at Swimbridge. The pack involved is not known.

More sporting success for Swimbridge! The 'Jim's Boys' skittles team, captained by Jim Westcott and based at the Jack Russell, were the 1965 winners of the Coronation Cup. Pictured, back row, l-r, are Ken Dennis, Eddie Dennis and Henry Smale. Front, l-r, Bill Squire, Jim Westcott and Stan Cann.

World War One cavalryman Ernest Dallyn of Hutcherton Farm lifts his cap to the master before the hunt moves off from Swimbridge Square.

and then went uphill to the railway station. The beast entered a house, without doing any serious damage and finally became entangled in wire netting near the Vicarage.

Local experts judged that had it not been for the netting, the stag, described as 'an exceptionally fine animal', would have escaped. As it was, it was the first 'kill' recorded in Swimbridge in living memory.

Various local hunts met in Swimbridge Square during the twentieth century, with local farmers riding to hounds and crowds of enthusiastic followers and spectators watching the huntsman and whippers-in marshal the packs.

Cheers!

With more and more pubs across the country calling time permanently, Swimbridge is fortunate to have the thriving Jack Russell at the very heart of village life.

Owned by the Darch family, the establishment has all the ingredients needed for success in the twenty-first century. It has a renowned restaurant, serving fine wines and food sourced wherever possible from local suppliers, but also retains a traditional pub atmosphere, with log fires, serving local beers and ciders in the bar, and is home to skittles, darts and pool teams.

Swimbridge in the mid-nineteenth century had six licensed premises – three in the village itself and three in the wider parish.

The village pubs were The New Inn (renamed The Jack Russell in 1962), The Coach and Horses, built to tap the coaching trade when the road through Swimbridge became the main highway from Barnstaple to South Molton and beyond, and The Lamb and Flag, tucked away from the main road in High Street.

In the southern part of the parish, the hamlets and scattered farms were served by The Travellers Rest, near Cobbaton, a coaching inn which lost its trade

The former Hare and Hounds pub at Swimbridge Newland. The building also once housed a Church of England Mission Room.

when services were diverted to the newer, more direct route from Barnstaple to the outside world.

Close to the parish's northern boundary was The Stone Cross Inn, situated on the road between Brayford and Goodleigh, a handsome Georgian building which was to continue to trade as a shop for some time after ceasing to be a public house. The Hare and Hounds was located at Swimbridge Newland.

By 1900, only the three pubs in the village itself survived to fulfil their original purpose. Swimbridge, and its thirsty tannery employees, quarrymen and farm workers (provided they were not strict nonconformists who had signed the pledge) provided sufficient custom to make the three licensed houses viable.

Although public houses became subject to licensing in 1872, opening hours were less restrictive than they were to become during World War One, when the easy availability of alcohol was deemed to be counter-productive to the war effort.

The police kept a close watch on licensed premises, at a time when every rural village had a resident constable who, in the case of Swimbridge, lived close to The New Inn.

After a fracas in 1908 the landlord of The New Inn, Arthur Eastmond, was brought before the magistrates in Barnstaple charged with allowing drunkenness on his premises. After hearing the evidence the justices dismissed the case, which resulted in a round of applause from the public seats in the courtroom!

The spotlight turned in 1909 to The Lamb and Flag, the conduct of which had caused the police concern

Former village policeman Tom Derges was landlord of the New Inn during World War Two and was noted for giving servicemen on leave their first pint free of charge.

for some time. The authorities claimed Swimbridge did not need three pubs, and were successful in persuading the licensing committee to refuse to renew the licence.

At the time The Lamb and Flag was owned by the Bridgwater-based brewers Starkey Knight and Ford and a couple of months after closure the licensing committee met again to consider the level of compensation due to the owners and to the landlord.

The committee was told that over the three years prior to the enforced closure The Lamb and Flag had sold an average of 57 barrels of beer each year (the number of pints in each barrel was not specified), 51 gallons of spirits and 22 dozen of bottled ales and stout.

The brewery company was awarded £480 in compensation and the landlord, a Mr C. Partridge, received £40, in both instances less than they had asked.

The pubs of the period particularly enjoyed polling times, whether for local contests or general elections.

In 1910 one particularly prominent local figure, George Norman, a Devon County Council alderman (a position he shared with Lord Fortescue) and vice-chairman of the Barnstaple Board of Guardians (the body responsible for delivering poor relief in the pre-welfare state era) blamed the influence of alcohol for the loss of his seat on the local district council.

Norman had been a councillor representing Swimbridge for thirty years and more and the local press had gone so far as to say that his re-election was 'a foregone conclusion'.

On this particular occasion his confidence – unlike his opponents he did not bother to carry out a full canvass – and that of the journalists was misplaced. In an election night bombshell, Norman finished bottom of the poll. He reacted bitterly to his defeat, with his denunciation of the role drink had played in the election hitting the headlines.

There had been no overtly political rancour in the election, as all three candidates were Liberals and on the radical wing of that party. Nevertheless, Norman effectively accused his colleagues of buying votes with drink.

Speaking after his defeat, at a meeting of the Barnstaple Board of Guardians, he said: "Many persons have expressed surprise at my being defeated but if they had been at Swimbridge and witnessed what took place, they would not have been surprised.

"A motor car hired by my opponents ran from the time the polling booth opened until the time it closed, running backwards and forwards from the polling station (at the village school) to the public houses.

"After the public houses were shut up, what was seen in the village was beyond description. Persons were lying down in the roads, while some were in the fields, so drunk that they could not possibly reach their homes."

Apart from his involvement in local politics, George Norman was a leading member of the Baptist chapel in Swimbridge, so his opposition to the public houses in the village and to alcoholic beverages was no doubt very deep-seated.

After the closure of The Lamb and Flag, the two remaining licensed houses, The New Inn and The Coach and Horses, continued to serve the village. In a case of the gamekeeper turned poacher, in 1931 former village policeman Tom Derges crossed the road from the police house to become the licensee of The New Inn, a position he held until 1953.

The New Inn was owned for half a century by the Wiveliscombe brewers Arnold and Hancock, whilst for many years The Coach and Horses was part of the empire of Starkey Knight and Ford.

The licensee at The New Inn at the time the name was changed to The Jack Russell was another long-standing landlord with a high reputation, Tom Snell.

Tom Snell was mine host at the New Inn when the name was changed to The Jack Russell. He is pictured in 1966 with a dispenser for Watney's Red Barrel, advertising material for the World Cup and a fine example of a Jack Russell terrier on the bar.

The Coach and Horses, situated on the main road, in front of Chapel Court, suffered a serious fire in March 1953, when its thatched roof was destroyed.

The premises were restored and remained open as a public house, but eventually closed around 1970, leaving The Jack Russell as the sole surviving public house in Swimbridge parish. The building was later an antiques centre, and is now a private house.

The Arnold and Hancock estate, including The Jack Russell was acquired in 1974 by Watney Mann West Ltd, a company which was itself eventually taken over by Grand Metropolitan Hotels.

For a while The Jack Russell came under the ownership of one of the pub companies established when the so-called 'Big Six' brewers (including Grand Metropolitan) were obliged by the government of the day to reduce their pub estates and abandon their bid for a virtual industry monopoly.

The government action also effectively stymied the attempt by the 'Big Six' to standardise their products by replacing traditionally brewed cask ales with keg beer – an action which prompted the creation of CAMRA, the Campaign for Real Ale.

Swimbridge would be a much poorer place without the modern-day Jack Russell. Even George Norman, were he to return to Swimbridge in the twenty-first century, might acknowledge its immense value to the community.

Fire destroyed the thatched roof of The Coach and Horses pub in 1953.

The Coach and Horses, a Starkey Knight & Ford brewery house, was restored with a slate roof.

The landlord of The Coach and Horses around the turn of the nineteenth/twentieth century was William Snell. He is pictured with his wife Emma and two of their children, Ern and Lena Snell. The identity of the man standing behind young Ern is unknown. In the 1920s Ern Snell pioneered a motor transport service to Barnstaple by placing wooden seats in a lorry.

Richard Bristow, landlord of The Jack Russell in January 1985 is surrounded by the coins from a Pile of Pennies pushed over by his Rotweiler Munchin. £222 was raised for Guide Dogs for the Blind.

The Jubilee Hall

For the first thirty-eight years of the twentieth century the main venues for indoor social and cultural events in Swimbridge were both linked to the parish church of St James.

The Jubilee Hall, opened in 1938, in its original form.

The foundation stone for the Jubilee Hall was laid by Mrs Barclay Black on 18 June 1938. The chairman of the Jubilee Hall Committee, Mr P. Williams is on Mrs Barclay Black's left and on the far left is the architect of the building, Bruce Oliver. On the far right is Mr W J Westacott, chairman of Swimbridge parish council and to his right, wearing a hat, is the vicar, Rev. C. A. Curgenven. The girl in the white dress is believed to be Rosie Dennis.

The Old Schoolroom close to the church, and the parochial school on Barnstaple Hill – still often described as the 'new schoolroom', despite having been in use since 1866 – played an important and valued role in village life, but both had considerable limitations in both size and scope.

As the 1930s progressed there was a growing feeling that Swimbridge needed a purpose-built hall.

In 1935 the village marked King George V's Silver Jubilee and after the bills for the celebrations had been settled a balance remained of £38, which it was agreed should be used to launch a fund-raising campaign for a new venue.

The initial financial target was £1,100 and although grants and loans were available from various national and local bodies, around half of the sum required was raised by local subscriptions.

Fundraising schemes included an invitation to local people to buy a brick for £1 – a substantial sum considering that a farm worker in the mid-1930s earned thirty two shillings and sixpence (£1.62p) a week.

In 1936 the influence of the vicar of Swimbridge, the Rev. Cecil Arthur Curgenven, enabled the purchase of a site for the hall from the Diocese of Exeter. The foundation stone was laid in June 1938 and from that point the project moved forward rapidly, with the official opening of what was to be the Jubilee Hall.

The name, still retained today, commemorates the fact that the movement towards providing the facility had its roots in the Silver Jubilee celebrations for King George V.

The opening ceremony was carried out by Captain D. M. Wills, the area representative of the National Council of Social Services, a body which had given a loan of £300 and a grant of £180 towards the cost of the hall.

The organisation co-ordinated charitable activities and gave advice to groups like Swimbridge's village hall fundraisers. It still exists today, merged with Volunteering England, under the new title of the National Council of Voluntary Organisations (NCVO).

A list of the organisations represented on the first Jubilee Hall Management Committee illustrated how completely the village had come together to make the facility a reality.

The parish council, the parochial church councils of St James church and the Anglican churches at Gunn and Cobbaton (Travellers Rest), representatives from the Methodist and Baptist churches of Swimbridge, Cobbaton and Gunn, the committees of the Women's Institute, the Men's Club, the local branches of the British Legion (Men's and Women's sections, the local lodge of the Royal and Ancient Order of Buffaloes (RAOB) and the Workers Educational Association were all represented.

The opening ceremony was followed by a public tea at which the vicar referred to claims in the local press about the 'dullness' of village life. The Jubilee Hall, he said, was likely to 'greatly reduce the trouble!'

The village turned out in force for the tea held in the Jubilee Hall in 1938 after the new facility had been formally opened.

There was certainly nothing dull about the evening entertainment that followed the public tea. The head-teacher of Swimbridge School, Mr F. H. Drew, was the master of ceremonies and introduced a stream of local talent, who sang, performed sketches, gave humorous monologues, and told stories.

The entertainment was followed by dancing to the Devonia Dance Band, which consisted of three well-known local men – New Inn licensee and former policeman Tom Derges (accordion and saxophone), Swimbridge railway station signalman Tom Way (piano) and butcher Harry Balment (drums).

The evening was to be the first of many thousands of occasions when the community came together in the original Jubilee Hall, now refurbished and enlarged (see Chapter Nine, *A Village in Transition*).

The hall has subsequently provided the backdrop for the more official aspects of village life, hosting parish council meetings and acting as a polling station for elections, as well as being the venue for meetings and social events organised by a vast number of organisations, including many groups that no longer exist, notably the Women's Institute, the cricket club, and the Young Farmers.

Thousands of people have attended events at the hall over the seventy-seven years of its existence and will have their own special memories.

Mervyn Dalling, who served first as treasurer and later as chairman of the hall management committee, recalled that as a child growing up in Swimbridge, it "always a great treat to go to something in the Jubilee Hall."

He remembered attending fêtes and taking part in various concerts organised by the parish church, the school and the football club.

"From time to time a concert party would put on a show, there were film shows and on one occasion Lord George Sanger's Circus set up its big top behind the hall."

Swimbridge Women's Institute, which met at the Jubilee Hall, planted a tree in the hall grounds in 1953 to mark the coronation of HM Queen Elizabeth II. Mrs Fleet and Mrs L. Dalling hold the post, while Mrs C. H. Balment holds the post. Mr C. H. Balment is pictured on the right. The woman holding the spade has not been identified.

Chapter 7

A Village on the Move

Swimbridge by road and rail

For the vast majority of Swimbridge residents, public transport up until the third quarter of the nineteenth century meant a jolting ride to Barnstaple on a carriers' cart with only rudimentary springs, or a near 10-mile round trip on foot along roads choking with dust in summer and clogged with ankle-deep mud in winter.

The gentry, the clergy and the professional classes had access to carriages, dog carts or other vehicles, either owned or hired for specific occasions, and the farmers had their traps and carts. For anyone else, a visit to the nearest market town was a difficult and tiring business.

The opening to Barnstaple in 1873 of the Devon and Somerset Railway, from a junction with the Bristol and Exeter mainline at Norton Fitzwarren, near Taunton, with a station provided at Swimbridge, brought an instant improvement in travel prospects for the villagers.

The line, which later became part of the Great Western Railway (GWR) system, opened relatively late in the development of the British railway network, at a stage when even third class passengers could expect reasonable comfort.

Swimbridge was also fortunate in that the station, unlike most of the others on the line, was fairly close (about a third of a mile) from the village centre. It was a stiff walk uphill from The Square to the station, situated to the north of the village itself, close to the hamlet of Yarnacott, but the gentle descent back to the village was a significant advantage when returning home from market or from the employment opportunities in Barnstaple made possible by regular and guaranteed public transport.

For late nineteenth century Swimbridge, the railway also opened up improved facilities for the carriage of livestock, agricultural feedstuffs and fertilisers, and general goods, including raw hides and other materials for the village tanning industry.

For around half a century, the railway, despite restricted services, reigned supreme as a means of public transport. This supremacy was not seriously challenged until the years following World War One.

The conflict had seen a huge rise in the development of motor transport, whilst the run-down of the military after the end of hostilities released on to the market large numbers of robust army transport vehicles, boosting the rise of road services for both passengers and goods.

Road passenger traffic grew extensively during these years, in the case of Swimbridge developing rapidly from ad hoc services provided by a local entrepreneur, who fitted reversible wooden seats to a lorry, to regular and relatively comfortable motor buses, which had the great merit of picking up passengers from the very centre of the village and depositing them in the town centres of both Barnstaple and South Molton.

The two decades that followed a second global conflict, World War Two, saw a major growth in private motoring. The 1950s and 1960s constituted the age of the family car, liberated the working classes from dependence upon public transport and at the same time delivered a death blow to the rural railway.

Early transport

Although North Devon enjoyed reasonably good rural rail and bus services for much of the twentieth century, it was by no means unusual right up to the 1960s and beyond to discover men and women who had never travelled farther afield than Bristol, and even some who had barely been out of their home county.

The story of transport and how it affected Swimbridge over the centuries is effectively an account of slow evolution, occasionally punctuated by revolutionary developments.

When the village first began to develop, there were no roads as such, merely tracks made by animals and humans continually passing and re-passing the same way.

Swimbridge, which grew up around first a ford and later a bridge across the Venn Stream, was from early days a significant contributor to North Devon's rudimentary system of communication, especially when compared to many of its neighbouring villages on the fringes of Exmoor.

One of the earliest revolutionary occurrences in the field of transport, the invention of the wheel, long pre-dated the birth of Swimbridge as a settlement. Even then, for long distance communication and the carriage of goods, four legs long outweighed two or four wheels in importance.

Given the rutted state of tracks and roads, pack animals were a more efficient and reliable form of

Original horse power. Jim (left) and Harry Yeo with their team of horses at Swimbridge.

transport than wagons and carts. Former village policeman and local historian Cecil Grimmett, in his 1950s essay on transport in the area, states that in North Devon a special type of horse was bred for use as a pack animal, becoming extinct when better roads were able to accommodate relatively speedy wheeled vehicles.

Even for the relatively prosperous, travel was drawn-out, uncomfortable and potentially dangerous.

A major development in the mid-eighteenth century was the development of turnpike roads. The establishment across the nation of turnpike trusts to create and maintain roads of a certain standard, financed through tolls, led to the appearance of regular stage coach services, drawn by four or six horses, and also made the carriage of goods swifter and more reliable.

The original turnpike route from Barnstaple to South Molton and on to Bristol and eventually to London passed through Swimbridge parish, although not the village centre.

The old road carrying the Barnstaple to Bristol and London stage coach services ran through Hannaford and along Devils Lane (at the top of Dennington Hill), continuing along a short portion of the present

Baptist minister the Rev. E. J. Burrows was one of the privileged few to have access to a pony and trap to provide personal transport in the early twentieth century.

highway alongside Kerscott, where a toll house was positioned, and on past the present-day Hales Garage to South Molton.

The connecting road from the turnpike to Swimbridge village was via the narrow and steeply inclined Dennington Hill.

The current main road through Swimbridge, the main A361 before the classification was transferred to the newly opened North Devon Link Road in 1988, dates from 1830.

From this point the stagecoach services ceased to use the high-level Devils Lane route in favour of passing through the village itself, and the now closed Coach and Horses public house is believed to date from this time.

Grimmett records that although communication between North Devon and London, Bristol and Exeter improved radically following the development of the turnpikes, the area was poorly supplied with local coach services.

At the start of the twentieth century carrier services between Barnstaple and South Molton, for goods, parcels and passengers, operated from two long-disappeared public houses, The Black Horse, in The Square, with a daily service, and The Golden Anchor, close to the former cattle market, which ran on Mondays, Wednesdays and Fridays.

The coming of the railway

The most remarkable thing about the Taunton to Barnstaple railway line, serving Swimbridge, Filleigh, South Molton and ten other small towns and villages in Somerset and Devon, was not the fact that it was built in the first place but that it survived into the 'Swinging Sixties', the mid-twentieth century age of The Beatles.

In its latter years, when a passenger alighting from a train would cause raised eyebrows among the staff, Swimbridge Station had become an anachronism. A delightful one, to be sure, but an anachronism nonetheless.

The station's small booking office, situated on the Barnstaple-bound or 'down' platform ('up' travel was always considered to be in the London direction), sold only a handful of tickets in the later years. It was generally considered that in the 1950s and 1960s, the income from passenger traffic hardly justified the wear and tear on the brake blocks entailed in stopping the trains.

Surviving rural rail services, including the former Southern Railway route between Barnstaple and Exeter (now dubbed by the marketing men as *The Tarka Line*) serve stations which have been reduced to unstaffed halts. Tickets are available from the booking offices at each end of the line, or from the conductor on the train.

Looking east along the valley of the Venn Stream, from the railway bridge at the top of Station Hill. The view, taken in September 1964, gives a good overview of the station in its final years. At this time the loop line through the goods shed was mainly used for the storage of redundant wagons. The station appears deserted apart from a small boy on the down platform, probably heading for the signal box.

An early 1930s view (in snowy conditions) of a Barnstaple-bound service at Swimbridge. Bulldog Class 4-4-0 John W Wilson *(named after a politician from GWR territory) was built in 1906 and withdrawn in 1936. In later years named engines were rarely if ever seen on the Taunton to Barnstaple line.*

Swimbridge, almost to the end, had its own station master, who was provided with a detached house situated at the junction of Station Hill with Road Lane, two signalmen, working shifts, and a lad porter. (The house was demolished to allow for widening when the North Devon Link Road was built through the station site).

The down (Barnstaple) direction had the main station building. This was reached by a ramp from the road, terminating in a small forecourt with space for a couple of cars. The platform was accessed by a gate and the building was just a few steps down the platform. The main frontage of the building was open to the elements, with the booking office to the right.

Much of the space in the draughty waiting area was occupied by a large weighing machine for parcels traffic.

The signal box, with its gleaming levers and equipment to facilitate the single line working, was situated along the Barnstaple platform from the main building, together with a galvanised iron shed where the oil for the signal lamps was stored and the lamps themselves trimmed.

The up and down tracks through the station (which joined again in the Barnstaple direction underneath the overbridge and at the other end just past the trolley shed on the single line route) were connected by a timbered crossing available for use by both passengers arriving from Barnstaple or departing for South Molton and Taunton (there was no footbridge) and for the luggage and parcel barrows

111

Tom Way, who later moved to a bigger box in Torbay, was a long-serving signalman at Swimbridge.

The waiting room on the Taunton-bound platform at Swimbridge was more substantial than at some other stations on the line, and was completely covered in. The allotments behind the access to the goods shed can be clearly seen in this view.

pushed by the porter.

The up platform had a small but fully roofed and enclosed waiting shelter. The platform was also flanked by the south wall of the quite extensive goods shed. This was served by a loop off the running lines. The goods yard – the site of which is now occupied by a large detached house called, appropriately, *The Sidings*, had a separate entrance, off Yeoland Lane, capable of admitting sizeable lorries, and there were pens for handling livestock.

After the withdrawal of goods traffic, the loop line was for some time used for the storage of redundant wagons.

The station was also the home base for a permanent way gang, who had responsibility for maintaining stretches of line in both directions, towards Barnstaple and South Molton. The gang, usually about six or eight strong, and their tools travelled along the route in a small petrol-engined trolley, kept in a wooden shed at the Filleigh end of the station.

The gang, which in the early 1960s was under the direction of Cliff 'Taffy' Grant, took a great pride in their work, which included keeping the permanent way tidy as well as safe.

In the days of steam locomotives, cutting back undergrowth to prevent it from being set alight by flying cinders from the engine, was an important part of the task, along with making sure the hedges and fences were strong enough to keep marauding sheep and cattle off the track.

In its declining years, the line was quiet, with a train in each direction at roughly two-hour intervals. It came to life to a certain extent on summer Saturdays, when it was used by seasonal holiday trains.

These hammered non-stop through the Swimbridge platforms, carrying thousands of holiday-makers, many of whom had travelled through the night, from the Midlands, the North of England and South Wales. Through coaches from London Paddington were also carried by one train.

The line was single track almost throughout, with passing loops at most stations. Tokens allowing a train to safely occupy the various sections of line were issued by the signalmen, and were exchanged with the firemen of the locomotives as trains ran into the station. Automatic token exchangers were installed to deal with the non-stop holiday trains.

By the mid-1960s the route was quiet enough to be chosen for location filming for The Beatles film *A Hard Day's Night*. The special train carrying the Fab Four only got as far as South Molton, where the only Beatle to venture on to the station platform was drummer Ringo Starr.

Trains to Swimbridge and Barnstaple started from a pair of bay platforms at the western end of Taunton Station. The bay also accommodated services for the Minehead branch and occasionally there would be confusion as to which train was which, leading to some unfortunate passengers eventually realising that they were heading for Williton and not Wiveliscombe.

The realisation would have dawned fairly soon after the train had re-started from Norton Fitzwarren station, on the edge of Taunton, where the Barnstaple and Minehead branches diverged.

The men responsible for maintaining the track between a point close to Barnstaple in one direction and to the other side of Filleigh in the other. Pictured l-r are George Yeo, Charles Sowden, Leonard Dalling, Fred Barrett (later a signalman), Percy Dennis, Les Slade, Cliff Grant (the ganger, or foreman) and Fred Parr. The track gang had a motorised trolley to transport themselves and their materials along the line, kept at the east end of the station, which was subject to the same safety system as the ordinary trains on the line.

The normal motive power for passenger trains in the '50s and early '60s was the ex-Great Western Railway 43XX 2-6-0 locomotive. Here 6372 pauses at Swimbridge with a three-coach train to Barnstaple circa 1963. There do not appear to be any alighting passengers, which was sadly often the case. 'Up' trains always ran in the Taunton (and eventually London) direction and 'down' trains ran to provincial destinations.

Looking west towards Barnstaple another ex-GWR 2-6-0 locomotive 7337 waits before departing for Taunton in July 1964, in the last days of steam on the line. The signal box on the down (Barnstaple) platform is the building on the left of the picture.

It is 1965 and diesel multiple units (DMUs) are now providing the regular passenger services in place of steam. Two services pass on the double track through Swimbridge Station (most of the line outside the passing stations was single track), one made up of two coaches and the one at the Barnstaple-bound platform (nearest the camera) composed of a two-car and a three-car unit.

Mervyn Dalling purchased the last ticket sold at Swimbridge Station, a single to Barnstaple Junction, priced at one shilling and three pence.

At the very end of services, in the mid-1960s, attempts were made to cut costs by removing staff from some of the stations (although not Swimbridge) and by the introduction of diesel multiple units to replace the combination of a steam engine and three or four carriages.

Even in the early 1960s the coaching stock for stopping services was of the non-corridor variety, which meant that for a journey between Taunton and Barnstaple lasting one hour and fifty minutes (five minutes less to Swimbridge) the only chance of a visit to a lavatory was for a desperate passenger to make a dash for the conveniences during a stop at an intermediate station, hoping that the guard would forbear to blow his whistle until the need had been fulfilled.

The gangwayed multiple units may not have been as romantic as the green-painted ex-Great Western Railway locomotives, but they at least gave access to essential facilities.

In the Barnstaple direction Swimbridge was the final stop before reaching North Devon's regional centre, with no station ever provided at Landkey. The Devon and Somerset's and subsequently the Great Western Railway's station in Barnstaple was at Victoria Road, on a site now occupied by Western Power. The sizeable goods shed is still visible, now providing a home for the Grosvenor Church.

The Great Western, later the Western Region of British Railways, had working arrangements with the London and South Western Railway (later the Southern Railway and finally the Southern Region of BR).

The LSWR had built the first line to reach Barnstaple, extended from Crediton in 1854, and also operated the routes that diverged at Barnstaple Junction Station (now the town's only rail link) to reach Bideford, Torrington, Ilfracombe and, via

Barnstaple Town Station and a narrow gauge line across the foothills of Exmoor, Lynton.

Until 1960 trains from Taunton, after stopping at Swimbridge, ran into Barnstaple Victoria Road station. The locomotive ran round its train and then hauled it over part of a triangular junction layout, across the River Taw and into the platforms of Barnstaple Junction. Some trains terminated at the Junction, while others continued to Ilfracombe.

After the closure of Victoria Road to passengers (it remained open for goods for several more years) the trains from Swimbridge used another leg of the triangular layout to run direct to Barnstaple Junction.

The railway timetables, at least in the latter years of the line, appear to have been devised to make it impossible for people employed or being educated in Barnstaple to make it to their work places or schools by normal starting times, or to return home at a convenient hour.

Rail travel was scarcely more attractive for shoppers. Even prior to 1960 Swimbridge rail passengers, unless they lived close to the railway station, faced a walk up the hill from the village and then a substantial walk from Victoria Road to Barnstaple's main shopping streets.

After the closure of Victoria Road, it was an even longer walk from the Junction, braving the elements in bad weather across the old Taw bridge, with the prospect of a return journey laden down with shopping, and followed by another walk from Swimbridge Station to their village homes.

In stark contrast, the Southern National buses stopped in Swimbridge Square and terminated on The Strand in Barnstaple, just a short distance from the shops and the Pannier Market.

With special buses laid on for the schoolchildren after Swimbridge had ceased to have an all-age school in 1947, the market for rail passenger travel from the village understandably shrank to almost invisible proportions before the ultimate withdrawal of services.

With the closure of the tannery in 1965 and the triumph of the motor lorry for delivering to farms, there was no longer any income from goods traffic to make up for the passenger deficit. In fact, goods services from Swimbridge ceased in August 1964, more than two years before the final passenger train ran on 1 October 1966.

Although the trains continued to run into the middle of the sixties, the killer blow to the rail service was actually delivered when, in the early 1960s, Harold Macmillan's Conservative government appointed the chairman of Imperial Chemical Industries (ICI), Dr Richard Beeching, to find a way of cutting the horrendous financial deficit incurred annually by the nationalised railway system.

Beeching's report *The Reshaping of British Railways* recommended that 6,000 miles of mostly rural lines – a third of the total network in 1963 of 18,000 miles – should be closed entirely, together more than 2,300 stations.

The Taunton to Barnstaple line, and with it Swimbridge Station, was on Beeching's hit list.

Local authorities, including Swimbridge parish Council, opposed the decision to abandon the railway line, but although some people argued that the Barnstaple-Taunton line was a less costly route to maintain than the surviving route through Crediton to Exeter, in their heart of hearts people must have realised that the old Devon and Somerset Railway had more or less been an economic lost cause throughout its life.

Economics are not the only justification for railways and socially, particularly during the two World Wars of the twentieth century, the Taunton to Barnstaple line had its moments and was well used by servicemen on leave and evacuees and, in later years, by national servicemen. The line can also claim credit for helping to boost the accessibility and popularity of the North Devon coastal resorts, and particularly of Ilfracombe.

Swimbridge Station had, over the years, seen quite substantial investment. There was a single platform only on the south side of the line until a second platform and passing loop were provided from 19 February 1904.

The goods shed was on a loop line opposite the original platform, and so from 1904 was behind the westbound (to Taunton) platform. The original small signal box was at the east end of the original platform, but was replaced by one in the middle of that platform when the loop was lengthened.

Throughout much of its working life, Swimbridge station had something of a reputation as an unofficial social centre for the village. The fact that there were considerable gaps between the arrival and departure of trains meant that staff had time for other activities, which from time to time included cutting hair and repairing clocks.

Although this was strictly against regulations, the life of a signalman on a sparsely-used line was a

1 October 1966 was the last day of passenger services at Swimbridge (freight had been withdrawn in 1964). Mr D. Shaddick was on duty in the ticket office to serve the very last passengers.

lonely one, and visits by friends and neighbours to 'the box' were welcomed.

The signal box was a cosy place, particularly when there was a fire burning in winter, and kept spotlessly clean by the men who worked there. Woe betide any visitor who unwittingly touched the polished signal leavers with bare hands, rather than with the tea towels provided.

Generations of young (and not so young) visitors enjoyed the life of country railway stations. The

Many Swimbridge residents rode on the very last train to Barnstaple Junction, returning by other means! Pictured, by the guard's compartment of the train, are l-r, Owen Dalling, Stella Dennis, May Adams and Stafford Marshall.

Railway dereliction. The site of Swimbridge Station after the tracks were removed to eventually make way for the North Devon Link Road. The platforms are still in place, although the buildings have been demolished. The separate entrance to the goods yard and shed can be seen to the right.

author David St John Thomas, one half of the well-known publishing firm of David & Charles, wrote extensively in his book *The Country Railway* of his experiences at South Molton Station as a young evacuee during World War Two.

He was allowed the run of the station, collecting tickets, pulling the signals off and on, and collecting from the fireman of incoming services the token which allowed the train to occupy a stated section of track.

South Molton was exceptionally busy by the standards of the line, with three lorries at one stage being used to deliver goods to the surrounding area, the livestock markets previously mentioned, and the existence of a cider house close to the station yard, the long-vanished Tinto Inn, which slaked the thirst of many travellers and railway employees.

My own experiences of being allowed to take part in the life of Swimbridge station came a couple of decades later, when the line was much quieter and staff – stationmaster and churchwarden Ken Cornelius, signalmen Fred Barrett and Ken Crook, and porter Ralph Sampson are the ones I best remember – generally welcomed distractions.

Given present-day health and safety regulations, one can imagine the horror with which authority would contemplate the idea of a fifteen-year-old non-employee being given detonators (intended to give warnings during fog or other exceptional operating circumstances) to place on the tracks.

The only comments made at the time after a Taunton-bound train had run into the platform to the accompaniment of a series of explosions would be of the 'what the 'ell's goin' on 'ere then' variety, shouted up at the open window of the signal box by a startled driver on his footplate.

What the passengers thought, I never discovered.

Perhaps it was a good thing that by this stage they were few and far between. As for the highly conscientious station master, I am sure he was away on business at the time of the explosions …

The rise of road transport

The arrival of the railway in Swimbridge in 1873 was undoubtedly a major advance in local communications, but as has been shown earlier in this chapter, its heyday was to prove relatively brief. By the mid-twentieth century the village station had become a little-used backwater.

The benefits of the creation of a direct road through the village to replace the old turnpike on high ground were not felt to their fullest extent until the development of the internal combustion engine.

Once effective road transport was introduced, running right into Swimbridge Square, the railway was simply unable to compete. In fact, for much of its later existence, it made no real effort to provide a realistic alternative to the buses.

In the morning it was impossible to arrive in Barnstaple by train by the start of normal working hours and and the area's schoolchildren and those who worked in the market town crowded on to both service and special buses in the village each morning. Many of the bus passengers had in fact already walked or cycled substantial distances to the Square, from outlying farms and cottages, and those from the north of the village actually crossed the railway bridge, passing the rather forlorn railway platforms.

Today, with the former railway line now occupied by the North Devon Link Road, the triumph of road over rail is complete.

Swimbridge's first taste of mechanised road transport was not supplied by the internal combustion engine, but by steam. Road engines travelling east from Barnstaple regularly filled their water tanks from the Venn Stream before embarking on the long climb up Kerscott Hill, throwing long hoses over the side of the bridge, connected to pumps on the engines.

This was a spectacle that continued to entertain the village children well into the late 1920s/early 1930s, especially when the equipment from Barnstaple Fair was being moved to its next event at Bridgwater.

As recorded earlier, the first faltering steps towards organised public transport for Swimbridge came when local man Ern Snell was quick to recognise the passenger potential of a motor vehicle. He installed wooden seats in the body of a lorry and ran a service to Barnstaple.

This photograph has not been positively identified but it is believed that the seats pictured with this group of workmen may have been the ones fitted on a lorry by Ern Snell to provide public road transport to Barnstaple.

Entrepreneur Ern Snell, seen on the right with village blacksmith Charles Gould, put wooden seats, made specially for the purpose, on to a lorry, to provide the village with its first public motorised road transport, at some point after the end of World War One.

The seats were made by village carpenter William Henry Holland, proprietor of a business that still exists today, having been passed down to his son Denzil and on to grandson Patrick.

Progress was also made during this period to establish motorised goods services based on Swimbridge. The Yeo brothers, carters, hauliers and agricultural contractors, whose teams of heavy horses were a familiar sight at the time in the village, bought their first motor lorry.

The major step forward as far as road passenger transport was concerned came in 1921, with the inauguration of the first regular Barnstaple-South Molton omnibus service, with the route number C5, run by Colwills of Ilfracombe Ltd.

Colwills originated as a coaching service run by Sam Colwill and based in Ilfracombe. From 1875 he built up a coach and four service, notably along the Exmoor coast to Lynton. The business passed to his daughter Laura, who was responsible in 1918 for motorising the concern in partnership with a retired

A Hardy Colwill single decker bus (the firm was a local predecessor to Southern National) waiting to leave Barnstaple for South Molton, via Swimbridge.

117

A reasonably sophisticated charabanc, complete with hood, provides the transport for an outing organised by St James'
church, Swimbridge, probably for choir members, in June 1923. In the front seats, next to the driver, are Miss Alma
Garman and the vicar, the Rev. Cecil Curgenven. In the second row of seats is the curate (unnamed), Miss Helen
Tatham, and Mr and Mrs F. H. Drew (school headmaster and his wife). In the third row are Mr W. Chown, Mr E.
Sampson, Mr A. Snell and Miss Ethel Holland. On the back seat are Mr F. W. Newton, Miss Ella Holland, Mr A.
Sturgess, Miss I. Chown and an apprehensive-looking Miss Elsie Holland.

Army captain, Geoffrey Cecil Shiers, who was the owner of two charabancs.

When the owner of the substantial Crossville Motor Co Ltd, Claude Crosland Taylor met Laura Colwill and Captain Shiers whilst on holiday in North Devon, he was persuaded to invest in an omnibus operation in the area, which ran a number of services in the area.

In 1924, after Taylor had withdrawn from Colwills (Ilfracombe) Ltd, the firm merged with another 'bus operator, the Hardy Central Garage Co Ltd of Minehead, to form Hardy Colwills. The merged concern established its headquarters at The Strand, Barnstaple, where a bus station had been constructed in 1922.

Hardy Colwills maintained the Barnstaple-South Molton service until the company was taken over by the National Omnibus Transport Company in 1927. The new operators adopted a new route number, 107, which was to endure for more than forty years and become familiar to Swimbridge residents.

The village stores and post office entered (literally) into the spirit of the new motor age, installing petrol pumps to supply the increasing number of motor vehicles on the Barnstaple-Taunton Road.

The parent company, by now the National Bus Company, split its West Country operations into

Western National and Southern National from the late 1920s. Southern National itself was divided into two sections, one covering Dorset and the other routes in North Devon and North Cornwall.

The two West Country rail companies as they existed in the late 1920s and 1930s, the Great Western and the Southern, had 50 per cent stakes in Western National and Southern National respectively and the bus networks in general followed the railway lines owned by the two private companies.

The Barnstaple to South Molton bus route through Swimbridge was an anomaly – a Southern National route following the Great Western Railway-owned Taunton to Barnstaple railway line.

A further service through Swimbridge (the 147) was introduced by the Southern National company in 1933, serving West Buckland from Barnstaple on the town's market days of Tuesday and Friday. The service was suspended on the outbreak of World War Two but resumed in 1945 (from 1969 with a new route number of 347). The service was later cut back to Fridays only and eventually ceased altogether.

It takes a stretch of the imagination given today's increased traffic to envisage service buses running along the narrow and winding Yeoland Lane to Riverton and beyond.

The Southern National buses took more than

The bus shelter, opened in 1952, may not be the most elegant structure in Swimbridge but for generations of passengers it has proved a blessing on wet days.

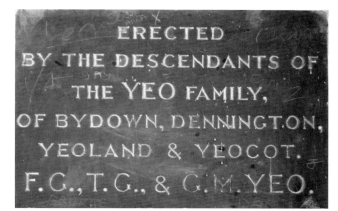

The Yeo family were the donors of the bus shelter as the plaque on the wall records.

The green double deckers operated by the Southern National Company were a familiar sight passing through Swimbridge on regular and special school services during the mid-twentieth century.

Its use as a bus station made The Strand a bustling place for many years, in contrast to the slightly abandoned feel the thoroughfare has in modern times. A signal on the adjacent Barnstaple-Ilfracombe railway line can be seen, and the curving metal railway bridge over River Taw is also just visible.

passenger traffic away from the railway line, as parcels were also carried.

From 1969 to around 1980 both the Southern and Western National concerns were effectively nationalised. This stage of public transport provision came to and end when Margaret Thatcher's government introduced deregulation of bus services, with extensive privatisation.

For a period of time services in North Devon were operated under the banner of Red Bus. After a spell in which services to Swimbridge were operated by minibuses, the once familiar double deckers returned to what is now the Barnstaple – South Molton (route number) service operated by Stagecoach.

Some of the services bypass Swimbridge village, using the North Devon Link Road as a fast and direct inter-town route. The village nevertheless benefits from the fact that buses (including double-deckers) use Station Hill to serve the Hooda Close housing development.

Swimbridge's position on both the the main road and the railway route from Taunton to Barnstaple

ensured that for much of the twentieth century public transport for villagers was at least adequate.

Rail and bus services, apart from the market day services to villages such as West Buckland, served the main centres of population. In the days before the wider availability of the motor car, travel to the more remote parts of the area was time-consuming and tiresome.

In the late 1920s my paternal grandmother, Mrs Minnie Dalling, decided to take her three youngest children to visit family in Stoke Rivers, an isolated settlement (really little more than a hamlet) on the edge of Exmoor. As the crow flies, Stoke Rivers is less

Mrs Minnie Dalling, pictured with her daughters Dorcas (Doll) and Norah at their home, 19 Station Hill, took her family on a roundabout rail journey to visit relatives in Stoke Rivers, as described in this chapter.

the services of two separate railway companies, the journey took three or four times longer to accomplish than it would take to travel directly between Swimbridge and Stoke Rivers today.

No doubt, for the children at least, it was an adventure, at a time when the horizons of the less well-off in rural areas were very considerably narrower than they are today.

At least the generous (many would say over-generous) provision of rural rail services made such an outing possible. For a family or individuals without personal transport in the second decade of the twenty-first century, the walking element would be substantially increased.

My grandmother lived long enough to appreciate the benefits bestowed by the motor car. Ironically, one of the first to offer her a ride to visit family and friends was her youngest son Ivan, a Great Western engine driver who at one stage of his career was often to be found at the regulator of a steam locomotive heading a Taunton to Barnstaple train.

Ivan Dalling had started work as a teenager in the 1930s, based at the Great Western Railway's locomotive depot at Victoria Road. The job entailed starting work in the early hours of the morning to clean and prepare the engines stabled at the shed.

than 5 miles from Swimbridge. Yet even in the second quarter of the twentieth century, it was a journey that required an amount of effort and planning almost incomprehensible to the present generation, virtually all of whom take car ownership for granted.

From her home at 19 Station Hill the first stage of the journey was a short walk to Swimbridge's Great Western Railway station. As the widow of a GWR platelayer, who had died in 1924 as a result of ill-health caused by service on the military railway lines on the Western Front during the 1914-18 war, she was able to take advantage of reduced fares, or privilege tickets.

The train took the family to Barnstaple Town Station, on the bank of the River Taw close to The Strand. Leaving the GWR train from Taunton to continue on its journey to Ilfracombe, Minnie and her children crossed to the other side of the platform to board the diminutive Southern Railway (ex-Lynton and Barnstaple Railway) narrow gauge train.

Climbing the Yeo Valley, past Snapper Halt, the train eventually crossed the towering Chelfham Viaduct, 6 miles from Barnstaple and ran into the picturesque Chelfham Station. From this point the family walked the 2 miles to Stoke Rivers.

Later in the day, the time-consuming journey was repeated in the opposite direction. On foot, and via

The rising standard of living as the 1950s progressed made it possible for better-paid workers to buy cars, which eventually took passengers away from the railways. Ironically, Ivan Dalling, one of the first to have a car, was a railway engine driver.

He later worked at such diverse depots as the GWR's main London shed at Old Oak Common and the tiny shed at Brimscombe in Gloucestershire, which provided banking engines to assist trains up the steep Sapperton Bank on the Gloucester to Swindon and London Paddington route.

Ivan returned to live in Swimbridge in the 1950s, at High Cross, and drove trains on the Barnstaple – Torrington service. He moved to Taunton for the latter part of his railway career.

Describing the considerable effort required for one family to travel even small distances as late as the 1920s highlights the fairly restricted lives led by both country and town dwellers well into the twentieth century.

The victory of road over rail became complete in 1988 with the opening of the Link Road, following exactly the line of the old railway through Swimbridge.

Whenever I drive along the route of the old railway, especially when heading from Barnstaple through the cutting on the approach to the old Swimbridge Station, memories flood back of the local men who made the station such a friendly, if ultimately doomed aspect of village life.

Returning to road transport, tractors became a common sight in the lanes around Swimbridge, particularly during World War Two.

Below: *Stop me and buy one? What appears to be an ice cream salesman's tricycle, with a refrigerated box at the front, has halted on the main road bridge at Swimbridge.*

Chapter 8

A Village at War

Swimbridge in times of conflict

The haunting strains of *The Last Post* and the sharp retort of rifle volleys disturbed the peace of Swimbridge churchyard on a July day in 1907.

Being laid to rest with full military honours was local farmer's son William Berry Rice, a trooper in the Royal North Devon Hussars.

Trooper Berry, twenty-two-years-old, had been in summer camp with his unit at Woody Bay when he became ill. Diagnosed as suffering from enteric fever, he was taken home to the family farm at Cobbaton, where he died three days later.

The path to the church door was lined by some 40 of his fellow troopers and the coffin was borne on a hand bier whilst the band of the regiment, with drums covered in black crape, played Handel's *Dead March in Saul.*

Following the service the firing party discharged three volleys over the grave, after which it was the turn of seven trumpeters to sound the solemn last farewell to their comrade.

The church was packed for the occasion, with the mourners including a large contingent of The Order of Foresters, of which the deceased had been a member. Trooper Rice was described as being `a man of a kind and genial disposition, much liked by the villagers and his fellow Hussars'.

Trooper Rice's family were later granted compensation amounting to a little over £4 by the War Office.

The congregation at the parish church of St James probably included young men and boys from Swimbridge parish who, within less than a decade of Trooper Rice's burial in home soil, would also meet their deaths while wearing the King's uniform.

In World War One and its immediate aftermath, in the years between 1914 and 1919, *The Last Post* would sound over the graves of no fewer than 23 men from Swimbridge parish. Unlike Trooper Rice, who died in the service of the Crown but close to home and in peacetime, the war casualties would find eternal rest not in their native soil but in places they had barely

North Devon Hussars riding through South Street, South Molton.

heard of before the start of hostilities.

Their graves, to be found in Northern France, in Belgium, on the Gallipoli Peninsula in European Turkey, in Mesopotamia (modern-day Iraq) and in Palestine reflect the fact that the 1914-18 conflict was truly a world war.

One local victim of the war died on a hospital ship and was buried at sea.

In July 1907, few of the villagers attending the funeral of Trooper Rice would have given much thought to the prospect of a world war.

Although the difficulties faced by the regular Army and volunteer forces in subduing the Boer farmers at the turn of the century had shaken British morale, and despite the well-reported arms race between the European powers, particularly in the field of warship construction, there was still little expectation among ordinary people of a major conflict.

Yet despite the public's feeling of complacency during the period often described as 'the long Edwardian summer', preparations were being made to improve Britain's military readiness.

The United Kingdom maintained one of the smallest professional armies in the world, a situation that was largely the result of the long-standing dominance of the Royal Navy. But lessons learned during the Boer War had led to recognition that there had to be a substantial and properly trained reserve force to back up the regular Army.

The tradition of raising volunteer forces to defend the homeland, with each town and village required to purchase weapons and carry out training and drill, became particularly relevant during the Napoleonic wars and the threat of invasion by the French Revolutionary government.

The cavalry arm of the home force, the yeomanry, recruited chiefly from the ranks of farmers' sons, who could ride and shoot and had their own mounts. In the years before the 1914-18 conflict Britain's Territorial Force was re-organised into fourteen infantry divisions and fourteen mounted yeomanry brigades, and recruiting began in earnest.

At first the young men of Swimbridge parish appeared to muster little enthusiasm for the new force. A recruiting drive saw the Barnstaple volunteer companies march to the village headed by their band, which then entertained the gathered crowds with two musical selections.

The great and good of the parish assembled on the platform to urge eligible young men to flock to the colours. The main speaker was Hugh, 4th Earl Fortescue, who had inherited the title from his father in 1905. Lord Fortescue was well-qualified to speak on military matters as a result of his own yeomanry service.

His oratory nevertheless failed to stir would-be martial hearts in Swimbridge. When the Barnstaple

North Devon Hussars from Swimbridge are included in this photograph, taken before they were posted abroad. Those definitely identified are Fred Elworthy, second from the left in the front row, and his brother Ernest Elworthy, far left on the back row.

Training for battle. Ernest Dallyn of Hutcherton Farm takes cover behind his prone mount.

units marched back to the market town, they had failed to increase their numbers by a single recruit.

One Swimbridge man did volunteer but on enquiry it was discovered that he was too old to be accepted. The failure to attract recruits in the village infuriated the vicar, the Rev. Henry Harrison, who told the reluctant young men that he would have signed up himself was he not too old.

Matters began to progress militarily in the village as the first decade of the twentieth century neared its end.

By 1911 the local mounted volunteer force had four squadrons, based on Barnstaple, South Molton, Torrington and Holsworthy with detachments in several parishes, including Swimbridge, where the enlistment of local men had increased considerably.

Among other measures taken in the first decade of the twentieth century to try to prepare Britain for any future war was a drive to improve marksmanship, a skill in which the British forces had been unable to match the Boer farmers in the South African conflict. Across the nation, the formation of rifle clubs was encouraged to help rectify the deficiency.

The Swimbridge Miniature Rifle Club met for the first time in 1911 at the Old Schoolroom, where a range had been created on the lower floor, with much encouragement from the tannery-owning Smyth family. A further shooting range was created in a tallet at Marsh Farm, the home of Rifle Club member Ernest Symons.

Local landowner, Robert Jameson, who had acquired the Bydown estate some years before, presented a cup for competition within the club, together with a rifle.

The Swimbridge club staged matches against neighbouring villages, with a special sense of rivalry being present in contests against Landkey.

The leading Swimbridge marksmen included a number of farmers' sons whose names will become familiar as this chapter unfolds; particularly good scores were recorded by Ernest Symons, Christopher Shapland of Newtown, and Arthur, Fred and Ernest Elworthy of Dennington Barton.

Other preparations for war were being made locally, well publicised in the local press. It was announced in 1913 that in the event of war, the Red Cross would take over the Albert Hall in Barnstaple for use as a hospital and in June of that year a major rehearsal was staged, with Red Cross members, helped by Boy Scouts, setting up the necessary equipment in the hall.

Once European (and eventually global) war had become a reality – Britain declaring war on Germany on 4 August 1914 – attention began to be given not just to building up the armed forces but also to the need to look after the welfare of the dependents of the men now flocking to join the colours.

W. H. Smyth, as chairman of Swimbridge parish council, organised support in the parish for the Devon Patriotic Fund, established to raise money to help the wives and children of those who called to the colours (whether they were regular soldiers or territorials), together with the inevitable sick and wounded.

Smyth called a meeting at the Old Schoolroom on 15 August, opening the proceedings by saying he believed the country was passing through the most serious time in its history.

The call for subscriptions to help the needy brought a substantial response. Mr and Mrs Jameson of Bydown House gave £25 and Smyth himself contributed five guineas (£5.25p). Mr Harding Nott of Tordown House undertook to collect subscriptions in the Gunn area and the Hole family of Hannaford House also made a generous contribution. By October the sum raised had exceeded £80.

In that same month the focus again turned to the need to stimulate recruitment to the armed forces. At a further meeting, also in the Old Schoolroom, Mr Smyth again took the chair and urged all those present to consider themselves to be recruiting sergeants.

He read out the names of the 16 men from Swimbridge, several of whom, as territorials, had been active as volunteers with the North Devon Hussars and as members of the Swimbridge Rifle Club for some years before the start of the war.

An early (1914) impression of life on active service was given in a letter from France, sent by Private W. Snell to his father Mr Alfred Snell, who was employed by farmer Mr T. Skinner of Riverton. Private Snell was a regular soldier serving with the Coldstream Guards – a member of the small British professional army dismissed by the German Kaiser as 'contemptibly small' – leading to the adoption by the survivors of that force of the name 'the Old Contemptibles'.

Each soldier at the front received a gift from Queen Mary – a box containing chocolate. This example, sent to Ernest Elworthy, is preserved at Bickle Farm, Swimbridge.

He wrote to his father: "It is rough out here now, but we can stick it. No doubt we will beat these dirty beggars before we are done with it. We see some awful sights but we take no notice of it, we are hardened into it, but I don't think anybody will be sorry when it is over. As I write this the shells are bursting all round us."

After the relative mobility of the first months of the war, fighting eventually stabilised as opposing forces dug in on a trench line running from the Swiss border to the Belgian coast.

The first three deaths of men either from Swimbridge or with strong connections to the parish

In 1914 tannery owner W. H. Smyth took the lead in making welfare arrangements for the families of Swimbridge soldiers. Smyth later volunteered and was killed in action. He is pictured spending his last peaceful hours with his family.

Three Hussars notable for their marksmanship died as a result of the Gallipoli campaign against the Turkish Empire. Pictured at a competition at Bisley before the war began are, back row, l-r, Christopher Shapland, Ernest Elworthy and Ernest Symons. The fourth man on the back row, Frederick Elworthy, survived the war.

occurred on what would become known as the Western Front, where the French army and British and Empire forces faced the Germans, who were also combating the Russians in Eastern Europe.

The parish's first death in action was a particularly poignant one. Private Walter John Turner, whose parents lived in Barnstaple, had worked on a farm in Swimbridge parish prior to the war. He enlisted with the 1st Gloucestershire Regiment and after basic training was sent across the channel.

He had been in the front line for just one day when, on 31 January 1915, whilst on watch in his unit's trench position at La Bassee, near Lille in northern France, he was shot and killed by a German.

The notification from the War Office of Private Turner's death arrived in the same post as a letter he had written to his parents. His letter read: "Just a few lines trusting to find you all in the best of health, as I am now. I am still alive and kicking."

The autumn of 1915 brought a number of deaths in action or from illness. The second man from Swimbridge parish to give his life for his country was Private Lionel Tucker of the 8th Battalion, The Devonshire Regiment, who was killed at Loos, in France.

Five sons of the Tucker family of Frogmore Farm, Cobbaton, served in the armed forces in 1914-18; Lionel was the first of three of the brothers to die on active service.

Rifleman Ernest Ridd (twenty-nine), from Swimbridge Newland, serving with the Rifle Brigade, became the third fatal casualty when he was killed in action and buried in Northern France in early October 1915.

The mounted territorial units from North Devon, including men from Swimbridge, had been mobilised on 4 August 1914. In the spring of 1915 locally-raised units were dismounted and embarked upon troop-ships, bound for a very different type of warfare to that for which they had originally trained.

Their destination was the Gallipoli Peninsula, which forms the northern bank of the Dardanelles, a strait that provided a sea route to what was then the Russian Empire. Russia, still a monarchy ruled by the Tsar, was an ally of Britain and France.

In contrast, the Turkish-dominated Ottoman Empire had thrown in its lot with Germany and its allies and was attempting to stir up a *Jihad* or Holy War against the British Empire, which contained millions of Muslim subjects.

The Gallipoli Campaign, encouraged by Winston Churchill, then First Lord of the Admiralty in the British wartime government, was seen by Britain and France as a way to aid their Russian allies and shorten the duration of the war. It turned out to be a disaster, costing the lives of thousands of Allied troops, British, French, Australians, New Zealanders, and men from the Royal North Devon Yeomanry.

Britain and France launched a naval attack followed by an amphibious landing on the peninsula, with the eventual aim of capturing the Ottoman capital of Constantinople (modern-day Istanbul). The naval attack was repelled and, after eight months' fighting the land campaign also failed and the invasion force was withdrawn to Egypt.

During the autumn of 1915 and the first week of 1916 the eyes of the community focused on Gallipoli and the North Devon soldiers fighting desperately for survival on the narrow and perilous foothold established on the shores of the peninsula.

Among the troops fighting in Gallipoli were three close friends from Swimbridge, whose exploits with the village Rifle Club have already been mentioned.

Swimbridge's renowned marksmen were told at Bisley that they were shooting for a young lady. This turned out to be a doll, now preserved at Bickle Farm, Swimbridge. Colin Elworthy, grandson of sharpshooter Fred, displays the doll, which to this day bears the cross-rifles badge of the crack-shot.

Ernest Symons of Marsh Farm, killed at Gallipoli. His platoon commander wrote to his own family saying that Symons had been 'a real topper – a very keen man'.

Ernest Symons, Christopher Shapland and Ernest Elworthy were the three crack shots of the regiment and in peacetime had been regular competitors in territorial shooting championships at Bisley.

On one occasion the trio, and Ernest Elworthy's brother Frederick, shooting as a team at Bisley, had been told that they were competing for 'a young lady'. They duly won the contest and were awarded the prize, a large doll!

The doll, in a glass case and adorned with the crossed rifles badge of the marksman, is kept as a prized possession at Bickle Farm in Swimbridge parish, by Frederick Elworthy's grandsons Colin and Christopher Elworthy.

The comradeship of Swimbridge's 'three musketeers' was split apart when Sergeant Ernest Symons was killed at Suvla Bay in the Dardanelles, on 2 November 1915.

A fellow member of the Hussars wrote to his own family in Tawstock to say that a shrapnel shell had burst over the unit's position, killing two men, including Symons, and wounding two others.

Ernest George Symons (twenty-six) was the eldest son of Walter Symons of Marsh Barton, Swimbridge. He had been educated at West Buckland School from

Like many other soldiers in Gallipoli, Ernest Elworthy died from illness, in his case dysentery, which was rife in the trenches of the Dardanelles.

the age of twelve, with a great uncle paying the fees.

Three days later another member of the sharp-shooting trio, Lance Corporal Ernest Elworthy (from the farming family at Dennington Barton) died from dysentery. Lance Corporal Elworthy's brother Frederick, another Bisley marksman, was also at the time serving with the Hussars in the Dardanelles.

A month later letters confirming Ernest Symons' great popularity in the Hussars were received at Marsh Barton Farm. The letters had been written by Symons' immediate superior, a Lieutenant V. Williams, to his father, Major Williams, the officer commanding the 1/3 Royal Devon Yeomanry.

Lieutenant Williams said: "My sergeant (Symons) has just been killed. He was a real topper. He was our musketry sergeant and a very keen man. On one occasion he carried out a reconnaissance, almost right up to the Turks' front line in the night time. At the time of his death Sergeant Symons was collecting letters from his troop for the homeward-bound mail."

Back at home in Swimbridge, memorial services were held in the parish church of St James for Sergeant Symons and Lance/Corporal Elworthy.

Conditions at Gallipoli were appalling in every sense. Another trooper with the Royal North Devon Hussars, William Marlow, wrote home to his father, a gardener employed at Swimbridge Vicarage. Marlow described how the Hussars were positioned to the right of a prominent point which the British soldiers christened Chocolate Hill, about 250 yards from the positions occupied by the opposing Turkish soldiers.

First of all, torrential rain flooded the Hussars' trenches to the depth of two feet. There was a shortage of food and drink, as the communication trenches leading to the firing line were also under deep water.

Worse was to come in the form of snow, in what was described as the great blizzard of November 26 1915. When the snow stopped falling, everything froze over, including the soldiers' clothing. The bolts of their rifles would not work. Trooper Marlow told his father: "We kept at it until we were relieved, and got praised for it by the Brigadier."

Marlow, like many other soldiers from North Devon, contracted frostbite and dysentery. He was taken on board the hospital ship *Panama* and, on arrival in Malta, transferred to hospital where, although he was at first well enough to write to his father, he eventually died.

Bisley marksman Frederick Elworthy was fortunate not to join his brother on the list of fatal casualties. Frederick wrote to his brother Arthur at Dennington Barton, describing a lucky escape.

Frederick Elworthy said: "I was taking aim at a Turk when I felt my rifle jerked up and I fell back in the trench wounded. I was taken to hospital. It seems that a bullet struck off the foresight of my rifle and buried the sight between my eyes. I have been four days in hospital."

A narrow escape. A bullet from a Turkish sniper was deflected by Fred Elworthy's gunsight.

The gunsight that saved Fred Elworthy's life at Gallipoli is displayed by his grandson, Colin Elworthy.

Christopher Shapland, from Newtown Farm, was the third of the famous Swimbridge Hussar marksmen to die. He contracted frostbite in the severe blizzard that hit Gallipoli on 26 November 1915 and died in hospital in Egypt in March of the following year.

Christopher Shapland died in Egypt and is buried in a war cemetery in Alexandria.

Below: *Gallipoli frostbite victims await evacuation to hospital in a dugout covered in straw and lined with Huntley and Palmers biscuit boxes.*

The sight that saved Fred Elworthy's life is also preserved today at Bickle Farm, together with a tin, which once contained chocolate, presented to each serving soldier by Queen Mary as a Christmas gift. The sight saved Fred's life but the light reflecting on its glass lens was probably what caused the Turkish sniper to fire at him in the first place.

Another narrow escape was that experienced by Private Herbert Thomas of Swimbridge Newland, serving with the Royal Army Medical Corps. The ambulance car of which he was in charge was smashed by a shell, his passenger being killed.

Following the final withdrawal of Allied forces from the Dardanelles on 8 January 1916 the North Devon troopers were sent to Egypt. The Hussars were to take part in the invasion of Palestine in 1917 and 1918, fighting in many engagements including the capture and defence of Jerusalem.

Inevitably, more casualties were to be incurred among the Swimbridge men.

The trio of Swimbridge marksmen, already shattered by the deaths of Ernest Symons and Ernest Elworthy, was finally eliminated when Corporal Christopher Shapland of the Royal North Devon Hussars, who had contracted frostbite during the great Gallipoli freeze, died in hospital in Egypt in March 1916, following an operation to his foot. He had enlisted in the Hussars in 1909, at the age of sixteen.

As 1916 wore on, there were further deaths to plunge Swimbridge into mourning.

In August Private G. Liverton of the 6th Battalion, Devonshire Regiment, died in hospital in India, another victim of illness contracted on active service.

In the same month Private Frederick Mears, also serving with the Devonshire Regiment, was killed in action in France. He had worked on a farm at Satterleigh before enlisting and had been at the front line for fifteen months, having celebrated his twenty-first birthday a few days before his death.

In November 1916 a veteran of the South African war was killed in action in France. Private Thomas Taylor of the Devonshire Regiment was the son of the late Mr Edward Taylor of Station Hill, Swimbridge. Private Taylor had served with the county regiment throughout the South African war, had been present at the relief of Ladysmith and had been awarded the Queen's and King's Medals during that conflict.

Back at home in Swimbridge, day-to-day life during the war, up to his retirement in 1916, was faithfully chronicled by the headmaster of Swimbridge School, Mr William Shelley. Since the early years of the century he had kept extensive scrapbooks of press cuttings relating to life in the village and in North Devon, particularly where national and local politics were concerned.

From the start of World War One until the volumes cease after his retirement, William Shelley meticulously recorded the war news. This ranged from

As war casualties mounted the military became ever more hungry for recruits. At the same time farmers, who had already lost sons to the Army, were under pressure to grow more food. This led to attempts to gain exemption for key workers at special tribunals. Although some requests were successful, farmers like Percy Tucker of Swimbridge (pictured here) continued to join the forces and do their bit.

enlistment drives, charitable efforts, including the collection of eggs for sale, wounds and deaths to local soldiers and sailors, and the return of servicemen on leave to their homes.

Two items he recorded in the summer of 1916 were the return to the village of a naval man, Ship's Steward Forrester, prior to rejoining his ship, a minesweeper. Forrester had previously been employed by farmer James Mortimer, at Accott.

Deaths of Swimbridge men must have been particularly painful for Shelley, who during his thirty-three years at the school would have taught the majority of them.

A further report in his scrapbook for 1916 mentioned the memorial service at Swimbridge for Private George Liverton and Private Fred Mears. Muffled peals were rung on the bells in the tower of St James' church before and after the service.

William Shelley's scrapbooks also record the regular sittings in Barnstaple of the tribunals whose task it was to decide whether or not men should be exempted from military service because of the importance of their jobs to the war effort or simply to the maintenance of something approaching a normal way of life on the home front.

The majority of applications for exemption naturally came from the farming sector, not only because of its dominant position in the local economy but also its role in producing the food urgently needed to counter the German submarine threat and save Britain from starvation.

In some tribunal cases farmers, often elderly men, appealed on the basis that a son or a worker wanted by the military was the only able bodied man left on the farm, with other sons or employees already away serving in the armed forces.

Exemptions, when granted, could be permanent or for a period of time. In some cases self-employed men, whose plea for exemption had failed, would be allowed a month or so to settle their affairs before being called up.

Henry Hammett, a thirty-year-old widower and sub-postmaster at Swimbridge, proved to be one such case. He told a tribunal that he was unable to provide satisfactory help for carrying on the work of the Post Office. He had four brothers in the armed forces, two of them regulars.

The tribunal members had little sympathy and described the case as one where women could do the necessary work. Hammett was allowed a month's delay of conscription (with no right of appeal) and told by the chairman of the tribunal that they 'hoped he would live to come back safely' to North Devon.

The services of skilled and experienced horsemen – desperately needed both on the land and at the front-line of the war – were constantly the subject of bitter contests between their employers and the military.

Some interesting details of the life of an agricultural worker were revealed at another local tribunal hearing. A farmworker at Stone in Swimbridge parish was said to earn seventeen shillings (85 pence) a week but also had as many rabbits as he liked, a quarter of an acre for growing potatoes, free milk and a cottage.

Despite the shortages and disruption caused by the war, Christmas continued to be celebrated in Swimbridge each year during the conflict, with a particular emphasis on ensuring that the children of the various Sunday schools continued to receive their treats and parties.

Christmas leave was highly prized among the front line fighting men and for the 1916 festive season L/Corporal George Luscombe, at thirty-three one of the oldest Swimbridge men serving, was able to spend a few days in the village.

When he returned to France after his furlough, his luck ran out. He became ill and on 8 January 1917 died in hospital from spinal cerebral meningitis.

George Luscombe had been a trustee and poor

steward at Swimbridge Methodist church and was very successful as a local preacher. He was for eighteen years a traveller for an outfitter's in Boutport Street, Barnstaple. A memorial service was held at the chapel he had served so well.

Another death affecting the parish occurred in December 1916 when Seaman Albert Boobyer (or Boobyear) – the only naval rating with connection to the village to die in World War One – lost his life.

The twenty-one-year-old signaller was serving on a minesweeper, HM Trawler *Lord Airedale* which was carrying out its dangerous task when a mine exploded and caused the vessel to sink. Boobyer had worked as a porter for the Great Western Railway at Swimbridge Station.

In June 1917 the Tucker family of Frogmore, Cobbaton suffered its second death on active service, when Private George Tucker of the Devonshire Regiment died of wounds in France.

Illness contracted on the front line claimed another victim the following month, when Private A. Cox (twenty), of the Devonshire Regiment, died in Mesopotamia.

On 11 November 1917, Private Frederick Sexton of the Devonshire Regiment died, aged twenty-four, in Palestine, from the wounds he had sustained in action. He was the fifteenth man from the parish to

Illness claimed another victim when twenty-year-old Private Alfred Cox of Swimbridge died on active service in Mesopotamia, modern-day Iraq.

John Tucker, the third member of the Frogmore, Cobbaton, family to die, had emigrated down under before World War One and fought with the Australian forces.

Tannery owner Lieutenant W. H. Smyth, the only commissioned officer from Swimbridge to die in conflict, had been active in urging young men from the village to join the volunteer forces before the 1914-18 war began. He volunteered himself and, at the age of thirty-nine, was killed in action at Neuve Eglise in April 1918.

be killed. The war would continue for exactly twelve months after the death of Private Sexton and was to claim several more victims from Swimbridge.

In April 1918 the Tucker family of Cobbaton suffered their third fatality of the war, when John Tucker, known as Jack, was in killed in action in France.

Jack Tucker had worked as a gardener at Arlington Rectory before emigrating to Australia. At the outbreak of the 1914-18 war he joined the Australian Imperial Forces, later finding himself in the Dardanelles. He was wounded in the head during the fighting on the peninsula and was evacuated to hospital in Malta. After Gallipoli his Australian unit fought in the Middle East before being transferred to the Western Front.

The oldest man from Swimbridge, and the most high-ranking from the village to die in World War One, also met his fate in April 1918. Lieutenant William Henry Smyth, the former owner of the

tannery in the village, was killed in action at Neuve Eglise, aged thirty-nine.

The death of Lieutenant Smyth also had its poignant aspects. Smyth had obtained a commission as Second Lieutenant in the 11th Battalion Devon Regiment towards the end of 1914 and at the time of his death was serving with the 2nd Battalion of the Worcestershire Regiment.

As chairman of Swimbridge parish council, he had been active in encouraging recruiting, putting his own life on the line by volunteering despite being thirty-five at the time.

Perhaps most ironic of all was the fact that it was Lt Smyth's wife who had fired the first shot when the miniature rifle range had opened in the Old Schoolroom, with the aim of encouraging marks-manship among young men likely to soon find them-selves in combat.

Above left: *Farmer Walter Symons of Marsh lost his second son, Albert, killed in action in France. It is believed he had advanced his age and was only eighteen when he died.*

Above right: *A nurse wrote to Elsie Symons, who had looked after her brothers and sisters following her mother's death in childbirth, to tell her of her brother Albert's last moments.*

Right: *The letter written by a nurse to Elsie Symons, telling her of her brother's death in hospital.*

The Tuckers of Frogmore, who lost three out of five serving sons, were not the only family from the parish to suffer more than one death in action.

On 21 April 1918 Ernest Symons' younger brother, Albert, serving with the 1st Battalion of the Somerset Regiment, was killed in action in France. Albert, officially aged nineteen, was probably only eighteen, as he had brought forward his age.

In almost all cases where soldiers were killed in action or died later in hospital from wounds or illness, the impersonal (and dreaded) official telegram of notification from the War Office was followed up by a handwritten letter. These came from a variety of sources, including commanding officers, regimental chaplains, or someone who had served alongside the dead man – often being present at the time of death.

Emily Symons, who after the premature death of her mother had assumed much of the responsibility for family affairs, received a letter in May 1918 from a nurse at a military hospital in France. The letter, typical of its kind, designed to reassure grieving relatives that the loved one had been cared for and had not suffered unduly, read as follows:

"Private Symons passed away at 6am, the 21st April. His were face and lung wounds. The lung wound made breathing very difficult but when we found he could not recover he was kept under the influence of morphine so that he should not suffer – it is best so.

"He did not realise that he could not get better. Few of the boys do and, naturally, we do not tell them. They are so wonderfully brave and bright and hopeful.

"I think if you write to the matron here in a few months there might be some arrangements made by which you could obtain a photo of his grave. At present the little cemetery is quite new but later will be well kept. With kind sympathy, sincerely, D. Webb."

Anyone who has visited a war cemetery in France will realise that the nurse's confidence that the place where the remains of Albert Symons had been laid to rest would be well kept was completely justified.

The Symons family, like the Tuckers, were badly hit by the war and the effects lingered long after the signing of the armistice. The deaths in action of his sons, on top of the earlier death of his wife in child-birth, proved too much for Marsh Barton farmer Walter Symons. He gave up the farm and moved to Landkey.

Between the end of April 1918 and the Armistice, two more serving soldiers from Swimbridge gave their lives for their country. At the end of August Corporal William Scott was killed in action in France and less than a week later Private Claude Alexander Shute, of the Gloucestershire Regiment, died of wounds.

Private Shute was one of a new draft of younger recruits sent urgently to France to stem the German's last great attempt to achieve a breakthrough on the Western Front before the Allies' overwhelming strength, bolstered by the arrival of thousands of fresh American troops, could bring the war to an end.

The final Swimbridge man to lose his life whilst the war was still in progress was Private Francis John Trute of the 2nd Battalion, the Devonshire Regiment, a married man, who died on 27 October 1918 aged thirty-one, just a little over a fortnight before the armistice was signed on 11 November.

Soldiers from Devonshire Regiment units were involved in the fighting until the very end. In October and November 1918 the regiment took part in the British Army's final advance in Artois and Flanders and by the time of the Armistice on 11 November it was located east of Tournai in Belgium.

The dawn of the New Year of 1919 heralded a new era of peace (however temporary) but it did not stop deaths as a result of the war. On New Years Day, Sergeant T. A. Lock of the 1st/6th Battalion The Devonshire Regiment died from illness and was buried at Kirechkoi-Hortakoi Military Cemetery in Greece.

On the last day of February 1919, Sapper Stanley J. Cook of the 10th Railway Company, Royal Engineers, died in hospital in France from double pneumonia. He had worked as a platelayer for the Great Western Railway.

A total of 23 deaths in World War One of men orig-inating from Swimbridge, or closely connected to the

T. A. Lock, promoted to sergeant before his death, died of illness in the middle east and is buried in Greece.

Royal Engineer Stanley Cook died in France from double pneumonia.

certainly caused directly by service in the trenches of Flanders or elsewhere.

The author's grandfather, Charlie Dalling, died in 1923, aged thirty-six. He, like Sapper Cook, had been a GWR platelayer. His death from respiratory problems, although occurring five years after the end of the war, was acknowledged to be due to his service in France.

No complete record survives of the total number of men from Swimbridge parish who served in the armed forces during the 1914-18 conflict.

The best guide to the numbers involved is a press cutting from August 1916 reporting a function held to mark the retirement of William Shelley as head-teacher of Swimbridge school. This records that "about 70 old boys are now in His Majesty's services."

Given that the war still had more than two years to run, it is safe to assume that the final figure of those who served probably topped three figures. And given that the final death toll was 23, it is possible that roughly one in five of the Swimbridge men who served gave their lives.

The memorial in the churchyard of St James', Swimbridge, soon after it had been dedicated.

parish, are recorded in this chapter. Of these, only 21 are recorded on the war memorial in St James' church yard, unveiled and dedicated nearly two years after the end of the conflict, on 26 September 1920.

Although no victim of the war is buried in Swimbridge churchyard, memorial services were held at St James', and at the village Methodist and Baptist chapels, at intervals throughout the 1914-18 period. These occasionally commemorated two soldiers, if their deaths had been separated by just a short period.

The two names of locally-connected war dead missing from the memorial are those of Private Thomas Taylor and Seaman Albert Boobyeer (or Boobyear). A possible reason why Taylor was not included on the memorial is the fact that as a regular soldier he had been away from the village for many years, and his father had died before the outbreak of war.

Where Boobyeer is concerned, he had not been at any time a resident of Swimbridge, although he had worked in the village.

Other deaths, not marked on the memorial, were

Like Sapper Stanley Cook, the author's grandfather, Charlie Dalling, was a Great Western Railway platelayer. He served on the military railways in France, where he contracted the tuberculosis that killed him.

William Shelley's notebooks, already referred to in this chapter, are useful not just as a source of information on the comings and goings of the war and the men who fought it, and the home front activities such as the military tribunals.

In addition to recording casualties up until the time in 1916 the head teacher ceased to keep the records, they also form a useful if not complete guide to local men who served and survived.

Some of the reports of deaths collected by Shelley mention other family members serving in the forces. The press report of the death of Private Frederick Mears in August 1915 mentions that three of his brothers were also serving at this stage of the war – Corporal John Mears of the Royal Engineers, Private Charles Mears of the 14th Devons and Private William Mears of the Royal West Kents, all of whom survived.

Other accounts of the wartime activities of Swimbridge men come from relatives; John Squire of Gunn has kept a careful record of his father's service history.

John Herbert Squire had been a sergeant in the Somerset Royal Horse Artillery (Territorial) prior to 1914 and subsequently served in the wartime army, eventually being commissioned and ending the conflict as a Lieutenant.

Wartime produces amusing as well as tragic stories

Training for war, and war itself, can produce both camaraderie and humour. John Herbert Squire's horse caused much amusement by constantly following his owner around various camps, as the photograph illustrates.

Former service men and others parade outside the New Inn at Swimbridge, on Remembrance Day between the two world wars of the twentieth century.

John Herbert Squire was a territorial sergeant in the Somerset Royal Horse Artillery before World War One. During service during the war itself he was commissioned, ending the conflict as a lieutenant.

and the Squire family tells the anecdote of how John Herbert was noted for the fact that his horse developed the habit of closely following his owner around camps. A photograph survives of the horse's devotion and is reproduced in this chapter.

First person memories of World War One remained vivid in the parish throughout much of the twentieth century. Photographs and other mementoes of those who failed to return were cherished and Swimbridge had two active branches of the British Legion – one for men, one for women – and Remembrance Sunday services were well attended.

The years between World War One and the 1939-45 conflict allowed sufficient time for another generation to grow up and reach an age in which they could play their part in the conflict.

John Herbert Squire's son John, educated at West Buckland School and Regent Street Polytechnic in London, joined the Territorial Army in the last days of peace.

"I was in the actual process of signing on just as a phone call came through ordering the TA to mobilise. Instead of going home I had to stay where I was – and eventually I was in the forces for seven years!"

First war veteran John Herbert Squire's son, also John, joined the Territorial Army in 1939 on the very day units were mobilised for the new world war. His service in the Royal Artillery eventually took him to Burma.

Despite being involved in the supply of food, which would have normally exempted him from active service, Harry Balment volunteered for the armed forces at the start of World War Two.

Like his father, John Herbert, John Squire became a gunner, serving in the Royal Artillery. His father had served in Mesopotamia (Iraq) and in Egypt in the 1914-18 war. John, after posting in the UK, found himself in the Far East in 1942.

"I was supposed to go to Singapore, where no doubt I would have been killed or captured when the city surrendered to the Japanese, but instead I was diverted to Burma."

John, who ended the war as a sergeant, returned to full-time education when he was demobbed from the army and later taught at Windsor Grammar School.

Given his North Devon roots, he later came to live in Swimbridge 'at the drop of a hat', buying Keepers Cottage in Gunn, where he and his wife Barbara have been strong supporters of the church of The Holy Name.

John retained a military link for many years. He had commanded the Cadet Force at Windsor Grammar School for eleven years, with the rank of major, and in 1985 returned to West Buckland, teaching and taking charge of shooting.

Many of the immediate recruits from Swimbridge to the forces in 1914 had little choice – they had joined the volunteer force to ride and shoot and were

quickly mobilised, while others were swept along by the war fever of the time.

There is evidence to suggest that public attitudes to war were very different in 1939 to those that had applied in 1914. The earlier generation may well have believed (at least for a brief period of time) that the German Kaiser was a figure of fun and that the war would be over by Christmas.

In 1939 there could have been few who were not already well aware of the threat to civilisation posed by Hitler and Mussolini. The war fever of 1914 as depicted on film had been replaced by a realisation of what probably lay ahead and a grim determination to resist fascism.

Young men and women from Swimbridge again volunteered to join the armed forces and auxiliary bodies, including men like Harry Balment, whose involvement in farming and the supply of food through the family butchery business would no doubt have justified classification as a reserved occupation.

The author's father, Aubrey John Dalling (always known as Jack) volunteered for the navy but, as a railwayman, was allocated to the Railway Operating Division of the Royal Engineers. Like many others,

Another of the many who volunteered for the forces at the start of World War Two was the author's father, Aubrey John 'Jack' Dalling. A railway employee before the war, he served in the Royal Engineers Railway Operating Division, in North Africa and Italy.

Sapper Dalling used a flimsy official forces Christmas card to send a greeting to his brother Owen at the end of 1944.

Below: *The first of mercifully few deaths of men with Swimbridge connections in World War Two did not occur until the conflict was three years old. Private James Wensley Eastmond (not Eastman as recorded by some sources), aged twenty-seven, of 164 Field Ambulance, Royal Army Medical Corps, died in November 1942.*

Right: *Farm worker Robert McDonald was in a reserved occupation but hitched a ride on a coal lorry to join the Army. He was killed fighting in Burma in 1944.*

including John Squire, his service career was to last for the best part of seven years, taking him to North Africa and Italy.

It would be wrong to minimise the human cost of World War Two, a conflict in which not only servicemen but civilians on all sides paid a terrible cost.

Nevertheless, the changing and more mobile nature of warfare meant fewer casualties among the fighting men. The 1939-45 commemorative tablet (placed alongside the existing 1914-18 war memorial) contains just five names.

Full details of the number of men from the parish who served in the second global conflict of the century are, unlike their counterparts from the earlier war, fully available. The names – 67 in total, plus the names of three of the five men who died – are inscribed on an illuminated scroll.

The war had been in progress for more than three years before the first recorded death of a Swimbridge man. He was Private James Wensley Eastmond (not Eastman as recorded by some sources), aged twenty-seven, of 164 Field Ambulance, the Royal Army Medical Corps, who died on 13 November 1942.

Two years were to elapse before further deaths. On April 11 1944 Private Robert Beattie McDonald of the 1st Battalion, the Devonshire Regiment was killed in action in Burma, four months before his twenty-first birthday.

McDonald, born in South Shields, came to Swimbridge in 1939, at the age of sixteen, from a childrens' home in Bristol. He lived with the Bartlett family at Tree Beech Farm, Gunn, worshipped at the local church and was baptised in 1940.

As an agricultural worker he could have remained a civilian, but hitched a ride to the recruiting office on coal merchant Walter Crook's lorry. After basic training he was posted with a batch of other replacements to the 1st Battalion the Devonshire Regiment, fighting to stem the Japanese invasion of India (which at that time included what is now the independent country of Burma (or Myanmar).

Robert McDonald was killed at Nippon Hill, the furthest point to which the Japanese invasion penetrated, and was last seen firing a light machine gun at the advancing enemy troops. He has no known grave but is commemorated on a memorial in Rangoon (Myanmar).

The material collected by Mervyn Dalling contains the story that Robert McDonald and a local girl had fallen in love prior to his joining the forces. The girl, who continued to live locally, never married and treasured the dead soldier's letters for the rest of her life.

Bandsman Arthur Frederick Douglas Cook of the 6th battalion, The Queen's Own (Royal West Kent) Regiment, who had been transferred from the Devonshire Regiment, died on 28 June 1944 at the age of twenty-seven. He was the son of Thomas and

Elizabeth Cook (née Ley) formerly of Swimbridge and had been born in Woolwich in 1917, where his father was stationed as a regular soldier stationed.

Exactly a month later the death was recorded of Captain John Kenneth Coward of the Indian Army Ordnance Corps. He was the son of Harry and Katherine Coward of Braunton and his exact connections with Swimbridge parish are obscure. Captain Coward, who had Indian nationality, was twenty-three at the time of his death.

The final death of a serviceman with (unspecified) Swimbridge connections was that of Flying Officer Capel Wilson Hogg of the Royal Air Force's 267 Squadron. Son of Edward and Stella Hogg, he was twenty-one at the time of his death in February 1946, presumably of wounds or illness. He is commemorated on the memorial in the Taukkyan War Cemetery in Burma (now known as Myanmar).

Not listed on the Swimbridge memorial tablet for the dead of the 1939-45 war is another member of the Tucker family of Frogmore, Cobbaton. John Tucker was the son of Fred Tucker, who had survived the

Not listed on the Swimbridge memorial tablet for the dead of the 1939-45 war is another member of the Tucker family of Frogmore, Cobbaton. John Tucker (pictured) was the son of Fred Tucker, who had survived the 1914-18 conflict in which three of his brothers were killed.

4th platoon, Swimbridge B Company, 4th Battalion Devon Home Guard, pictured at the Jubilee Hall in October 1944. Front, l-r, Frederick Hosegood, J. Isaac, R. W. Holland, Sid Pugsley, Ivan Harris, Frank Mears, Major F. Tomkins (Commanding Officer), William Hubber, Sid Scrivens, William E. Mearles, Sid Lock, William Squire, Owen Dalling, R. Turner. Second row, l-r, Leonard Skinner, Walter Huxtable, Stan Stanton, Reg Rice, Sid Cottle, John Shapland, Wilfred Kivell, Fred Dallyn, Tom Tucker, Albert Dibble, Arthur Dallyn, Roy Westacott Third row, l-r, Horace Dalling, George Houle, Ernest Wheaton, Redvers Tucker, John Westacott, Bill Cox, Albert Phillips, John Newton, Percy Wheaton, Bill Greenslade, Jim Westcott, Alan Heard, George Steer, fourth row, l-r, John Broadrib, Walter Isaac, Fred Elworthy, Murray Hutchens, Albert Dennis, Jim Webber, Ron Smith, Bill Balment, Back row, l-r, Harry Squire, Tom Folland, Walter Snell, Leonard Dennis, Herbert Snell, Bill Holland, Francis Joslin, Charles Elworthy.

conflict in which three of his brothers were killed.

The 1939-45 war, as mentioned earlier in the chapter, involved the civilian population of Britain in a manner quite unprecedented.

Swimbridge had a large Home Guard unit, comprised of able-bodied men either too young or too old for active service in the regular forcesor in reserved occupations. The force was commanded by Major Tomkins of Riverton and there was a Cobbaton detachment, based at the hamlet's former school, drilled by a Sergeant Hubber.

In Swimbridge the unit at one stage of the war was based at one of the cottages that formerly stood on The Square. This was nicknamed 'Fort Knapper' after the name of a previous resident.

Former parish council chairman Ray Liverton grew up in Swimbridge during the war years and his reminiscences of the village at war have entertained many audiences. Ray's father, tannery general foreman, attempted to enlist in the RAF at the start of the 1939-45 war but was refused permission because of his value to the tannery, now involved solely in the production of leather for Army boots.

Although the Home Guard unit initially had only a few shotguns as armament, while many members had at first to drill with broomsticks, the force eventually became well respected and well armed. Members guarded important communications, including the Taunton to Barnstaple railway line, and kept a close look out for German paratroopers, considered a genuine threat in the dark days of 1940.

Charles Elworthy's big Humber vehicle transported sackfuls but also carried Home Guard members around Swimbridge parish.

Members of Swimbridge Home Guard, believed to have been photographed at Cobbaton.

Swimbridge played its part in the drive to boost the production of munitions, with houses giving up their iron railings, whilst tin cans and newspapers were collected for salvage.

Ray himself joined the Air Training Corps and managed to secure for himself flights in aircraft, some official and some, particularly one in a Wellington bomber, highly illegal.

On one occasion, preparing for a flight over the English Channel, he was issued with a parachute. The young woman in charge of the stores did little to reassure the cadets, telling Ray: "If it doesn't work bring it back and I'll issue you with another one!"

Life for citizens on the home front was very controlled during World War Two, with strict rationing and an enforced blackout. Farmers and

Ray Liverton, for decades active in district and parish council affairs in Swimbridge, was a member of the Air Training Corps during World War Two and was adept at obtaining flights, some official and some not!

other food producers were subject to government regulation, with farmer Albert Westaway of Combe chairing the local War Agriculture committee charged with enforcing the rules (as described in an earlier chapter).

Despite the regulations, the fact that the village economy was still largely agricultural meant that food shortages were not felt as badly as in industrial regions of the country.

The author's mother, Sheila Dalling, who spent her life in the East Midlands industrial conurbation of Derby and Nottingham, passed wartime holidays in Swimbridge whilst my father was serving abroad and in later years often spoke of enjoying meals that were quite unobtainable at home.

She also recalled climbing to the top of Hooda hill in the late evening summer twilight with her sisters-in-law Rose and Winnie Dalling and seeing a glow in the west which represented burning buildings in badly-bombed Plymouth, more than 60 miles away.

My father's favourite wartime memory (before being posted overseas) was of the free first pint given to servicemen by the New Inn landlord Tom Derges when they came home to Swimbridge on leave.

Having grown up in the village in the 1920s and early 1930s, the returning servicemen were probably more accustomed to being given a stern lecture or even a clip around the ear by Derges in his earlier role as village policeman!

For at least a century since the outbreak of World War One in 1914, British forces have been involved in active service somewhere across the globe. Action for

Bob Shearer from Swimbridge Newland (standing on the left) served with the Royal Engineers during the campaign to recapture the Falkland Islands after they had been invaded by Argentinian forces. In July 1982 the parish council marked twenty-one-year-old Bob's service with a commemorative tankard, presented by chairman Ray Liverton.

Guardsman Christopher King, of the 1st Battalion Welsh Guards, who as a child lived in Swimbridge, was killed in Afghanistan in July 2009.

Britain's servicemen has varied from major conflicts such as the Korean War in the early 1950s to police actions in either far-flung posts of the Empire such as Malaya (modern-day Malaysia) or on home soil, fighting terrorists in Northern Ireland.

Servicemen from Swimbridge and neighbouring parishes have inevitably taken part in post 1939-45 operations, particularly during the era of compulsory National Service, which extended into the early 1960s.

More recent conflicts in the Middle East have also involved local men. Bob Shearer from Swimbridge Newland served with the Royal Engineers during the campaign to regain the Falkland Islands after they had been invaded by Argentinian forces. In July 1982 Bob (then twenty-one) was presented with a commemorative tankard, on behalf of the parish council, by its chairman, Ray Liverton.

In 2008 Corporal Ross Austen, who earlier in the year had married his wife Sarah at St James's church, Swimbridge, was severely injured in an explosion in Afghanistan whilst serving with the Chivenor-based 24 Commando Engineer regiment.

Less than a year later, Guardsman Christopher King, of the 1st Battalion Welsh Guards, who as a child lived in Swimbridge, was killed in Afghanistan. Serving in Helmand Province; he died whilst on foot attempting to clear a vulnerable area to allow a patrol vehicle to pass through. An improvised explosive device went off, killing him instantly.

A book of remembrance was placed in St James' church by the then vicar, the Rev. Peter Bowers. It was the latest item to commemorate the death of a local serviceman, joining two memorials marking World War One dead – the oak litany desk in memory of Ernest Symons and the brass plaque in honour of

Lieutenant William Smyth – together with the top half of the belfry screen, a gift to preserve the memory of Flying Officer Capel Hogg, who died in World War Two.

Time alone will tell if Guardsman King will be the last serviceman whose death will be marked in Swimbridge's parish church.

For anyone with an interest in military matters, particularly relating to the 1939-45 war, a visit to the Cobbaton Combat Collection is a must. Founder Preston Isaac, who lives in the former coaching inn at Traveller's Rest describes the Collection as 'a runaway hobby that just kept on growing', has always been an avid collector, starting with flint tools found on an uncle's farm, progressing to old hand tools and later old farm implements and machinery.

His first military items were bits and pieces his father, Walter Isaac, author of a volume of reminiscences *The Way Twas*, had saved from his Home Guard days, a Devonshire Regiment cap badge, and a real prize, an anti-tank grenade. The Cobbaton Combat Collection has exhibits from the Boer War right up to the First Gulf War.

On site is a large shop stocking collectors' items, de-activated guns, inert ammunition, clothing, hats, badges, survival equipment, books, CDs, toys, souvenirs and much more. There is a working

Parson Jack Russell is not Swimbridge's only tourist attraction. Preston Isaac's Cobbaton Combat Museum is extremely popular with visitors to North Devon. Preston is pictured in front of a Russian T34 tank from World War Two. From May 2015 Cobbaton was transferred from Swimbridge parish to Chittlehampton.

Norah Claye (third from the left), who lived at Gunn for many years, nursed British soldiers in both the 1914-18 and 1939-45 wars. During the struggle against the Japanese in Burma in World War Two she was matron of a field hospital. When she died in the year 2000, at the age of 105, she was the oldest surviving member of the Burma Star Association and was given a Guard of Honour at her funeral.

NAAFI canteen wagon with seating area, serving hot and cold drinks and snacks seasonally, and a picnic area.

The collection which is now run by Preston Isaac's son Tim, has disabled facilities and wheelchair access. Only guide dogs are allowed in the buildings.

A heroine of two world wars

Norah Claye, who lived at Gunn for many years, nursed British soldiers in both the 1914-18 and 1939-45 wars.

During the struggle against the Japanese in Burma in World War Two she was matron of a field hospital. When she died in the year 2000, at the age of 105, she was the oldest surviving member of the Burma Star Association and was given a Guard of Honour at her funeral.

She was born in 1895, in Macclesfield, Cheshire, on the edge of the Peak District, where with her younger sister Joyce she walked extensively in the wild countryside around Kinder Scout.

The daughter of Army officer, Major Albert Sandford Claye, Norah joined the Territorial Army Nursing Service in Leeds in 1915. In later life she recalled that the nurses were called at 6am, were on duty an hour later and worked a fourteen-hour day, until 9pm.

The war claimed the life of her brother Jeffrey and Miss Claye herself served in France, eventually being promoted to Lieutenant in the TA Nursing Service,

working as a nurse in France.

Between the wars she worked as a hospital matron at the Leicester General Hospital and in Barnstaple.

When Word War Two began she was called up as a Major and sent to run a hospital in Scotland, recalling: "The nurses there were all regular Army and very suspicious of a conscripted civilian."

In 1942 she went to the Far East as a matron, working in Bangalore and then Ranchi in India. Her involvement with Burma began in 1943 when she became matron of the Commilla Hospital on the war front and she remained there until the end of the conflict.

At the end of the war she left Burma for India where, by now a Lieutenant Colonel and the senior woman officer in the country, she worked as matron in Hyderabad, turning a barracks into a 1,800-bed hospital. She was demobbed in 1946 with the rank of Lieutenant Colonel, returned to Leicester and then, in 1950, to North Devon and Gunn with her father and sister.

In her later years she and her sister lived at the Lilian Faithfull Nursing Home in Cheltenham, but paid visits to Gunn, attending services at the church of the Holy Name organised by the Burma Star Association.

At the time of her death the President of the Cheltenham and Cotswold branch of the Burma Star Association, Major John Edwards, said: "She was one of our great characters – a lovely lady but an old-fashioned matron, the kind who had you standing to attention by your bed when she did her rounds."

Chapter 9

A Village in Transition

Swimbridge changes with the times

The people of Swimbridge, gathered together in the Jack Russell or in private homes on the evening of 31 December 1999, were commemorating an event of even greater significance than the passage of time marked by their predecessors a hundred years before.

A lot of water has flowed down the Venn Stream and under the bridge at Swimbridge in the 115 years since the start of the twentieth century. Nevertheless, the view of bridge, stream and church is essentially unchanged.

On the eve of the same day in 1899 the villagers had greeted not just a new year but a new century. For the modern-day revellers who raised a glass and a cheer as the midnight chimes struck at the end of 1999, there was a third reason to celebrate – the fact that they were witnessing an event, a new millennium, that would not occur again for a thousand years.

On that evening in 1999, at least one group of merrymakers welcomed the millennium in some style. A number of families had put aside £10 each month over the previous year and found themselves holding a kitty of around £1,200 to fund their New Year's Eve celebrations.

Simon Dyer, who was present that evening, recalls. "The champagne was flowing and at midnight we went outside to let off fireworks. We had bought a display which read '2000'.

"But because we were standing directly underneath we could barely see anything. It was the rest of Swimbridge that apparently got the real benefit!"

Had the villagers of 1899/1900 been able to return

for a few hours on the last evening of the twentieth century they would have found a great deal to recognise in modern-day Swimbridge.

The small bridge across the Venn Stream remains as popular a meeting place as ever, although the villagers of more than a century ago would have noted the absence of cottages on The Square.

The sounds of conviviality coming from the bars of the Jack Russell would have been much the same as would have been heard a century before from the tap rooms of the village's three active public houses, The New Inn, The Coach and Horses and The Lamb and Flag.

The lead-covered steeple of the parish church of St James would also have showed little change, although anyone returning from a century before would have noticed that the churchyard in 1999 was somewhat fuller than it had been in their day.

The cottages in High Street, Church Lane and Station Hill would also have been largely unchanged, at least on the outside.

Here the differences would have been noticeable only on the other side of the front doors, where the level of comfort enjoyed by ordinary families at the start of the twenty-first century would have been unthinkable in 1899.

Another modern sound – one beyond people's comprehension in 1899 – would have been the hum of noise from television sets, as those who chose to mark the millennium in the comfort of their own homes watched at first hand celebrations from around the world.

Swimbridge immediately after World War Two was not so very different in a physical sense to the parish of half a century before, as described in Chapter One, *A Village and its People*. So much of what had been familiar in 1899 was still visible a hundred years on and, equally, the composition of the people who made up the community in 1950 was broadly similar to the social structure of 1900.

Some of the more impressive residences in the village and in outlying hamlets, still privately owned at the start of the twentieth century, were now used as schools or for other purposes. But in the late 1940s and 1950s there was still a sizable number of properties occupied by a middle class composed largely of people living on inherited capital or military pensions.

Swimbridge is twinned with St Honorine du Fay in Normandy. Pictured is the signing of the twinning agreement at the Old Vicarage in 1976. Swimbridge parish council chairman Mr W. R. Shapland has just signed the charter, watched by Ray Liverton, the vicar, the Rev. Nigel Jackson-Stevens and North Devon MP Jeremy Thorpe (far right).

Parish council member Colin Wadsworth says the quality of life in Swimbridge improved dramatically following the opening of the North Devon Link Road. The absence of vehicles on the now unclassified road through the village – once the A361 main holiday route into North Devon – in the middle of a weekday, proves his point.

Directories published in all of the first five decades of the twentieth century show how popular the parish was with retired brigadiers, colonels, captains, and majors, one or two retired naval officers, and a substantial number of maiden ladies, with groups of two or three sisters often living together in a genteel, if not always a particularly prosperous manner.

The latter group was particularly common in the years between the two world wars, when the slaughter on the western front and elsewhere had greatly reduced the marriage prospects for many women.

In the middle of the century the rest of the population continued to be divided between the self-employed and the employers of labour – the farmers, the tannery, local quarries and the Great Western Railway (British Rail Western Region after nationalisation in 1948) – and the employed.

Well into the twentieth century almost all the working people of Swimbridge occupied unmodernised cottages with primitive facilities – mains electricity only reached the village in 1937, and came even later to farms and cottages away from the village centre, which often relied on a generator until the 1960s. With mains water only being connected to the village in 1951, other essential facilities frequently consisted of an Elsan chemical toilet, or even a simple bucket in a shed or outhouse.

The construction of council houses, at High Cross in 1933 (four properties built for just over £1,500) and at Archipark in 1951 (twelve homes built for less than £20,000) improved standards for those fortunate enough to be allocated one of the properties.

Farming and working families tended to be large by later standards and most of them had roots in Swimbridge or in surrounding parishes. "We never did our courting any further afield than we could cover on a bicycle," was a common explanation for the tightly-knit village community still remembered today.

Real change in the social make-up of the village came only in the last quarter of the twentieth century. The popularity of working in town and living in rural surroundings made Swimbridge increasingly attractive to professional people.

A modern directory would show as many doctors, lawyers, senior local government officials, lecturers and teachers as it would farm labourers and industrial workers.

In the 1950s agriculture in the parish was still conducted on a traditional basis. Most farmers employed full-time labour and called in extra part-time helpers for specific jobs, particularly at harvest times.

Farmers today, especially in an area where the raising of livestock is predominant, generally rely on their own labour and expertise and that of family members, supplemented by the use of specialist contractors.

During the same time period, more property of the type sought by professional people was becoming available. The steady reduction in the number of working farms in the later decades of the twentieth century led to farmhouses being sold off with just a small amount of land (with the rest of the acreage combined into bigger agricultural units or rented out).

Barn and mill conversions, many of which can be seen today in Swimbridge parish, also increased in popularity.

Several factors contributed to Swimbridge's surge in popularity as a place to live and to its present-day reputation as a lively village with a community which makes things happen.

Many of today's residents regard the opening of the North Devon Link Road as the prime catalyst for change.

Colin Wadsworth and his wife Lee, originally from Birmingham and London respectively, moved to Swimbridge in 1985. Today, after thirty years in the village, bringing up a family, Colin is a member of the parish council and Lee is its clerk.

"We liked living here from the start but soon discovered that life in the village was blighted by the

Ray Liverton, former district and parish councillor for the village and chairman of the parish council on many occasions, is 'Mr Swimbridge'. Ray's years of service to the village were marked by the naming of the road into the new housing development as Liverton Drive. Ray is now a North Devon Council Honorary Alderman.

The opening of the North Devon Link Road, pictured running through what were until 1966 the platforms of Swimbridge railway station, removed overnight the bulk of traffic from the main road through the village centre.

The new housing development off Barnstaple Hill has fitted well into the village environment.

traffic on what was then the A361. This was the main road into North Devon for thousands of holidaymakers, including lots of caravans, and the only route for heavy lorries the whole year round," Lee explained.

"It could take ten minutes at least to cross the road, making it difficult if you lived south of the A361 to do simple everyday things like take the children to school, or visit the post office in its present situation. We got to the point where we didn't even think of going anywhere at weekends in the summer. It was almost impossible to pull out on to the main road."

The opening of the Link Road changed the situation dramatically. "Quite apart from being able to go to Barnstaple and elsewhere, we were given the freedom to move around our own village," Colin Wadsworth recalls. "A village has to move with the times and attract new blood. The Link Road certainly played a major role in making Swimbridge attractive to newcomers."

A second factor during the latter years of the twentieth century and in the first couple of decades following the millennium has been the increased availability of housing. Colin Wadsworth explained: "Apart from some infilling, there had been little expansion of housing in Swimbridge since the construction of Archipark in the early 1950s.

"The development of private housing schemes at The Orchards and Bestridge Meadow, at Hooda Close and Oakdale Avenue and mixed private and social provision at St Honorine du Fay Close and later off Barnstaple Hill, at Liverton Close, changed the residential character of the village.

"We have moved from a combination of quite substantial but relatively expensive houses and small cottages, to a mix of cottages, often refurbished and remodelled, bungalows and now modern housing of various sizes.

"At the same time the essential character of the village has been retained, which I think reflects credit on the parish and district councils."

A third major catalyst for change in the village has proved to be the school. As the nature of the population changed in the 1970s, with more retired people moving into the village, younger people moving out because of a shortage of affordable housing, and families getting smaller, the school was threatened with closure.

When the current headteacher Garry Reed was appointed in 1981 there were just 33 pupils on the roll. Today, with 115 pupils, Swimbridge is the top primary school in the county of Devon and ranked 30th out of 17,000 primaries in England as a whole.

The school's renaissance has not been achieved without a certain amount of controversy. More than half of its pupils live outside the parish, a situation which has brought some criticism.

Garry Reed is nevertheless unequivocal in his belief that without the influx of children from Barnstaple and neighbouring parishes, the school would have closed its doors long ago.

"There was no choice but to accept children from out of the parish. Adopting this policy meant that the number on the roll rose to 50 after two or three years. The argument was put forward at the time that having reached this number, we could restrict entry to children from the parish.

"Had we done so the school would not exist in 2015. A total of 50 pupils would simply not be enough for survival in today's educational world."

Colin Wadsworth, before his retirement deputy principal at Petroc in Barnstaple, believes the school has played a huge role in ensuring the popularity of Swimbridge as a place to live. "Swimbridge was an ordinary school, without anything to distinguish it from a great many others, relying wholly on a more or less static village population.

"It could not continue to exist simply as a service to one village. It had to break the mould and under Garry Reed's leadership it did just that. It is now so popular and has established such a glowing reputation that people will move to live in the parish just to ensure that their children get a place at the school."

Garry Reed himself is clearly extremely and justifiably proud of what the school has achieved under his leadership, although modest in his comments. "I discovered that people liked my style of teaching," he says.

One admirer of that style over the years that his grandchildren were pupils at Swimbridge was a former senior education officer from Birmingham. He commented that he wished the city schools for which he had been responsible could match the village school's standards of education and behaviour.

When Garry Reed does eventually retire he will leave behind a school with 'a wonderful future'. His only cause for concern is accommodation. Despite all the alterations and additions to the fabric of the school made in recent years, it is still essentially a product of the mid-nineteenth century.

Ranking alongside Swimbridge's reputation as a place with good communications by the standards of many rural settlements (thanks to the Link Road again, plus a regular bus service), its attractiveness as a place to live, and its reputation as a centre of educational excellence, is the reputation the village has forged as a leading centre for culture and entertainment.

As an earlier chapter showed, the football and cricket teams of the post-World War Two period, despite success on the field, always struggled to maintain adequate facilities. When an attempt to revive both sports was made in the 1980s, the lack of somewhere to play was a major handicap.

Before the millennium a group was formed to campaign and raise funds for a recreational facility for the village, operating under the title of SNAP – Swimbridge Needs a Park.

Julie Whitton, pictured by the enlarged and refurbished Jubilee Hall which she helped to create, says that once Swimbridge people are convinced they have useful skills they are all too ready to get involved in village projects.

Any criticism that all new initiatives in the village were prompted by newcomers was deflected by the fact that SNAP was inspired by farmer and then parish councillor John Bartlett, whose family has been established in Swimbridge for more than 100 years.

SNAP struck an instant chord with many residents of the village, particularly those with young families, and became one of the first projects to attract a highly talented organiser and fund raiser in the person of Julie Whitton.

Colin and Lee Wadsworth now look back to the success of SNAP in eventually securing the land for the park (it took a long time to overcome a succession

With great hopes for new sporting glory when Swimbridge's new park is fully in operation, villagers still retain memories of past triumphs. Sid Facey of Station Hill is pictured with the YMCA Cup, which he helped Swimbridge FC to win in the 1951-52 season. The holders of the trophy at the time of writing were Landkey Town FC, who stage their after match get-togethers at the Jack Russell.

The church and the community as a whole remember those who have given their lives for their country each Remembrance Sunday. The war memorial was re-dedicated by the vicar, the Rev. Shaun O'Rorke, in August 2014, to commemorate the start of World War One.

of obstacles) as being the start of much that has subsequently happened for the good in Swimbridge.

Colin Wadsworth has no doubts about the effect of the SNAP campaign. "It probably kick-started everything else, including the transformation of the Jubilee Hall, that has happened since SNAP got off the ground," he said.

Julie Whitton, at the heart of both the SNAP movement and the achievement of the magnificent refurbishment and extension of the Jubilee Hall, agrees that the park campaign was of great importance.

"It got people used to the idea that things could be achieved, no matter how difficult the process seemed to be.

"People in the village could sometimes be reluctant to get involved, not because they did not want to help, but because they felt they didn't have anything to offer.

"Once they were convinced that they had skills which were useful to the projects going on in the village, there was no stopping them. You just need to ask – and people rarely say no!"

Julie cites as examples of people's willingness to get involved in such events as Lightquest, which produced 300 volunteers, and various runs organised in the village.

"If we organise a run of some kind, we get 60 marshals. People in Swimbridge are willing to work together, which is always a good start. Because we have like-minded people we make things happen.

"We are a dynamic community and having facilities such as the new hall and a park will only make it

Lady Arran cuts the ribbon to formally open Swimbridge's Streamside Garden.

easier to whip up enthusiasm in the future."

Although newcomers and new initiatives have helped maintain Swimbridge's community spirit during the time of huge social change either side of the millennium, the village's oldest institution, the parish church of St James, is still a lively centre of activity and the chapel of ease of the Holy Name at Gunn has a loyal congregation.

The tradition of carrying the cross to the top of Hooda on Good Friday is still faithfully observed.

Right: *Each Christmas farmer John Ackland of Yarnacott and helpers erect an illuminated star on John's land at Hooda Hill. Former parish councillor and airline pilot Yves Clarke has confirmed that the star is visible from the air and welcomes him home to North Devon on incoming flights.*

Manufacturing still takes place on the former tannery site, thanks to Bill Hedge – Bill the Potter.

The first recorded wheelbarrow races in Swimbridge were before the start of the 1914-18 War. Featured in this shot from the modern version are Stuart Swanson and David Harrison.

Right: *Swimbridge is fortunate to retain its village post office, run for the last decade by Syd Pring-Ellis and family. Syd has also introduced a range of grocery and other items, giving Swimbridge a retail outlet which many villages of similar size lack.*

The parish church embraces not only regular churchgoers, but the wider parish too, particularly on occasions such as the annual November Remembrance service.

St James' church is today frequently used for talks, concerts and other social occasions. This is not a lowering of standards, but a return to the usage of earlier centuries, when the church was the only public building in the village.

Many parishioners play a major role not just within the church but also in the wider community. David Netherway, who has lived in the village for thirty-nine years, played a significant role in the extension and refurbishment of the Jubilee Hall and was the project director for the acclaimed Swimbridge Church Streamside Garden.

The Streamside Garden occupies land to the north of the path which runs from the footbridge across the Venn Stream to Watergate.

The area of land, known to many as the Old Churchyard, despite the fact that it had never been used for burials because of its proximity to the stream, had become overgrown.

In 2006 in his role as a parochial church councillor David Netherway suggested to his fellow PCC members that the area should be cleared and turned into a public open space.

Several years after the initial concept had been announced, work began on the garden in August 2011. It is today an attractive and much appreciated facility.

David Netherway explained: "Church land which had been an under-used asset in the heart of the village is now an attractive open space for everyone's enjoyment." The total project cost was over £50,000, which was met mainly from a successful bid to the National Lottery Community Spaces Programme

Features of the garden include a granite artwork by North Devon-based sculptor and monumental mason Gabriel Hummerstone. The Elworthy family of Bickle Farm had donated an old granite roller to enhance the garden. Gabriel Hummerstone added text to the roller, with the well known words from the 23rd Psalm, 'In pastures green he leadeth me, the quiet waters by', scrolling across the granite.

Benches in the garden were made by Swimbridge resident Yves Clark, with the timber taken from a spalted beech tree from Chittlehampton that blew down in a gale in 2006.

The garden is also home to a horse-drawn plough donated by Sid Bartlett, a former church warden at St James. The implement featured in the Plough Sunday service each January, when prayers are said for the success of farming in the parish for the coming year.

The second decade of the twenty-first century sees Remembrance Sunday strictly observed in the parish.

The war memorial in St James' churchyard was re-dedicated in August 2014 after refurbishment. The

In 2015 John and James Bartlett milk some 200 Friesians at Sandyke Farm.

Formerly neglected land alongside the Venn Stream, which forms part of the churchyard of St James' church, has been transformed into a much appreciated community facility, the Streamside Garden. The project was driven by parochial church council member David Netherway, who is pictured at the garden.

church congregation, parish councillors and other members of the community joined together and prior to the service had an opportunity to look at displays in the church commemorating the soldiers who lost their lives in the First World War.

The main panels, researched and assembled by Mervyn Dalling, are displayed each year around the time of Remembrance Day.

The then churchwarden, John Hayes, carried a British Legion standard to the war memorial. The service was led by the vicar, Rev. Shaun O'Rourke, veteran Mat Bluge, a former Guardsman, read out the names on the war memorial and Geoff Dodd, chairman of the parish council, laid a wreath.

For several years the *Last Post* was played at Remembrance services by Eleanor Elworthy from Dennington Barton. Eleanor, who now lives in Gibraltar, first played for the service at the age of fifteen.

No fewer than four of Eleanor's great-uncles died

in World War One and are commemorated on the Swimbridge War Memorial – Ernest Elworthy, Ernest and Albert Symons and Thomas Lock.

David Netherway is now engaged on another interesting project, to commemorate the gift to Swimbridge of a reliable water supply, donated by the 9th Duke of Bedford in 1870.

"We rediscovered part of the stonework that surrounded a tap which used to stand between the bus shelter in The Square and the Jubilee Hall - one of the six taps that the Russell family donated to supply water to the in the village.

Three generations at the Jack Russell in 2015. Licensee Paul Darch holds his daughter Amelia, next to him is his wife Mellisa, with Paul's mother Jill on the right.

"The stone will be re-erected on the original site and the present Duke of Bedford has made a generous contribution to the project. It is planned to involve children from the village school in the project."

The village in the twenty-first century is much more environmentally-friendly than during the twentieth century. Black smoke from the tannery and the stench of hides being delivered to the site, heavy traffic on the main road, and the cowpats that were once a regular feature on The Square, have all vanished.

One of the most recent initiatives to boost the appearance of the village has been the creation of the Swimbridge Parish Green Team, a group of volunteers to help maintain and enhance the outdoor community assets in the parish.

Equipment for the Green Team – high visibility vests are still necessary, despite the reduction of road traffic – was supplied as a result of a successful funding application by the parish council to improve the village environment.

The group is funded and led by the parish council and supported by The Jack Russell, the second eldest institution in the village after the parish church.

The Green Team will tackle tasks including include litter clearing, the cleaning of street signs, grass cutting, the planning of bulbs and trees, maintenance of the churchyard, the Streamside Garden and the network of public rights of way.

The grounds of the Jubilee Hall will be maintained by the group, which will also undertake cleaning of the bus shelter and work in the new park.

David Netherway explained: "The Green Team is yet another example of the people of Swimbridge joining together to not only provide the best possible community facilities but also to ensure that they are properly maintained.

"And once the cleaning up is completed, the project has a social side, with a bite to eat being provided courtesy of The Jack Russell."

As this book went to press Swimbridge was celebrating the reopening of the extended and refurbished Jubilee Hall, a project which will provide a splendid facility to enhance the social life of the village well into the twenty-first century.

The new look Jubilee Hall was formally re-opened by former parish council chairman John Bartlett, a driving force behind the transformation of the hall. He is pictured at the ceremony with project co-ordinator Julie Whitton.

Conversation piece at a coffee morning in church. In the foreground is stallholder Maureen Hayward. Behind Maureen is churchwarden Vera Knight, talking to PCC treasurer Nick Arthurs. In the background David Netherway has a conversation with Ray Liverton.

After a thousand years the parish church of St James is still at the heart of Swimbridge life. In recent times the church has begun to play host not only to worship but also to events of many kinds, including concerts, talks organised by its new Friends organisation, driven by Mark Haworth-Booth, and social and fund-raising activities such as the Christmas coffee morning illustrated here. Pictured l-r, at one of the stalls are Margaret Meade, Janet Balment and Phyllis Netherway.

Julie Whitton at the microphone at Devon County Show 2015, during the presentation to Swimbridge of the Prince of Wales Award, which recognised the redevelopment of the Jubilee Hall, the creation of the Streamside Garden and the activities of the Green Team. Also pictured, l-r, are David Netherway, Lady Arran, and County Show chairman David Parish.

The £630,000 project was funded by a £500,000 Lottery award and by many other grants and community fund raising.

The official opening of the new Jubilee Hall was carried out by former parish council chairman John Bartlett, who encouraged and sustained the project over many years, being particularly supportive especially at times when problems arose.

The modern hall and its facilities will be used by the village school, for weddings, a dance and craft clubs and many other events, including theatre and music shows.

Jubilee Hall Chairman Colin Wadsworth said at the opening ceremony: "It is great to be able to show what can be achieved by commitment, hard work, good design and quality building and the generosity of our funders."

Project Leader Julie Whitton said: "I am so excited to have reached this result, a fantastic new hall for our community to enjoy."

The housing development off Barnstaple Hill – named Liverton Drive in honour of long-serving parish and district councillor Ray Liverton – has blended well into the village environment.

Further development was on the cards at the time of writing, with plans for housing on the former tannery site.

Manufacturing on a modest scale is still carried on in Swimbridge in the twenty-first century. The former tannery company offices on Hannaford Lane are occupied by Bill Hedge – Bill the Potter as his website proclaims – who learnt the skill of the potter's wheel and the kiln as a member of a monastic order, the

The Feoffees, an organisation which once funded its support for local charities from the income from properties it owned in the village, is still active. Pictured are villagers enjoying a free lunch in 2015.

Cistercians of the Strict Observance at Mount St Bernard Abbey in Leicestershire.

When he joined the community Bill had no previous experience at all of pottery.

After being thrown in at the deep end to learn the craft, he became enthusiastic about his role, and completely re-vitalised the monastic pottery, eventually making it a key component of the life and economy of Mount St Bernard Abbey.

Although Bill was eventually ordained to the Roman Catholic priesthood as Father Bernard, he eventually left the monastic life for the wider world, teaching pottery in a school he discovered to have a defunct pottery which he restored to life.

151

Volunteers from Swimbridge's Green Team help keep the village looking immaculate. Pictured, l-r, are Bob Bateman, Tess Bateman, Colin Wadsworth, Martin Fry and David Netherway.

He then spent some time in the craft's spiritual home, Stoke on Trent, and was then involved in a large-scale enterprise in the South of England, selling products to garden centres, before discovering that he was being ripped off by his business partner.

Bill eventually found lasting fulfilment working for eighteen years for CARE, Cottage and Rural Enterprises, based at Blackerton near East Anstey on the southern edge of Exmoor. He explained: "Working with adults with learning difficulties allowed me to combine pottery with the counselling and other social skills I had learnt whilst in the monastery. I stayed for eighteen years and found the atmosphere quite monastic – what I suppose I was born to do.

"When I retired at sixty-five I bought what had been the old tannery offices and turned it into a home and a place where I could make pots and meet people!"

Bill has used his monastery-honed skills to been make high-fired pottery for more than forty-five years, with a product range including cook, table and kitchen ware, porcelain medallions, green man and other character masks for gardens, and special one-off pieces for more decorative use.

Those closely involved with public life in Swimbridge see a bright future for the village and the wider parish as the twenty-first century unfolds.

Colin Wadsworth summed up the vision of the future he shares with many other councillors and community workers when he said:

"There are times when transition from one era to the next can cause difficulties. The strong community spirit evident over the decades in Swimbridge has helped to ensure that our village remains united.

"With so good ideas constantly being put forward, so many enthusiastic workers and a continuing flow of new projects, we believe the future is set fair."

Swimbridge parish council has been looking after the interests of the village since 1894. Pictured are chairman, Geoff Dodd (centre) and, clockwise around the table, Lee Wadsworth (clerk), Ian McLaughlin, David Luggar (district councillor), Richard Edgell (county councillor), Gavin Coulstock , Rosemary Haworth-Booth, Colin Wadsworth (vice-chairman).

Appendices

Appendix 1

Priests of Swimbridge from 1443 (Source the Rev. J. F. Chanter)

1443: John Hoigg

John Brase

John Henton

John Baker

1530: John Rouck

1532: Robert Bulpayne

1535: John Powell

1536: John Grodson

1538: William Alley

1540: John Proute

1540: John Vele

1541: Thomas Hodge

1548: Richard Canne

1564: Christopher Thorne

1588: John Brook

1600: Henry Hatswell

1604: Matthew Hammond

1608: Edward Dawson

1612: Morgan Davy

1617: William Leigh

1649: William Leigh

1662: Daniel Cory

1676: Thomas Yeo

1685: John Jenkins

1686: Thomas Yeo

1695: William Beare

1719: Henry Elmestone

1727: William Palmer

1730: William Ward

1731: Joseph Clarke

1735: William Prince

1781: Charles Hill

1787: William Hole

1787: Nicholas Dyer

1821: Hugh Northcote

1832: John Russell

1880: Richard Martin

1887: Jose Fortescue Lawrence Gueritz

1889: Henry Harrison

1911: Henry John Freke Van

1915: Cecil Arthur Curgenven

1939: Henry John Allen Rusbridger

1949: Eric Robotham

1953: A. P. R. Mayne

1963: John Read

1969: Richard Gilpin

1973: Nigel Jackson-Stevens

1985: Alasdair MacKeracher

1989: Peter Bowers

2012: Shaun O'Rourke

Appendix 2
Swimbridge Parish Council Chairmen

The first meeting of Swimbridge parish council took place on 31 December 1894.

1894:	Mr H. Chichester of Tree	**1960:**	T. J. Holland
1901:	Mr George Norman	**1961:**	Mrs L. E. Dalling
1910:	Mr W. H. Smyth		Cecil W. Trigger
1917:	W. R. Shapland	**1962:**	W. R. Shapland Junior
1919:	Captain F. E. Phillips of Bydown	**1966:**	C. G. Huxtable
1927:	Mr W. B. Burgess	**1968:**	O. C. Dalling
1934:	Mr W. J. Westcott	**1971:**	Mr R. J. Liverton
1946:	Albert Westaway	**1980:**	W. R. Shapland
1949:	W. R. Shapland Senior	**1982:**	R. J. Liverton
1953:	F. R. Joslin	**1995:**	John Bartlett
1954:	H. Smale	**2002:**	Robbie Moyse
1955:	A. Sturgess	**2003:**	R. J. Liverton
1956:	C. H. Balment	**2011:**	Andy Comerford
1957:	W. R. Shapland Junior	**2012:**	John Hayes
1958:	T. E. Spencer	**2013:**	Geoff Dodd

Appendix 3
Headteachers of Swimbridge School

Mr E. W. Hicks 1861-66

Mr T. Grace 1866-69

Mr W. E. Turner 1869-76

Mr B. T. Jones 1877-78

Mr S. Cater 1878-79

Mr W. E. Turner 1879-80 (second spell)

Mr J. Raw 1880-83

Mr W. Shelley 1883-1916

Mr C. J. Pickford 1916-20

Mr F. H. Drew 1921-44

Miss R. L. Burgess 1945-66

Mr D. V. M. Harvey 1957-62

Mr M. E. N. Holmes 1962-1981

Mr G. D. Reed 1981 -

Appendix 4
Licensees of the New Inn/Jack Russell

Date	Licensee	Owner of premises
1850.	John Smallridge	
1857.	John Bond	
1870.	Abraham Rice	John Gaydon
1878.	James Hooper	"
1883.	John Salter	"
1884.	John May	John Burgess
1885.	Robert Clarke	"
1896.	William Henry Harris	William Hancock Wiveliscombe
1904.	Frederick Thomas McDermott	John Crang-Smyth
1907.	Arthur Eastmond	"
1919.	Charles Albert Freeman Baldwin	Arnold & Hancock Ltd
1923.	Stephen Cooper	"
1931.	Thomas Edward Derges	"
1953.	Lavinia Frances Derges	"
1953.	William Samuel Edwards	"
1960.	Thomas Snell	"
1971.	Stanley George Phelps	"
1974.	Frederick Robert Chapman	Watney Mann West/Chef & Brewer
1981.	Barry George Davis	"
1983.	Richard Frederick Bristow	Ushers Limited
1986.	John Prince	"
1988.	Michael Jeffrey	Grand Metropolitan
1990.	Maureen Hayward	"
1996.	Hugh Lloyd Johnston	Phoenix Inns Ltd
1996.	Susan Ann Carey	"
1998.	Bill & Debbie Furnifer	Free house
2004.	Ian & Rose Ford	
2006.	Paul Darch	Free House

Selected Further Reading

Devon by W. G. Hoskins (Collins 1954)

Old Devon by W. G. Hoskins (David & Charles 1966)

Devon and its People by W. G. Hoskins, (Exeter: A Wheaton 1959)

Devon by L. Russell Muirhead (Ed)(Penguin Guides 1947)

The Making of the English Landscape by W. G. Hoskins (Leicester, 1955)

The Buildings of England: Devon by Bridget Cherry & Nikolaus Pevsner (Yale University Press 2002)

The King's England: Devon by Arthur Mee (Ed)(Hodder & Stoughton 1938)

England's Thousand Best Churches by Simon Jenkins (Penguin Books 2009)

The Church of St James Swymbridge by The Rev. J. F. Chanter

A Guide to the Parish Church of St James Swimbridge (2006)

Swimbridge Methodist Church Jubilee 1898-1948 (Pamphlet 1948)

Swimbridge Baptist Church 150th Anniversary (Pamphlet 1987)

Methodist Church Swimbridge TER-Jubilee 1816-1966 (Pamphlet 1966)

Look at the Past of Swimbridge by Lois Lamplugh (Wellspring 1993)

The Parish of Swymbridge in North Devon by Mervyn C. Dalling (Dalling 1965)

Notes on the History of the Village & Parish of Swimbridge by Cecil Grimmett (Manuscript circa 1950)

Bydown, Kerscott and Dennington by Lois Lamplugh (Manuscript 1991)

The Way Twas (A Country Boy's Memories) (Cobbaton & Traveller's Rest) by Walter Isaac (1993)

School Heritage: 125 years of a Devon Village School seen through the annals of the School Log Books by G. Reed & others (Swimbridge School May 1991)

West Buckland: The Diary of an Edwardian School by Berwick Coates (Ryelands Publishing 2008)

West Buckland School by Berwick Coates (Halsgrove Publishing 2000)

The Natural History of a Country School: A Celebration of the 150-Year History of West Buckland School in Devonshire by Berwick Coates (Woodfield Publishing)

Parson Jack Russell The Hunting Legend 1795-1883 by Charles Noon (Halsgrove Country Classics 2000)

Memoir of the Rev. John Russell and his Out-of-Door Life by E. W. L. Davies (1878)

◇ SELECTED FURTHER READING ◇

Parson Jack Russell of Swimbridge by Lois Lamplugh (Wellspring 1994)

Echoes of Exmoor Pa'son Jack Russell (Simpkin, Marshall, Himilton, Kent & Co 1925)

Yesterday's Exmoor by Hazel Eardley-Wilmot (Exmoor Books 1990)

Simonsbath The Inside Story of an Exmoor Village by Roger A. Burton (Burton 1994)

Days of Renown The Story of Mining on Exmoor and the Border Parishes by J. M. Slader (West Country Publications 1965)

My Life as a North Devon Farmer by Pat Pidler (Edward Gaskell 2006)

The Taunton to Barnstaple Line by C. Maggs (The Oakwood Press)

The Barnstaple & Ilfracombe Railway by C. Maggs (The Oakwood Press 1978)

The Country Railway by David St John Thomas (Penguin Books 1979)

The Lynton & Barnstaple Railway by G. A. Brown, J. D. C. Prideaux & H. G. Radcliffe (David & Charles 1964)

Last Train Excursion Brochure (Barnstaple Round Table 1966)

Us be Goin' to Barnstaple Fair by Maureen E. Wood (Edward Gaskell 2001)

Subscribers

Ali, Pete, Rosie and Lin-Li, Hannaford Barton

Shirley (née Smart), Nigel and John Ashelford, Fremington

Anna Averns, Station Hill, Swimbridge

Mrs Alison Ayre (née Bartlett), Home Farm, West Buckland

John and Margaret Bartlett, Sandyke Farm, Swimbridge

Mrs M. L. and Mr A. J. Bartlett (Bert), Coombe Farm, Swimbridge

Mr and Mrs S. Beedham, High Cross House, Swimbridge

Janet Bell, Cheltenham
Louise Bond, Rock House, Swimbridge

Rev'd Prebendary Peter and Jane Bowers, Swimbridge Rectory 1989 to 2010

Joan Brayley

Mr Royston Buckingham, Rosscarbery, Ireland

Mary Burgess (née Shapland)

Doctor Roger Burland

Mrs Julie Burnage, Callington, Cornwall

K. J. Burrow, Bucks Cross, Devon

Brian and Anne Chapman (née Grant), Barnstaple

Michael and Connie Chown, formerly Dennington Lodge, Swimbridge

Kevin, Annie, Myer and Leif Clark, Swimbridge

Christine Clark and Richard Clifton

Mo and Mike Clift, Church Cottages, Swimbridge

Patricia A. Cook, Youings Drive, Barnstaple

Michael and Joyce Cork, The Travellers Rest, Cobbaton

Mr and Mrs J. Cox (Jane Buckingham), Abbotsham

Marlene Dalling

Stuart Dallyn, Hutcherton Farm, Gunn

Sue Davie, Northam, Bideford

Nige de la Cour Smith

Mary de la Cour Smith

David Dennis, Station Hill, Swimbridge

Jacqueline Dennis, Swimbridge

The Dennis Family, Archipark, Swimbridge

L. Down, Archipark, Swimbridge, North Devon

Simon Dyer, Swimbridge

Brenda Dyer (née Huxtable)

Eddie Dymond, Bishops Tawton

County Councillor Richard Edgell, Garliford, Bish Mill, South Molton, Devon

Charles Elworthy, Dennington Barton

Colin Elworthy, Swimbridge

S. W. and H. E. Elworthy, Dennington Barton, Swimbridge

Richard and Mary Fardon, Barnstaple

Bill Folland

June Folland (née Grimmett)

Folland family, Barnwell, Landkey, North Devon

Rachael Gooch, The Mill House, Hannaford Lane, Swimbridge

Ivy Grant, Youings Drive, Barnstaple

Christine Gubb (née Bartlett), Barnacott Farm, Stoke Rivers

Tobias and Clare Hall, Under Hooda, Station Hill, Swimbridge

Jessica, Charlotte, Freddie and Millie Hall, Under Hooda, Station Hill, Swimbridge

Kim Hampshire (née Dennis) of Archipark

Trevor Hampton, Moorfields Farm, Swimbridge

Mark and Rosie Haworth-Booth, Swimbridge

Anne Hayes, Hawthorns

Bill Hedge, Tannery Lodge, Hannaford Lane, Swimbridge

Mrs Marilyn Holland, Mulberry Way, Barnstaple

S. Huxtable-Selly, Cobbaton

The Isaac Family, Cobbaton

Martin James, Bydown

Christopher James, Tree Close, Gunn

Dave and Rosalyn Jordan, Hooda Close
Mrs Vera Knight, The Orchard, Swimbridge

Margaret J. Knight, Landkey, North Devon

Hilda Lavercombe (née Yeo), Barnstaple

Lawre and Marg who were evacuated to Kerscott Farm, Swimbridge in WWII

Hon. Alderman Ray Liverton, Swimbridge, Devon

Hannah L. Lloyd, Barton Manor Farm, Berrow, Burnham-on-Sea, Somerset

Edwin R. Lowe, Northam

Councillor David G. Luggar

Colonel Martin Maxse, Great Fisherton, Bishops Tawton, Devon

David and Phyllis Netherway, Swimbridge
K. O'Hanlon, Gunn

Alan Sampson, St Austell, Cornwall

Eric Sampson, now at Northampton

Judy and Keith Sanders, Bydown, Swimbridge

Archibald Thomas and Jenny Sanders, Tannery Cottage, Hannaford Lane

Linda Sanders (née Shapland), Bishops Tawton
Mrs Julia Scott (née Bartlett), Morna Cottage, Landkey

George H. Shapland

Stanley Smith, Barnstaple

Martin Sowden, Oakdale Avenue, Swimbridge, Devon

Vera Stables (née Cox), Greenmoor Road, Egremont, Cumbria

Peter and Janine Stern, Tannery House, Swimbridge

Ann Stoneman, Kerscott, Swimbridge

Swimbridge Twinning Association, twinned with St Honorine Du Fay, Normandy

Roger and Tracy Taylor, High Street, Swimbridge

Phillip, Matthew and Cameron Taylor, High Street, Swimbridge

Louvain Thorne (Dilly) née Grant

Jacquie Thwaites, Gunn

Aaron W. Thwaites-McGowan, Gunn

Nathaniel J. Thwaites-McGowan, Gunn

Mrs Rosalind Tucker, East Bradninch

Raymond and Ruth Vellacott, High Cross, Swimbridge

Colin and Lee Wadsworth, Mill Court, Swimbridge

Jim and Doreen Wheaton, Georgeham, Devon

Mrs Susan Wheaton (née Bartlett), Oatlands Avenue, Bishops Tawton

Julie Whitton, The Yews, Barnstaple Hill, Swimbridge

Julie Wilkins, Barnstaple

Maurice and Sheila Willis, 2 Watergate

Martin and Theresa Winter, Yeoland House, Swimbridge